Raymond Miller is Professor of Politics and International Relations at the University of Auckland. He frequently analyses politics in the media and is a past recipient of the Wallace Award for his contribution to the public understanding of electoral matters. Miller is the author or editor of, among other books, *New Zealand Government and Politics* (Oxford University Press), *Party Politics in New Zealand* (Oxford University Press), *Political Leadership in New Zealand* (Auckland University Press), and, with Ian Marsh, *Democratic Decline and Democratic Renewal: Political Change in Britain, Australia and New Zealand* (Cambridge University Press).

Democracy in
New Zealand

Raymond Miller

AUCKLAND
UNIVERSITY
PRESS

First published 2015
Reprinted 2015

Auckland University Press
University of Auckland
Private Bag 92019
Auckland 1142
New Zealand
www.press.auckland.ac.nz

© Raymond Miller, 2015

ISBN 978 1 86940 835 0

A catalogue record for this book is available from the
National Library of New Zealand

This book is copyright. Apart from fair dealing for the purpose of private study, research, criticism or review, as permitted under the Copyright Act, no part may be reproduced by any process without prior permission of the publisher. The moral rights of the author have been asserted.

Cover design: Spencer Levine

Printed in Wellington by Printlink Ltd

Contents

Lists of Figures and Tables		vi
Preface		ix
1.	Democratic Society	1
2.	Political System	26
3.	Constitution	45
4.	Parliament	61
5.	Electoral System	85
6.	Cabinet Government	106
7.	Leaders and Leadership	129
8.	Political Parties	157
9.	Māori Electoral Politics	184
10.	Elections and Voters	204
11.	Future of Democracy	230
Appendix		250
Bibliography		252
Index		263

Lists of Tables and Figures

Table 1.1: Free Trade Agreements with New Zealand	6
Table 1.2: New Zealand Population	9
Table 1.3: Ethnic Composition of New Zealand Population	10
Table 1.4: Ethnic Composition by Region, 2013	11
Table 1.5: It is a Citizen's Duty to Vote (Voters)	16
Table 1.6: My Vote Really Counts (Voters)	16
Table 1.7: Voter Turnout, as Proportion of Registered Voters	17
Table 2.1: Democratic Models	36
Table 2.2: Attitudes to the Monarchy (Voters)	39
Table 4.1: Composition of the 2014–2017 Parliament (as of March 2015)	64
Table 4.2: Parliament's Select Committees, 2014–2017	69
Table 4.3: Number of Seats and Population per Seat, 1896–2014	75
Table 4.4: New Zealand Parliament in Comparative Perspective	77
Table 4.5: Number of Three-year Parliamentary Terms, 1935–2017	81
Table 5.1: National Party List, 2014	94
Table 5.2: Labour Party List, 2014	95
Table 5.3: Results of the 2011 Referendum (Percentage of Total Votes)	100
Table 6.1: Alternative Governing Options under MMP	109
Table 6.2: Types of MMP Government	110
Table 6.3: Potential Governing Blocs under MMP	112
Table 6.4: John Key Ministry, 2014–	115
Table 6.5: Key Government Cabinet Committees, 2014–	116
Table 6.6: Clark and Key Ministries Compared	120
Table 7.1: Postwar New Zealand Prime Ministers	131
Table 7.2: Langer's Personality Traits of a Leader	139
Table 8.1: Party Support in General Elections under MMP, 1996–2014	165
Table 9.1: Results in Māori Seats, 1996–2014	191
Table 9.2: Māori Party and Labour Party Competition in the Seven Māori Seats, 2005–2014	195

Table 9.3: Voter Attitudes Towards Future of Māori Seats by Party (per cent)	199
Table 9.4: Māori Representation, 1990–2014	200
Table 10.1: Results of the 2008, 2011 and 2014 Elections	225
Table 10.2: Two-Party Results in Auckland, 2014	226
Table 10.3: Two-party Results by Region, 2014	227
Figure 1.1: Satisfaction with Democracy in New Zealand	13
Figure 2.1: The Political System	28
Figure 2.2: Attitudes to Monarchy by Age (Voters)	39
Figure 5.1: Māori Representation in the New Zealand Parliament	96
Figure 5.2: Women's Representation in the New Zealand Parliament	97
Figure 5.3: Referendum Ballot Paper, 2011	99
Figure 5.4: Knowledge of Electoral Systems by Age	101
Figure 5.5: Support for MMP by Age	101
Figure 5.6: MMP Vote by Party	102
Figure 6.1: Preferred Majority or Minority Government	111
Figure 7.1: Feelings Towards Major Party Leaders	141
Figure 7.2: Intensity of Feelings Towards Major Party Leaders	141
Figure 7.3: Feelings Towards the Small Party Leaders	152
Figure 8.1: Ideological Dimensions Matrix	167
Figure 8.2: Ideological Dimensions and Political Parties	169
Figure 9.1: Electoral Support for Labour–Rātana, 1946–1993	190
Figure 10.1: Influences on Voting Choice	216
Figure 10.2: Average Last Four Polls, 20 August to 15 September 2014	223
Figure 11.1: Very Interested in Politics, 2014	246

Preface

The aim of this book is to provide an easily digestible introduction to New Zealand democracy and politics. While it has been written with an undergraduate readership in mind, its content should appeal to any with a general interest in recent and future developments in New Zealand politics.

The book is a product of more than two decades of teaching and writing about democracy in New Zealand. Although there is a natural progression to its overall structure, it has been designed in such a way as to enable course conveners and readers to approach individual chapters in a sequence that best suits their own particular needs.

I am deeply grateful to those who provided assistance in the writing of this book. Sam Elworthy of Auckland University Press commissioned the project and was an invaluable source of encouragement. The quality of the finished product benefited greatly from the expertise of his staff, particularly Anna Hodge and Katrina Duncan. I would also like to thank Ginny Sullivan for copy editing and indexing; Dylan Matthews for his work on the graphics; and Rebecca Lal for proofreading. The book's cover was designed by Spencer Levine. Jack Vowles kindly granted me access to data from the New Zealand Election Study; Colin James gave permission to use a graph; and the New Zealand Electoral Commission website was a rich source of information on New Zealand voters and elections. I am indebted to Jennifer Curtin, a congenial co-author and co-teacher in New Zealand politics, and Peter Aimer, Ann Sullivan and Thomas Lundberg, who offered helpful feedback on parts of the manuscript. Above all, I wish to acknowledge an intellectual debt to Richard Mulgan, whose work on New Zealand politics, especially his three highly successful editions of *Politics in New Zealand*, inspired me to write this book.

Finally, I thank the thousands of students, both undergraduate and postgraduate, and the scores of teaching assistants and tutors who have sat through my lectures on New Zealand government and politics. I have been humbled by their enthusiasm, forbearance and goodwill.

Raymond Miller
The University of Auckland, March 2015

Chapter One

Democratic Society

New Zealand is one of the world's oldest and most enduring democracies. In 1852, the young colony adopted the United Kingdom's Westminster system of government, including an elected lower house and small upper house. In 1867, separate parliamentary seats were created for its indigenous Māori population. Although intended as a temporary measure, separate ethnic representation has been a feature of the New Zealand Parliament ever since. Universal male suffrage was introduced in 1879, and in 1893 New Zealand became the first country to extend the vote to all women.* Beginning in the 1890s, a party system slowly took root. In the heyday of the mass party era, up to one in four voters were party members. Further opportunities for participation occurred at each general election, when approximately nine out of every ten registered voters cast a vote. These unusually high levels of citizen engagement owed much to the size and distribution of the population, which was located largely in small rural and urban communities. Bolstered by a sense of belonging, relations between the government and governed were characterised by feelings of reciprocity and goodwill, leading an American scholar, Leslie Lipson, to observe that 'democracy in the literal sense of government by the people has come as near to fruition as in the Athens of antiquity' (Lipson, 1948: 481).

---

* Australian women received the right to vote in 1902. The United States followed in 1920 and the United Kingdom in 1928.

Despite presenting the outside world with an image of close democratic involvement, New Zealand follows the practice of much larger countries in having an indirect or representative system of democracy. The reasons are simple and largely concerned with the scale and complexity of the modern nation-state. Representative democracy has been defined as 'a form of government in which, in contradistinction to monarchies and aristocracies, the people rule' (Held, 2006: 1). Among the characteristics of this form of democracy are universal suffrage, 'one person, one vote', regular elections, the independence of political parties, and the right of all citizens to put themselves forward as the people's representatives. Although rule *by* the people in any literal sense is an unrealistic goal when applied outside the parameters of an election, representative democracy does imply government *of* and *for* the people, albeit indirectly expressed through the elected parliament.

At the heart of New Zealand's system of representative democracy is a commitment to free, fair and inclusive elections, with eligibility to cast the two votes offered under the mixed-member proportional (MMP) electoral system – one for a party and the other for the preferred electorate member – more liberally applied than in many other democracies. The country's electoral laws extend the right to vote to all residents, including non-citizens who have been present in the country for at least twelve months. The only other general restrictions are that all eligible voters be registered on the electoral roll and have lived in the same electoral district for a minimum of one month. Following on from decisions taken by the United Kingdom and United States, in the late 1960s and early 1970s the minimum voting age was progressively reduced from 21 to twenty years, followed by the current age of eighteen.* A Bill before Parliament in 2007 proposed that the voting age be further reduced to sixteen years, on the grounds that this would bring it into line with the school leaving age and a number of other individual rights, including the right to marry and have children. The Bill's sponsor later allowed it to lapse, believing that it lacked

---

* A number of countries, including Brazil and Malta, have reduced the voting age to sixteen years. Scotland lowered the voting age to sixteen for its independence referendum in 2014.

sufficient parliamentary and public support to become law. Those citizens and residents who have moved overseas remain eligible to vote providing they have returned to the country during the preceding three years and one year respectively. From time to time, other restrictions may apply. When considering the future of separate Māori seats, for example, the Royal Commission on the Electoral System recommended that any decision to abolish or retain the seats be restricted to those on the Māori electoral roll (Wallace, 1986: 113). The National Party disagreed, believing it to be a matter on which all New Zealanders should have a say. In contrast to the residency provision for voters, parliamentary candidates must be citizens.*

While the particular form of democracy practised in New Zealand is largely derived from elsewhere, especially Westminster's 'mother' Parliament, it is also a product of the country's particular physical and social environments, three aspects of which will be discussed in this chapter: geographical remoteness, small population base and brief history as a fully independent state. The paradoxes contained within each add layers of interest and complexity to what is a distinctively New Zealand system of democracy.

Remoteness

> 'All people think that New Zealand is close to Australia or Asia, or somewhere, and that you cross to it on a bridge. But that is not so. It is not close to anything, but lies by itself, out in the water. It is nearest to Australia, but still not near.' – MARK TWAIN

A recurring theme in the debate over national identity and what it is to be a New Zealander is the impact of geographical remoteness on New Zealand's sense of place and view of the outside world. Every generation has been challenged by its effects, which may include a sense of distance, leading to

---

* In 2002 a newly elected United Future MP, Kelly Chal, was forced to give up her parliamentary seat when it was found that, despite having been a New Zealand resident for some eight years, she had not taken out citizenship.

feelings of isolation and disengagement. In the early 1960s, a small group of scholars examined the impact of remoteness on the New Zealand way of life (Sinclair, 1961). Writing with the consequences of the Second World War still vivid in their memories, they acknowledged the dislocation felt by young soldiers as they returned from Europe. But they also noted some positive effects, including a heightened sense of national consciousness, together with an ability to understand and engage with the outside world (Chapman, 1961: 43). In the view of one contributor, 'New Zealanders, despite their physical remoteness from New York, London and Paris, are part of the world-wide dialogue of European civilization' (ibid.: 44).

From today's perspective, it seems almost fanciful to have been referring to a 'world-wide dialogue' in the early 1960s, decades before the advent of an integrated global economy, political union in Europe, the easy availability of international air travel and the inter-connected world of the internet. But in fact, post-colonial New Zealand was remarkably well connected with the outside world. As well as enjoying the benefits of a steady inflow of migrants annually from a diverse range of cultures and societies,* successive generations of young New Zealanders embarked on 'The Big OE', with the most popular destination being the cosmopolitan city of London. Yet further opportunities to travel and experience other cultures were made possible by the government's devotion to Empire, and later its commitment to the American-led alliance system, the consequences of which have been lengthy periods of overseas military combat for some New Zealanders in Europe, the Middle East, North Africa and South East Asia.

In recent times, there has been growing appreciation that New Zealand's remote location gives it and its populace a number of distinct benefits, including political autonomy, secure borders, low threat of terrorist attack, and the possibility, in theory if not in practice, of achieving a cleaner domestic and regional environment. Together, these benefits provide opportunities for self-determination barely imaginable in the crowded and disputed territories of the Northern Hemisphere. On the other hand,

---

* In 2014, one in four New Zealanders were immigrants.

unlike more strategically located states, New Zealand has at times struggled to maintain an international profile and identity, especially in comparison with its closest neighbour, Australia. During its early development, it was regarded as little more than a distant and inconsequential outpost of the British Empire. More recently, it has realigned its identity to fit with its location as a nation of the South Pacific, a decision that was reinforced by its opposition to French nuclear testing and the occasional visit of nuclear-armed and/or -powered American ships. In the view of critics of New Zealand's foreign policy stance under the current National-led government, independence is no longer guaranteed, and indeed is being compromised by the country's renewed involvement in Western military activities and intelligence networks, especially its 'Five Eyes' surveillance partnership with the United States, Britain, Canada and Australia.

Beginning in the colonial period, New Zealand's predominantly pastoral economy was well placed to compete in distant markets. Perishable food could be sent to the other side of the world by refrigerated shipping from as early as the 1880s. In an arrangement that proved highly beneficial for New Zealand producers, the United Kingdom took up to 90 per cent of the country's agricultural exports. In return, it sent disproportionately low levels of imported goods to New Zealand. This favourable arrangement lasted until 1971, when the United Kingdom government announced its decision to join the European Union (then referred to as the European Economic Community or Common Market). While European farmers were prepared to accept, if grudgingly, British access to the European Economic Community (EEC), they were adamant that any long-term arrangement would not include the Commonwealth. As well as being largely excluded from Europe, New Zealand's trade prospects with the Asia-Pacific region appeared similarly bleak, especially since its large national populations consumed comparatively little of what New Zealand produced.

To help compensate for these losses, in 1983 New Zealand forged a free trade agreement with Australia (see Table 1.1, overleaf). Within a matter of years, Australian investment in New Zealand's commercial and retail sectors had intensified to a point where all of the major banks and many of the large retail chains were owned by Australian companies.

Table 1.1: Free Trade Agreements with New Zealand

Australia	1983
Singapore	2001
Thailand	2005
Chile	2005
Brunei	2005
China	2008
Malaysia	2009
Hong Kong	2011
ASEAN	2011
Taiwan	2013
South Korea	2015

Source: Ministry of Foreign Affairs and Trade, 2015.

Between the 1980s and the early 2000s, the United States and Japan also emerged as significant partners, followed by South Korea and Singapore. The signing of a free trade agreement with China proved to be a landmark event in relations between the two countries. Within five years, China had replaced Australia as New Zealand's largest two-way trading partner. Export commodities included dairy, especially milk powder, timber and wool. In return, New Zealand imported machinery, electrical goods, clothing and apparel, and furniture.

New Zealand exporters continue to be susceptible to a number of risks, including rising oil prices and other transportation costs, international unrest, fluctuating exchange rates, and the sensitivity of markets to food quality and safety, as illustrated by China's temporary ban on infant formula in 2014, a decision that threatened the future of some 3 per cent of all exports to that country. As well as having to produce food of the highest quality, New Zealand exporters must be highly efficient, selling in distant markets at prices that compete with those of local producers. In the absence of significant forms of government assistance, such as subsidies and tariffs, New Zealand's open economy is particularly vulnerable to competition from other, more protected markets.

While periodic interruptions to bilateral trade may prove costly, they hardly compare with the challenge posed by the growing phenomenon of economic globalisation. Some observers claim that we now live in a 'borderless world' in which the nation-state has lost both any meaningful identity and its capacity for autonomous action. Isolated and heavily dependent economies, such as New Zealand's, are deemed to be especially vulnerable to the world's great powers, notably the United States and China, as well as major trading blocs and multi-national investors. Economic nationalists, whether they come from the social democratic left or the populist right, express concern whenever attempts are made to privatise state-owned assets or sign up to free trade agreements in situations that might prove disadvantageous to New Zealand, a recent example of which is the Trans-Pacific Partnership Agreement between twelve countries, including the United States and Japan.

Whilst acknowledging that economic globalisation poses a threat to the continuing existence of the nation-state, sociologist Anthony Giddens adopts the view that globalisation can have the reverse effect of empowering the nation-state by providing fresh opportunities for the development of greater national self-awareness and assertiveness (Giddens, 1998: 28–33). According to this argument, rather than the nation-state gradually disappearing, what we are witnessing is a flourishing of sub-national identities and independence movements, such as those found in Quebec, Scotland, Catalonia and elsewhere. And despite its earlier colonial identity, modern New Zealand, it can be argued, has developed a clearer sense of its own national character, while at the same time seeking to extend its influence through a growing network of bilateral free trade agreements and multilateral forums and associations. These include the Commonwealth, the United Nations (UN), the Association of Southeast Asian Nations (ASEAN) and the Asia-Pacific Economic Cooperation forum (APEC). As a small but independent voice internationally, New Zealand has gained a reputation for 'punching above its weight', as illustrated by the appointment of a former Prime Minister, Mike Moore, as Director-General of the World Trade Organization (WTO) (1999–2002), Don McKinnon as Secretary-General of the Commonwealth (2000–8), and Helen Clark as Administrator of the UN Development Programme (2009–). Perhaps most notable of all, New Zealand has twice been elected as a non-permanent member of the UN Security Council (1994–1995; 2015–2016).

No study of remoteness is complete without reference to the large number of predominantly young graduates and skilled workers who choose to live and work in 'greener pastures' overseas. With as many as half a million New Zealanders preferring the buzz and bustle of life in Australia's big cities, especially Sydney and Melbourne, and with many thousands more located in the United Kingdom and North America, the so-called 'brain drain' has been something of a political football, with opposition parties blaming the government for failed economic policies, limited employment opportunities, especially for the young, and low public morale. In 2000, for example, a newspaper advertising campaign partly funded by influential pressure group the Business Roundtable made the claim that young New Zealanders were heading overseas as a result of the failed policies of the new Labour-led government. According to the government's opponents, the alleged exodus of young New Zealanders constituted a 'generation lost'. Shortly before the 2008 election, the National Party leader, John Key, revisited the same theme with his complaint that 'the equivalent of this entire [Westpac] stadium and more leaves every year' (O'Brien, 2014). He was referring to a total of 52,500 permanent and long-term departures in that year. Three years after he took office, departures peaked at over 80,000 (Ministry of Business, Innovation and Employment, 2011). As the statistics confirm, blaming the brain drain on the policies of a particular government not only ignores patterns of migration established over many decades, but also the impact of the global economy and communications revolution on the lure of international travel and employment.

Smallness

Although there are approximately 80 nations with fewer people than New Zealand, its population of 4.6 million qualifies it as a small state (see World Atlas website). Its slow and incremental population growth over time can be explained by at least two factors. First, the country is far away from its preferred sources of immigrants, which has made the decision to leave the United Kingdom or Ireland a difficult one, especially since a vast majority of new immigrants had little prospect of returning to visit their families and friends once they had made the long journey. Second, government policy has tended to place tight controls on the number of new immigrants, especially from countries outside the white, English-speaking Commonwealth. In their defence, successive governments stressed the need to protect the small domestic economy, especially in the event that there were housing shortages or surplus workers. Those prepared to travel the 18,000 kilometres from the other side of the world to the ports dotted around New Zealand's long coastline were either great adventurers or from the middle and lower levels of the United Kingdom's class-based society. In either case the primary motivations were better financial prospects and a more desirable way of life (Sinclair, 1980: 101). For those unable to pay the fare, beginning after the Second World War the New Zealand government provided 'assisted passage' on one of its immigrant ships, the most well-known of which were the liners *Captain Hobson* and *Captain Cook*. A similar arrangement was first introduced by the New Zealand Company a century earlier as a means of establishing settlements in Wellington and Wakefield (near Nelson). As part of this new twentieth-century wave of assisted passage, those who undertook the six-week voyage were required to work for two years following their arrival in New Zealand (Hutching, 1999).

Table 1.2: New Zealand Population

1900	0.8 million
1920	1.3 million
1940	1.6 million
1960	2.4 million
1970	2.9 million
1980	3.2 million
1990	3.4 million
2000	3.8 million
2010	4.4 million
2015	4.6 million

Source: Statistics New Zealand, http://www.stats.govt.nz/browse_for_stats/population/estimates_and_projections/dem-trends-landing-page.aspx.

Whereas increases in the size of the population have been relatively modest (see Table 1.2), the same cannot be said for the distribution of the population, especially in relation to age and ethnicity (Research New Zealand, 2014). Consistent with trends elsewhere, the population is ageing, as illustrated by the rise in the median age, from 26 years in 1970 to 38 years today (ibid.). The most obvious explanation is increased life expectancy, with the average male living for close to 80 years and the average female 83 years. As a result, the proportion of the population reaching the retirement age of 65 years has increased from 11.7 per cent in 1996 to close to 15 per cent today (ibid.). Among the inevitable outcomes of this trend are a gradual shrinking in the size of the productive workforce and a corresponding rise in the cost of state-funded pensions and health care. Even more significant has been the gradual decline in the proportion of the population describing themselves as European (see Table 1.3). This decline has been most marked in the distinctly multi-ethnic city of Auckland, where Asians make up some 23 per cent of the population and Pacific peoples almost 15 per cent, compared with 59 per cent who are European. Two out of every three Asian and Pacific New Zealanders live in Auckland, and one in three Aucklanders were born overseas. In the much more homogeneous province of Canterbury, in contrast, Asians make up only about 7 per cent of the population and Pacific peoples less than 3 per cent, compared with virtually 87 per cent whose identity is European (see Table 1.4).

Table 1.3: Ethnic Composition of New Zealand Population*

	2001	2006	2013
European	80.1	67.6†	74.0
Māori	14.7	14.6	14.9
Pacific	6.5	6.9	7.4
Asian	6.6	9.2	11.8

Source: Statistics New Zealand, 2013.

* Because respondents may nominate more than one ethnicity, percentages total more than 100 per cent.
† In 2006, a significant 11.1 per cent of respondents identified themselves as New Zealanders.

Table 1.4: Ethnic Composition by Region, 2013*

	Auckland	Wellington	Canterbury
European	59.3	77.0	86.9
Māori	10.7	13.0	8.1
Pacific	14.6	8.0	2.5
Asian	23.1	10.5	6.9

Source: Research New Zealand, 2014: 18.
* Because respondents may nominate more than one ethnicity, percentages total more than 100 per cent.

Unlike the consistently upward trajectory in the proportions of self-identified Asian and Pacific New Zealanders, the Māori population took a long time to recover from the dramatic decline that occurred in the late 1800s and early 1900s. In 1858, its numbers were almost equal to those of the European population.* By the turn of the century the Māori population numbered only 43,000, or 5 per cent of the total, the reasons for which are said to include the ravaging effects of settlement, notably the introduction of European diseases and the social dislocation that accompanied the sale of tribal land (Sorrenson, 2014: 90–105). Following the introduction of universal welfare in the mid- to late 1930s, particularly improvements in the availability of medical care and adequate housing, numbers steadily increased. With projections suggesting a gradual rise in the Māori population at the rate of 1.3 per cent per year, by 2026 it is likely to exceed 800,000, or some 16 per cent of the overall population (Research New Zealand, 2014). In part, this reflects the fact that Māori life expectancy rates are also improving, although, at 73 years for men and 77 years for women, they are still some seven years behind those of Europeans.

The changing composition of the population has been a catalyst for renewed debate over questions of fairness and equity, especially in relation to public policy and the allocation of state resources. Successive governments have long accepted the importance of targeted provision

---

* Keith Sinclair has estimated that when Captain James Cook first visited in 1769 the Māori population may have been as large as 200,000 (Sinclair, 1980: 25).

for disadvantaged minorities, especially Māori, despite the opposition of some conservative groups. In a speech to the Orewa Rotary Club in 2004, for example, the National Party leader, Don Brash, alleged that Māori were beneficiaries of a 'government-funded culture of welfare dependency' and that there had been a 'drift towards racial separatism' to the point where 'the minority has a birthright to the upper hand' (Brash, 2004). More than a decade later, rising levels of inequality and child poverty have provoked calls for a stronger and more effective government and community response (see, for example, Boston and Chapple, 2014). One government initiative resulting from the National government's support agreement with the Māori Party is Whānau Ora, a scheme designed to empower whānau, or extended families, to access help in such areas as health care, education and employment. Also influencing the public policy debate has been the impact of immigration and an ageing population on the question of inter-generational fairness, especially in relation to the availability and cost of housing for first-home buyers in Auckland and Christchurch, health care and retaining the age of retirement at the current 65 years.

In their study entitled *Size and Democracy*, two American scholars explored the relationship between a nation's size and the quality of its democracy (Dahl and Tufte, 1974). Is citizen participation a more viable proposition in small states than large ones? Clearly, the early Greek thinkers imagined that it was, with Plato and Aristotle both claiming that the ideal state was the city-state, a territory sufficiently small to ensure high levels of direct citizen involvement in the decision-making process. But could the principles of direct democracy be adapted to the requirements of the modern nation-state, the population of which may be a hundred times greater than the largest city-state? Furthermore, is it reasonable to assume that participation rates and feelings of political efficacy are greater in societies that are smaller and more cohesive? While some studies find evidence of a causal link between smallness and enhanced democracy, especially in more remote island states, such as those in the Caribbean and South Pacific (e.g., Anckar, 2008; Ott, 2000; Srebrnik, 2004), others are best described as inconclusive. Anckar's study of democracy in small states concludes: 'In small communities, it is presumably easier for citizens to agree upon a

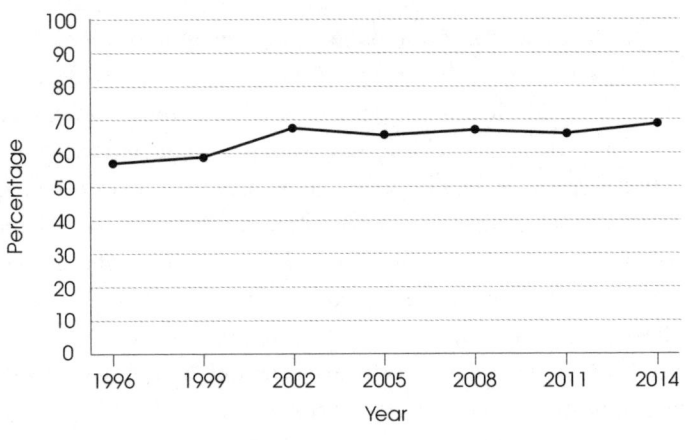

Figure 1.1: Satisfaction with Democracy in New Zealand
Source: New Zealand Election Study, 1996–2011.

common interest, but this also means that there is little need for a strong opposition. Thus, power is concentrated in the hands of a single, dominant political organization ... This, in turn, enhances the position of the leader of the executive branch, at the expense of the legislature and the parties' (Anckar, 2008: 435).

International ranking systems consistently place New Zealand among the world's most democratic countries. For example, the Democracy Ranking Association for 2013 placed New Zealand eighth, just below the Scandinavian countries, Switzerland and Germany, but ahead of Canada, the United Kingdom and the United States (Democracy Ranking Association website). The BBC News Magazine's 2014 index of 167 countries ranked New Zealand fifth, behind most Scandinavian countries, but again, ahead of Australia, Canada, the United Kingdom and the United States (Baptist, 2014). When viewed from the perspective of the New Zealand voting public, it is clear that levels of satisfaction remain high, despite the fact that, at any given election, approximately half of all voters are denied the government they most want (see Figure 1.1).

It is frequently said of small societies that they are better placed than large ones to develop a national community based on commonly held interests, values and aspirations. Although geographically diverse, New Zealand benefits from having a complex network of roads, transportation and communications. Together with an educated public and skilled workforce, this physical infrastructure has facilitated the growth of a collective identity or togetherness that incorporates all but the most isolated communities. Reinforcing this sense of cohesion is New Zealand's centralised system of government, especially its role in setting national standards in education and achieving some consistency in the provision of public health, housing and welfare. Yet further opportunities for developing a sense of national community are provided by the news media, especially the one-hour prime-time television news, the coverage of which often focuses on local personalities and events to the virtual exclusion of an international dimension. News producers clearly assume that a vehicle accident in Northland, or a murder in Dunedin, is of interest to the whole nation, a perspective that effectively shrinks the country into one small and decidedly parochial community.

There are obvious benefits to be derived from this narrow sense of community. To an extent not possible in much larger societies, smallness contributes to a sense of intimacy, a by-product of which is the expectation that politicians will be accessible to the public. Among the most popular leaders have been those who, rather than conveying a sense of superiority, are content to adopt the lifestyle of ordinary voters. While this could be said of the relationship between leaders and followers in many parts of the world, New Zealand's small settler society and egalitarian tradition make displays of openness and accessibility particularly important. Prime Minister Keith Holyoake (1957; 1960–72) was fondly referred to as 'Kiwi Keith', so devoid was he of the 'airs and graces' of a prime minister. As his biographer, Barry Gustafson, has pointed out, 'He insisted on his home phone number, 44-797, being listed in the phone book, and he received many trivial calls at home' (Gustafson, 2007: 127). These included helping a rail passenger with lost luggage, even going down to the Wellington railway station to help find it (ibid.). Holyoake's successors continued with the same 'everyman' tradition. Members of the public who called Robert Muldoon's (1975–84) home phone number could talk to the Prime Minister or his wife (they refused to install an answer phone). The couple's bach at Hatfield's Beach, north of Orewa, was one of the most modest in the bay. David Lange (1984–89) regularly ate with his family in a fast-food restaurant, and the warmth of his exchanges with members of the public, including passersby, helped mark him out as a popular, even charismatic, leader. Shortly after Helen Clark (1999–2008) became Prime Minister, the *Sunday Star-Times* newspaper featured a picture of her Auckland residence, along with a map showing how to get there. Clark objected, on the grounds that it potentially compromised her security and right to privacy. Rather than issue an apology, the newspaper pointed out that the Prime Minister's address and phone number were readily available in the Auckland telephone directory (Clark, 2000). Perhaps most interesting of all is Prime Minister John Key's reputation for ordinariness, especially given his extreme wealth and ability to maintain a lifestyle far beyond the reach of voters. Unlike all previous prime ministers except Clark, who was Prime Minister during the 9/11 terrorist attacks in the United States, Key is accompanied by plainclothes police officers at all times, something that might conceivably limit the public's access to him. Also quite unlike earlier prime ministers, Key has acquired the status of a 'celebrity' figure, although he is carefully framed as being 'star-struck' on meeting figures as diverse as singer Katy Perry, fellow golfer Barack Obama and All Blacks Daniel Carter and Richie McCaw. Despite these clear examples of exclusivity, Key has developed a persona of approachability and down-home ordinariness that make him an exceptionally popular leader.

Where New Zealand's system of representative democracy is most effective is in the strength of the public's satisfaction with democracy,[*] as well as its belief in the importance of participation, with 85 per cent of respondents to the New Zealand Election Study (NZES) (2011) agreeing that it is a citizen's duty to vote (Table 1.5, overleaf). The strongly held view that voting is both relevant and important (Table 1.6, overleaf) has

---

[*] The lower level of satisfaction in the late 1990s is probably due to some initial doubts as to the stability of multi-party government under MMP. The National–New Zealand First coalition finally collapsed in mid-1998.

Table 1.5: It is a Citizen's Duty to Vote (Voters)

	1999 %	2002 %	2005 %	2008 %	2011 %	2014 %
Agree	79.9	87.7	84.9	88.4	84.6	80.6
Neutral	11.8	7.3	9.2	7.0	8.7	12.1
Disagree	8.2	5.0	5.8	4.6	5.1	5.6

Source: New Zealand Election Study, 1999–2014.

Table 1.6: My Vote Really Counts (Voters)

	1999 %	2002 %	2005 %	2008 %	2011 %	2014 %
Agree	79.9	76.6	75.4	79.9	72.5	72.0
Neutral	11.8	14.8	14.8	11.7	15.1	16.2
Disagree	8.2	8.6	9.9	8.4	9.4	9.0

Source: New Zealand Election Study, 1999–2014.

its roots in the link between parliamentarians and the voting public. With electoral districts averaging only 45,000 voters, and with an additional 50 Members of Parliament (MPs) elected from the party lists, the level of representation in New Zealand (24,500 eligible voters per MP) compares more than favourably with those levels found in the United Kingdom (70,000), Canada (77,000) and Australia (91,000).* Satisfaction with democracy is also reflected in the historically high levels of voter turnout. Prior to the mid-1980s, over 90 per cent of all registered voters regularly participated in the election process (see Table 1.7). Clearly, the smallness and intimacy of New Zealand society played a role in instilling a sense that participating is important (see Table 1.5). It may also help account for the similarly high feeling of efficacy, or belief that the act of voting really counts (Table 1.6). Despite the frequency of elections and the limited choice available to voters in New Zealand's former two-party system, in the period soon after the Second World War National and Labour could call on the support of many

---

* Calculations are based on Britain's 646-member House of Commons, Canada's 308-member House of Commons, and Australia's 150-member federal House of Representatives.

Table 1.7: Voter Turnout, as Proportion of Registered Voters

		Movement
1981	91.4	
1984	93.7	+2.3
1987	89.1	-4.6
1990	85.2	-3.9
1993	85.2	0.0
1996	88.3	+3.1
1999	84.8	-3.5
2002	77.0	-7.8
2005	80.9	+3.9
2008	79.5	-1.4
2011	74.2	4.3
2014	77.9	+3.7

Source: New Zealand Electoral Commission, 2014b.

thousands of campaign workers, as well as an organisational structure capable of conducting door-to-door canvassing and mobilising the vote across the entire national electorate (Marsh and Miller, 2012). However, with the decline of mass-membership political parties and the advent of the modern election campaign, with its emphasis on a permanent campaign dominated by the electronic media, rates of voter turnout began to go into slow but steady decline.

Following the decision to adopt the MMP electoral system, an independent Electoral Commission was formed with a view to administering important aspects of the electoral process, such as allocating broadcasting funds, as well as promoting public awareness. In the months preceding the 2014 election, the focus of much of the commission's attention was the rising incidence of voter disengagement, particularly among 18–24-year-olds, and in Māori and Pasifika communities. Education and information activities included a mass media campaign on television and radio, as well as in print and online, on how to register and cast a vote. The commission also conducted research on the reasons for the decline in participation. It resulted in a conference aimed at raising awareness among political parties, journalists and members of the academic community (see New

Zealand Electoral Commission website). Although there was a slight rise in the proportion of registered voters at the 2014 election, many eligible voters failed to register, with the result that the estimated turnout was some six percentage points lower (71.9 per cent) than the official figure of 77.9 per cent (Table 1.7). As recent research has pointed out, far from the benefits of smallness and intimacy insulating New Zealand from international trends, at best they have merely slowed the inevitable process of disengagement (see, for example, Vowles, 2014: 53–74).

As well as the rise in non-voting, there appears to be a growing tendency for the voting public to become inattentive to campaign developments, as illustrated by the events that unfolded shortly before and during the 2014 campaign. In looking for broader explanations, analysts are likely to focus on the gradual shift of emphasis away from values and policies and towards more 'presidential' elections. Such elections are largely devoid of traditional meet-and-greet methods, such as public launches and campaign meetings, and instead employ the tools of political marketing, including branding, political 'spin', and promoting the image and style of the leader. Rather than conducting a campaign of any real substance, in 2014 the politicians were effectively side-swiped by a series of allegations coming from other sources, any one of which, if found to be correct, posed a serious threat to New Zealand's reputation as one of the world's most democratic and least corrupt societies. The most serious of these charges were: first, that there had been an orchestrated dirty tricks campaign against political opponents from inside the Office of the Prime Minister; second, that there had been unlawful mass surveillance of New Zealand citizens by the government's spy agency, the Government Communications Security Bureau (GCSB); and third, that the Labour Party's emails had been hacked by its political opponents. Despite the seriousness of these allegations, a number of which went largely unchallenged, popular support for National as measured by opinion polls flat-lined at around 50 per cent, with no perceptible shift in support either before, during or following the debates that accompanied each fresh allegation. Similarly, support for the two parties most likely to benefit from any fallout from these charges, Labour and the Greens, failed to show any increase, suggesting that the public remained unmoved by events, either because they did not believe them, or that they trusted the Prime Minister more than his accusers, or – perhaps more likely – because they were paying little or no attention to what was going on.

Youthfulness

Although the constitutional transition from colony to independent state was completed by the middle of the twentieth century, remnants of the country's colonial past remain. Perhaps most visible of these are the national flag, featuring the Union Jack, an imperial awards system that creates knights and dames in recognition of personal achievement, and, most important of all, retention of the British monarch as New Zealand's head of state.

During the early 1800s, New Zealand was administered from New South Wales, an arrangement that suited a somewhat reluctant British Colonial Office already stretched by the expansion of its Empire to the far corners of the globe. Over time, this arrangement proved unsatisfactory, creating a vacuum of power that an assortment of traders and land speculators were more than willing to exploit (Sinclair, 1980: 51–57). With the imminent arrival of large numbers of new British settlers, greater protection was required. In 1839 the British government installed Captain Hobson as Governor. Hobson was under orders to 'deal fairly with the Maoris, to appoint a Protector to guard their welfare once his government was established, to guarantee their rights to the land and, in order to prevent European purchasers from defrauding them, to provide that all European land titles must derive from a Colonial grant' (ibid.: 68). The following year the founding document of New Zealand statehood, the Treaty of Waitangi, was signed between Hobson and some 50 tribal leaders. As far as Hobson was concerned, British sovereignty had now been established (Durie, 2000: 415). While the meaning and significance of the Treaty has been debated ever since, the vast body of contemporary scholarship now accepts the Māori interpretation as signalling a partnership between Māori and the British Crown.

The 1852 Constitution Act was passed by the British Parliament and granted the young colony a limited form of self-government. While the Governor (then Sir George Grey) retained significant powers on behalf of the British Crown, the Act established a representative system of government, with an elected House of Representatives of 37 members and an upper house, the members of which were appointed for life by the Governor (Martin, 2004: 11–12). An initiative that only lasted for 24 years was a provincial system of government, with councils fulfilling certain responsibilities on behalf of the six provinces. At the first national election, which was held in 1853, only property owners with individual title were permitted to vote, a restriction that effectively excluded Māori, most of whom owned property in common. Until the formation of the first political party, the Liberals, in the early 1890s, obtaining a legislative majority required the support of independents and factions, the composition of which might change from issue to issue. Despite having achieved a measure of control over the decision-making process, the new settler society retained a deep loyalty to the 'Mother Country'. During the Australian federation debate of the late 1890s, for example, it was suggested that New Zealand consider becoming a state of Australia. Following a nationwide consultation process, the New Zealand government declined. One of the main reasons given was that it might weaken the country's close bond with Britain.

The next major milestone in the development of an independent state was the somewhat reluctantly taken decision in 1907 to endorse the status of a Dominion. Although some considered it to be more about semantics than matters of substance, replacing the designation 'Colony' with 'Dominion' put New Zealand on a similar footing with Canada and Australia, both of which had assumed greater control over their affairs, on the understanding that the British monarch was retained as head of state. While accepting somewhat greater autonomy with respect to domestic decisions, on foreign affairs and defence, the Dominions continued to defer to the leadership of the Westminster Parliament and government. As well as suggesting a commitment almost devoid of independent judgement, the promise 'where Britain goes New Zealand goes' provided a ready justification for New Zealand involvement in two major European wars.

The Balfour Report of 1926 declared the Dominions to be 'autonomous communities within the British Empire, equal in status, in no way subordinate one to another in any aspect of their domestic and external affairs, though united by a common allegiance to the Crown, and freely associated as members of the British Commonwealth of Nations' (Balfour Declaration, 1926). When the resulting Statute of Westminster was adopted in 1931, New Zealand was not a signatory, on the grounds that it remained satisfied with the level of independence already being offered (Sinclair, 1980: 246). There was also a sense in which the statute was seen to jar with the colonial government's aspiration that it be considered the most devoted and acquiescent of Britain's Commonwealth partners (ibid.). When the statute was finally signed in 1947, some sixteen years after Canada and five years after Australia, it marked a final step in New Zealand's constitutional progress towards full independence.

By the early 1950s it had become clear that Britain no longer had the military reach of a world power, and thus could not be relied upon to offer assistance to its former dependencies in the South Pacific. The ANZUS (Australia, New Zealand, United States Security) alliance with the United States and Australia, which was drawn up in San Francisco in 1951, not only marked the end of New Zealand's longstanding dependence on Britain, but also the beginning of a more regional approach to foreign affairs and defence. As we have seen, the transition to a more independent economic stance began much later and was largely a product of Britain's decision to enter the EEC. For many observers, however, the most important, even defining event in the emergence of an independent New Zealand was the 1984 ban on nuclear-powered and -armed ships, a decision that not only marked the end of ANZUS, but, more importantly, seriously damaged New Zealand's relationship with some of the world's most formidable nuclear powers, notably Britain, France and especially the United States.

Of the lingering symbols of British colonialism, by far the most important is New Zealand's continuing attachment to the monarchy. Of course, it can be argued that, under the Westminster system of democracy, the monarch has a severely restricted constitutional and political role, being little more than a titular head of state. Moreover, under the present monarch, Queen Elizabeth, the role has been largely localised, with a New Zealand-born and domiciled Governor-General fulfilling all the functions the Queen would carry out were she able to visit more regularly. For some, the most compelling arguments for retention are the popularity of the monarchy with the New Zealand public and the fact that it costs taxpayers virtually nothing to maintain. In contrast, an elected president may well incur significant costs, both in being elected and in maintaining an attendant executive and advisory staff. For opponents of the monarchy, the most pressing reasons are concerned with the undemocratic and unaccountable nature of the selection process, with succession being determined by birthright, as well as the symbolism that is associated with an advanced democracy under the leadership of a foreign potentate. Whether retention of the monarchy or its replacement with a republic is considered of purely symbolic or major importance is something that will continue to be debated. As it stands, however, neither major party is likely to initiate a referendum on the subject during the lifetime of the present Queen. Republicans are optimistic that this will change when Prince Charles becomes King.

A second remaining feature of New Zealand's colonial past is the use of an imperial awards system in recognition of personal achievement. Under the government of the former Prime Minister, Helen Clark, not only was the right of final appeal to Britain's Privy Council suspended, a decision that resulted in the creation of the New Zealand Supreme Court, but imperial awards were replaced by those deemed more appropriate for modern New Zealand. In making this decision, Clark noted that awarding the titles of knight and dame of the realm had been discontinued by Canada and Australia several decades before the New Zealand government made its decision. However, on taking office in 2008, Prime Minister John Key announced the reintroduction of imperial titles, a decision that was greeted with enthusiasm by previous recipients of Clark's most prestigious Order of Merit awards, more than 70 of whom accepted Key's offer of re-designation with the imperial titles of knight and dame. However, the Australian government's decision to reintroduce imperial titles proved much more controversial than that taken by Key. Tony Abbott's Australia Day 2015 announcement that the Duke of Edinburgh would be the recipient of an

Australian knighthood was widely condemned and contributed to calls for his replacement as Prime Minister.

Somewhat ironically, given his strong support for retention of the monarchy and reintroduction of imperial titles, in January 2014 Key announced that his government would hold a referendum on whether to retain the national flag or replace it with one that might more accurately represent New Zealand's status as a fully independent country. Debate on the future of the flag had waxed and waned over the preceding years, with periodic competitions to propose a design that would meet with the approval of most New Zealanders. Key's own initially stated preference was for a silver fern on a black background, a suggestion that, while seeking to exploit the successful branding of New Zealand's most prominent sports teams, including the all-conquering All Blacks, was criticised for its similarity to the black standard of the notorious Islamic State. Although Key's main motivation appeared to be concern that the Union Jack was little more than a 'relic' from New Zealand's colonial past, this was precisely the reason for its support among returned soldiers and other conservative groups, especially on the hundredth anniversary of the commencement of the First World War (see, for example, Editorial, *Bay of Plenty Times*, 2014). As with earlier referenda on the electoral system, it would be a two-stage process, with the first referendum offering a choice between several alternative designs nominated by a group known as the Flag Consideration Panel, and the second referendum serving as a run-off between the most popular alternative and the existing flag.

Conclusion

Rather than impeding development, New Zealand's remote location, small population and brief history as an independent state have reaped significant benefits. To compensate for the problem of distance, for example, successive governments have created a network of constructive relationships, often with much larger and more powerful states. These have included bilateral and multilateral trade agreements, membership of international bodies and cooperation agreements on everything from international aid and technical assistance through to environmental cooperation and defence. One study has observed that the resilience and access to resources of small democracies can give them an advantage over much larger countries, particularly in the competitive environment of the global economy (Keating and Harvey, 2014: R55). In New Zealand's case, any deficiencies in the availability of resources have been offset by the resourcefulness and adaptability of the people – skills that are colloquially referred to as the 'number-8 wire' approach to problem-solving.

It has been said that, while small states have the virtue of being able to reach outward to international bodies and communities, they are also well placed to reach inward, thereby enhancing the opportunities for effective representation and citizen engagement (Dahl and Tufte, 1974). Unlike more populous states, New Zealand has been able to achieve a degree of intimacy in the way its citizens interact with their elected representatives, a convention that has been endorsed by the nation's leaders, all of whom go to great lengths to make themselves accessible and accountable to ordinary voters. Levels of satisfaction with New Zealand democracy are high, and a vast majority of voters endorse the importance of elections and regard voting to be a duty they must continue to uphold. That said, New Zealand is hardly immune to the gradual decline in participation rates found elsewhere. These include declining voter turnout, albeit less severe than in some larger democracies, notably the United States; declining numbers of people joining and becoming active in political parties; and declining direct involvement in election campaigns, including fundraising, canvassing and mobilising the vote, as well as engaging with the unfolding events of the campaign, as illustrated by the lack of any obvious public response to the events that preceded the 2014 election.

During its two great periods of legislative activism in social welfare and workers' rights (1890s and 1930s), New Zealand was frequently described as a 'social laboratory'. In more recent times it has been more appropriate to call it a 'political laboratory', especially in relation to the decisions to abolish the upper house, introduce a free market economy, pass a Bill of Rights, grant citizens the right to initiate referenda, and move to proportional elections, with coalition and minority government being the most significant outcomes. It is tempting to assume that this experimentation was a product of public demand. In fact, in almost every case the changes were initiated from above, generally from government ministers, together with their bureaucrats and advisers. The one notable exception was the referendum vote to switch to MMP, although the matter only came to the public's attention several years after the Justice Minister, Geoffrey Palmer, appointed a Royal Commission on the subject. Rather than public demand, a more credible explanation for the scale of change is to be found in New Zealand's brief history as an independent state. In developing its own separate identity, it has been prepared to exploit the powers of a highly centralised system of government to overturn a number of inherited cultural, constitutional and institutional traditions.

Chapter Two

Political System

New Zealand was long considered a near-perfect example of the Westminster model of democracy. In keeping with their new country's strong links with the British monarchy and government, the early European settlers adopted Britain's constitutional arrangements, centralised government and two-house Parliament. Some variations to the Westminster system were tried and later abandoned, including provincial parliaments and factional politics, the latter surviving until the emergence of the first political party in the 1890s. While rule *by* the people is largely restricted to the act of voting, Westminster democracy provided opportunities for public engagement, partly through the presence of two mass-membership parties, but also according to the principles of single-party majority government.

Despite continuing public affection for Britain's cultural and political tradition, it is timely to ask if New Zealand's membership of the Westminster 'club' of nations is now effectively at an end. The purity of its Westminster heritage has been challenged by a number of developments, beginning with the abolition of the upper house and including the end of the two-party system and the advent under the mixed-member proportional (MMP) system of coalition and minority government. The introduction of citizens'-initiated referenda (CIR) represents a further departure from the Westminster model. Contrary to the spirit of representative government, voters are now able to challenge the authority of their elected representatives on any issue deemed to be of public interest or concern. Although occurring much later than it did in Canada (1888) and Australia (1986), the right of judicial appeal to the Privy Council was ended in New Zealand in 2003, a decision that leaves the monarchy and the Commonwealth as the only remaining political institutions explicitly linking New Zealand to its colonial past.

This evolving story of New Zealand's engagement with the Westminster system must include some consideration of how power is distributed among the three branches of government: the legislature, executive and judiciary. In the absence of an entrenched constitution, parliament is deemed to be sovereign. As in Britain, however, scholars tend to focus less on the powers of the sovereign parliament than on the lack of effective checks on the executive, with one constitutional expert, Geoffrey Palmer, once alleging that it exercised 'unbridled power' (Palmer, 1979). While it can be argued that one of the potential benefits of multi-party government under MMP is to empower small parties to hold the executive to account, this has to be balanced against the public demand for stable and effective government. As we will see in future chapters, while MMP has resulted in a more inclusive and consultative style of politics, questions remain over its success at increasing the powers of the legislature relative to those of the executive.

The best way to understand our political system, and the approach to be followed here, is to measure the extent to which we are in or beyond the Westminster system we began with.

Institutional Framework

The state has been described as either a defined physical territory (a nation-state) or a collection of political institutions that operate within and control that territory (Bevir, 2009: 199–202). In the case of the former, the state claims the sovereign right to pass and enforce laws, as well as dispense the proceeds from its physical and financial resources. Those who occupy the nation-state assume a collective identity, which may give rise to feelings of nationalism, even patriotism. When disputes arise with other nation-states over questions of territorial ownership and control, the movement of people, or political or commercial sovereignty, recourse may take the form of military conflict or peaceful resolution through a network of international agencies. With the advent of the global economy, including the emergence of large trading blocs such as the European Union and the planned Trans-Pacific Partnership, there is a growing sense that the nation-state has lost much of its power of autonomous action, hence the suggestion that the powers of the hitherto sovereign state are in the process of being 'hollowed out' (ibid.).

Although more commonly associated with a defined geographical area, the notion of 'state' that will be considered here is the collection of institutions that together make up the political system. While they may lack the constitutional separateness of America's three branches of government, the legislature, executive and judiciary together form the backbone of New Zealand's political structure (see Figure 2.1).

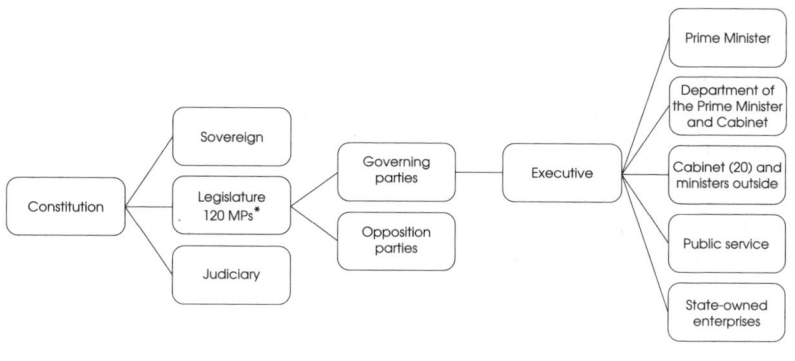

Figure 2.1: The Political System

* Due to the overhang provision, the 2014–17 Parliament had 121 members.

Sovereign

At the apex of power, at least symbolically, is the sovereign, or the British monarch, who has been conferred with the title of 'Queen of New Zealand' and who, on the rare occasions she visits the country, assumes the functions consistent with her role as head of state. In Queen Elizabeth's absence, the Governor-General fulfils a number of political duties, including: the opening and closing of Parliament; appointment, resignation and dismissal of ministers (at the behest of the Prime Minister); appointment of diplomats; and presiding over regular meetings with ministers, who together make up the Executive Council (New Zealand Government, 2008). Perhaps largely because of the constitutional role the Governor-General may be required to fulfil in the event that a government falters or fails to maintain its parliamentary majority, almost all recent appointees to the role have been former members of the judiciary. Although the Governor-General has never been called upon either to ask the opposition parties to form a government or to advise Parliament on the need for an early election, such powers do rest with the Governor-General should a government fail to retain the confidence of Parliament. The Governor-General is appointed for a five-year term by the Queen, on the recommendation of the Prime Minister.

Legislature

In the absence of an upper house,* the House of Representatives is the sole law-making body, although the Governor-General does play the necessary and impartial role of signing all legislation into law. Parliament can pass any laws, including those that reverse decisions made by any previous Parliament. Of course, the converse of this provision is that it cannot bind its successors, with the result that legislation passed by one Parliament can be revoked by the next. Presiding over parliamentary business is the Speaker, who is normally chosen from the ranks of the governing parties, although there is no constitutional requirement that this be the case.† While the powers of the legislature *vis-à-vis* the executive have increased, especially since the advent of minority government, they are not always sufficient to withstand the actions of a determined government. For example, while the need to allocate positions on Parliament's select committees to MPs from as many as six small parties has made those committees somewhat less susceptible to

---

* The Legislative Council was abolished in 1951.
† Hon. Peter Tapsell is the only Speaker to have been appointed from outside the government. A Labour MP, he was appointed by the 1993–96 National government with a view to preserving its one-seat parliamentary majority (at the time the Speaker was not entitled to vote).

government dominance, there has been a corresponding increase in the incidence of government Bills bypassing the select committee process, on the grounds that they are sufficiently pressing or important to be treated with urgency.

Executive

Under the Westminster system the pool of candidates for appointment to Cabinet and the wider executive is restricted to current Members of Parliament (MPs). While most prime ministers settle on a Cabinet of twenty members, there is no constitutional requirement that Cabinet be of that size – indeed, in the late 1990s, Prime Minister Jenny Shipley appointed a Cabinet of nineteen. Ministers who are appointed to positions outside Cabinet tend to be either junior ministers or members of the government's support parties. As we have seen, when it meets with the sovereign or her Governor-General, the executive is referred to as the Executive Council. One of the reasons for the dominance of the executive branch within the governing structure is the vast network of government departments and ministries that both implement government policy and provide research and advice. These include the core government departments, such as Social Development, Education and Health, as well as Treasury and the State Services Commission. Departments that are not deemed to be part of the public service include the New Zealand Police and Defence Force, together with the Security and Intelligence Service. In addition, the government is able to call on the expertise and advice of the Department of the Prime Minister and Cabinet. Opposition parties, in contrast, must rely on the services of small research units, the budgets for which are provided by an agency that is fully independent of ministerial overview, namely Parliamentary Service.

It is the role of the public service to implement the policies set by the incoming government. New ministers are likely to be briefed by officials on the ongoing issues that concern the department, and will in turn receive direction on the government's policy agenda and priorities. Consistent with the Westminster tradition of political neutrality, officials are required to offer the same standards of loyalty and impartiality to every elected government, regardless of the particular composition of that government or its ideological hue.

Judiciary

Although appointment to the judiciary follows a rather arcane process, it is free from the political interference that is associated with judicial appointments in many other countries. While a government minister, the Attorney-General, recommends and the Governor-General confirms new appointments to the various courts, there is a long tradition of non-political and independent appointments. This contrasts with the United States, where the credentials of potential appointees are scrutinised with a view to establishing what political and moral values will inform their decisions, especially with respect to their interpretation of the constitution. While the Chief Justice is appointed on the recommendation of the Prime Minister, as with other appointments, there is consultation with relevant individuals and agencies, including the New Zealand Law Society. Helping to manage any disagreement between government ministers and the courts, especially over the administration of justice, is the Attorney-General who, although a member of the executive, is given sufficient independence from the collective decisions of Cabinet to be able to defend the judiciary, especially in the event of attacks from individual ministers or sections of the public (New Zealand Government, 2008: 48–49). Although there is an understanding that government ministers should respect the independence of the courts and refrain from criticising their decisions, they are permitted to comment on policies that impact on crime and the administration of justice.

At the apex of the judiciary is the Supreme Court, which has been in existence only since 2004, when it replaced the Privy Council as New Zealand's highest appellate court. The Supreme Court is made up of the Chief Justice and four or five other justices. Below this is the Court of Appeal, a body of some nine members, including its most senior member, who is given the title of President of the Court of Appeal. The High Court sits in Auckland, Wellington and Christchurch, as well as travelling on circuit to a number of provincial cities and towns. In most circumstances, High Court judges sit alone. Below the High Court are the District, Family and Youth Courts.

Westminster System

The most immediately obvious feature of the Westminster democratic model is its simplicity. At its core is a centralised or unitary state, with the nationally elected government the unchallenged locus of political power. Unlike more pluralistic structures, such as that of the United States, there are no state or provincial governments with which to share power, nor is there significant devolution of responsibility to local government. Those few activities that are delegated to local councils are subject to tight external and fiscal constraints.* By creating a vast array of regional, district and borough councils, all of which have been granted a limited range of functions, the government is able to maintain its control. To this end, it is assisted by geographical proximity – as the examples of the United Kingdom, New Zealand and the nations of the Caribbean suggest, unitary governments are most effective in countries that are either sparsely populated or confined to relatively small land areas.

Implicit in this notion of a unitary state is the concentration of power in the hands of a small, homogeneous elite. Of the interlocking variables that contribute to this centralisation of political power, four stand out: first-past-the-post (FPP) or plurality elections, the strength of the two-party system, the incidence of one-party government and the role of a dominant executive. Writing in the 1960s, the French political scientist Maurice Duverger described what has become known as 'Duverger's Law' (1964: 217). It consists of a causal link between FPP or plurality voting and the emergence and consolidation of two-party systems. When the outcome of a plurality election is finely balanced, as tends to be the case in two-party systems, a party on less than 50 per cent of the vote may end up winning a clear majority of the seats, thereby guaranteeing it an absolute hold on power. In the New Zealand elections of 1978 and 1981, for example, not only did National win a majority of the seats with less than 50 per cent of the vote, it did so with even fewer votes than Labour. Distortions of this kind are quite common under plurality voting systems and reflect the distribution of party support from electorate to electorate. With the

---

* For an explication of the Westminster model, see Lijphart, 1999: 9–30. A summary of the main features of the Westminster system is provided in Bevir, 2010: 123–25.

growth of small parties, support for which tends to be widely dispersed, distortions can become even more pronounced. At the 1993 election, the last under plurality voting, National won 50 per cent of the seats with 35 per cent of the vote. Despite attracting a combined vote of 30 per cent, the small parties were rewarded with a mere 4 per cent of the seats.

As well as experiencing the favourable effects of plurality voting, two-party systems also benefit disproportionately from their appeal to a broad socio-economic base of electoral support. Whereas Labour derived the bulk of its electoral support from unionised workers, beneficiaries and the self-employed, National looked to farmers and their business associates in the provincial towns and cities, together with professionals and the well-to-do living in affluent city suburbs. Given the absence of other social divisions, for much of the postwar period the two parties enjoyed an electoral monopoly of up to 99 per cent of all votes cast. In this respect New Zealand's experience was little different from the two-party dominance found in other plurality voting systems. In societies with a largely one-dimensional social structure, that of socio-economic class, small parties have always struggled to retain their electoral support for more than one or two elections. In contrast, the multi-party systems of Europe are sustained by multiple cleavages, such as geography, language and religion.

With its guaranteed parliamentary majority, the winning party under the two-party system could expect to implement most if not all of its policy agenda. To this end, it relied upon the loyalty and support of each and every one of its duly elected MPs. While it is not uncommon to hear members of the public advocating for a parliament of independents, and while MPs themselves will sometimes claim to be mere 'delegates' of the voting public, what developed in New Zealand was a highly disciplined party system of government, with Harry Atmore of Nelson (b. 1870, d. 1946) having had the distinction of being the last independent elected at a general election under FPP. Not surprisingly, governing majorities in two-party systems are remarkably easy to maintain. Quite apart from the stigma attached to defecting to the other main party, loyalty has its rewards, not least promotion to Cabinet or the outer executive. Moreover, under two-party systems internal party control is strictly enforced, with the party caucus acting as an enforcer of party discipline and control. Its success can be illustrated in a number of different ways. For example, only one government in the postwar two-party period, Robert Muldoon's National government in 1984, could legitimately claim to have lost its legislative majority part way between elections.* As well as providing electoral stability, disciplined political parties offer electors a rational basis upon which to make their voting choice, as well as a measure of accountability in the event that they wish to apportion blame at the next election.

Perhaps the most important feature of the Westminster system is the power of the executive. A former British politician, Quintin Hogg (later Lord Hailsham), aptly coined the phrase 'elective dictatorship' in relation to the power of the executive. The reasons for this dominance are simple and have to do with the government's ability to control Parliament's legislative agenda. Most new policy is initiated by the executive, which is well placed to dictate the terms of the legislative process. Under New Zealand's majoritarian system, it was not uncommon for an executive of 24 or 25 ministers inside and outside Cabinet, together with two or three senior parliamentary officials (including the party's two Whips) to constitute a majority or a near majority of all the party's MPs. Given the seniority of its members and their ability to speak with one voice, not to mention their control over future promotions, it is hard to over-estimate the influence of the Cabinet on the direction of government policy. From this dominant position it was virtually assured of a parliamentary majority for all new legislation. Even a number as small as 24 or 25 ministers can be seen as something of an exaggeration, however, since every government is spearheaded by an inner Cabinet of six to eight of the most senior ministers. The informal influence of this small group on the wider executive and, beyond that, on the entire parliamentary caucus can be profound.

---

* In June 1984, Prime Minister Muldoon called a snap election on the grounds that he could no longer be assured of maintaining his two-seat parliamentary majority.

Durability of the Westminster System

Despite its dominance over postwar politics, in recent years the Westminster model has been described as being 'threatened' (Bevir, 2010: 123) and in its 'twilight' years (Dunleavy, 2006: 340). The reasons are numerous and include: the emergence of more socially diverse and pluralistic societies; the continuing decline in the electoral bases of the two major parties; growing public demand for direct involvement in the decision-making process; the greater incidence of constitutional checks on the ability of government to encroach unnecessarily in the lives of ordinary citizens, in New Zealand's case including the Official Information Act 1982, Bill of Rights Act 1990 and Human Rights Act 1993; and, of course, the substitution of plurality voting with voting systems more conducive to the electoral sustainability of small parties.

In his study of developments in British politics, Patrick Dunleavy (2006) observes that, even in the case of the British archetype, there have been a number of important departures from the Westminster model, including the introduction of devolved parliaments for Scotland and Wales; the advent of proportional representation in those same two countries, as well as in Northern Ireland, together with local government elections and election to the European Parliament; the decline of the two major parties and emergence of alternative electoral movements representing a range of social and nationalist divisions; and the introduction of new statutes on individual freedoms and rights that potentially curb the powers of Parliament and the executive. To these developments could be added the formation of a Conservative–Liberal Democrat coalition government in 2010.

Even more than in the United Kingdom, events in New Zealand have been described as representing 'a radical shift away from the Westminster model' (Lijphart, 1999: 9–47). According to this argument, over the passage of time the defining features of the Westminster model have been either diluted or replaced by those characteristics commonly associated with the pluralist or 'consensus' democratic model (see Table 2.1, overleaf). While New Zealand retains its representative system of democracy, any increase in the influence of the instruments of direct democracy,

Table 2.1: Democratic Models

Westminster model	Pluralist model
1. Representative democracy	1. Participatory democracy
2. Unitary state	2. Decentralised state
3. Sovereign parliament	3. Constitutional supremacy
4. Strong executive	4. Power-sharing executive
5. Two-party system	5. Multi-party system
6. Simple plurality elections	6. Proportional elections
7. One-party government	7. Coalition government

Source: Adapted from Lijphart, 1984.

including citizens'-initiated referenda, has the potential to curb the decision-making powers of the duly elected representatives. And while the power of the unitary state remains largely intact, the adoption of a 'super city' model for local government provides an interesting counterpoint to the hitherto unchallenged authority of central government. As the example of Auckland has shown, on major public policy issues such as housing and transport, central government must devolve some of its powers to locally elected councils. While New Zealand continues to have a strong executive, it now has a greater power-sharing role by virtue of the combined effects of proportional representation, a multi-party Parliament, and coalition and minority government. Finally, although New Zealand continues to have a sovereign Parliament, a number of its constitutional powers have been weakened by virtue of two major developments: the independence that was given to the central bank by the Reserve Bank Act 1989, especially over interest rates and the circulation of currency; and the increased use of judicial review, especially with respect to the provisions of the Bill of Rights Act 1990 and upholding indigenous rights as part of the Treaty of Waitangi settlement process.

One of best ways to get to grips with New Zealanders' current understanding of their political system and its future is to look at the debate over whether New Zealand should retain the monarchy or become a republic.

Future of the Monarchy

The transition from what British scholar Richard Rose once described as 'the only example of the true British system left' (quoted in Lijphart, 1999: 25) to a distinctly New Zealand adaptation of the Westminster system gives rise to the question of what should be done about the last significant institutional link with Britain, namely the monarchy. There is a common misconception that to sever ties with the monarchy is to forfeit a country's membership of the British Commonwealth. As the examples of South Africa and India show, there are precedents for opting for a republican system of government, including an elected president, while remaining an active member of the 53-member Commonwealth.

What might prevent New Zealand from following a similar route? For supporters of the monarchy, the fact that the position of Governor-General has been localised provides a powerful argument for retention (Cox and Miller, 2010). During the late nineteenth century and first half of the twentieth century, the role was filled by a succession of aristocrats and retired military commanders, all of whom were British and virtually none of whom had any direct link with New Zealand prior to their appointment.* Without exception, all returned to life in Britain following their term of office. The first New Zealand-born Governor-General, Sir Arthur Porritt, was appointed in 1967. A former Olympic bronze medalist and Rhodes Scholar, Porritt served as the Queen's personal surgeon prior to taking up the post of Governor-General. He was followed by the first New Zealand-domiciled Governor-General, Sir Denis Blundell (1972–77). Since then, every person to serve in this role has been New Zealand born and domiciled at the time of his or her appointment. Appointments have included the first Māori Governor-General, Sir Paul Reeves (1985–91), and the first woman, Dame Catherine Tizard (1990–96).

Those supporting retention of the monarchy also claim to be reassured by its reputation for being removed from party politics and the political debates of the day. In contrast to a republic, where presidential candidates

---

* Although born in Britain, Lord Bernard Freyberg (1946–52) spent part of his childhood in New Zealand.

tend to be closely identified with a particular party or ideological position, the British monarch refrains from expressing personal views or being seen to prefer one government to another. In her regular meetings with the British Prime Minister, the Queen is careful to avoid comments that may be misconstrued or in any way compromise her constitutional and ceremonial independence. On the other hand, the Governor-General is not always capable of maintaining this same level of political disinterest, with one, Sir Keith Holyoake (1977–80), having previously led a National government, and another, Tizard, having come from a prominent Labour family. These past affiliations and attachments notwithstanding, all who hold the office are expected to maintain the political independence of the monarchy in all that they say and do.

A related argument concerns the financial costs associated with adopting a presidential system of government, especially in the event that New Zealand opted for an elected president with genuine political power. As well as the constantly rising costs of election campaigns, creating an executive presidency is likely to require a significant budget, the size of which will depend on several requirements: building space; staffing, including legal and political advisers, researchers and managers; and travel and entertainment costs commensurate with the position of head of state. In contrast, maintaining the royal household is the responsibility of the British government and taxpayers. While New Zealand is responsible for all vice-regal expenses, these are minuscule by comparison and include: the Governor-General's relatively modest stipend; the costs associated with maintaining two properties, one in Wellington, the other in Auckland; and a small management team of approximately five staff, including a secretary, deputy secretary and public affairs manager.

These arguments notwithstanding, perhaps the most significant deterrent to New Zealand becoming a republic in the immediate future is public opinion (see Table 2.2). Surveys have consistently revealed that approximately half of all New Zealanders want to retain the English monarch as their head of state. While it might be expected that support for a republic has grown over time, on the grounds that a New Zealand head of state is more likely to win support from a generation of younger, more nationalistic voters, this has not been the case; indeed, whereas in 2005 slightly

Table 2.2: Attitudes to the Monarchy (Voters)

	2002	2005	2008	2011
Retain monarchy	51.2	48.7	49.6	53.2
Become republic	31.3	33.9	32.8	29.3
Don't know	17.5	17.1	17.5	17.5
	n=4859	n=2762	n=2700	n=3060

Source: New Zealand Election Study, 2002–2011.

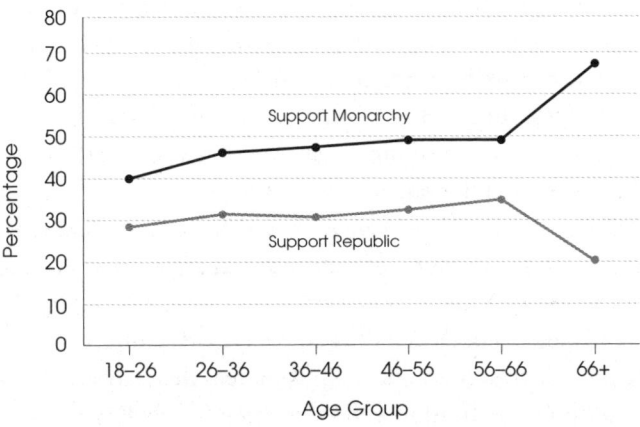

Figure 2.2: Attitudes to Monarchy by Age (Voters)
Source: New Zealand Election Study, 2011.

more 18–24-year-olds supported a republic than the monarchy, by 2011 there had been a dramatic shift, with some 59 per cent of young voters who expressed an opinion* preferring the monarchy, compared with 41 per cent opting for a republic. In the absence of other factors, the most plausible explanation for this shift in the opinion of young voters is the 'Duke and Duchess of Cambridge effect', with the marriage of the young couple having taken place only a matter of six months before the 2011 survey was conducted. Support for the monarchy among older age groups followed a predictable pattern, with the highest levels being found among those over the age of 65 (see Figure 2.2).

---

* 'Don't knows' were not included in this calculation.

The obvious affection for the Queen and her family felt by many older women is reflected in the gender breakdown, with 67 per cent of women who expressed an opinion favouring retention of the monarchy, compared with 61 per cent of men. Not surprisingly, those born in Britain expressed greater support for the monarchy (77 per cent) than New Zealand-born respondents (65 per cent), and those without a university education were more likely to be monarchists (68 per cent) than those with (58 per cent). Finally, the 2011 survey results reveal a significant difference in attitudes based on party vote, with some 63 per cent of Labour voters supporting retention of the monarchy, compared with 73 per cent of those who voted National. Strongest support for a republic was found among Green voters, most of whom were in the younger age groups (52 per cent).

Despite these and other pro-monarchist arguments, there is an equally strong set of reasons why New Zealand should become a republic. The first is concerned with the question of *relevance* and argues that the monarch is rarely in the country and that ties with Britain are attenuating. During her fifty-year-plus reign, Queen Elizabeth has made a total of ten visits to New Zealand, the most recent in 2002.* Whereas the early visits provided cause for national celebration and were attended by large and rapturous crowds, more recent visits have been low-key affairs, sometimes with a particular purpose in mind, such as the 14th Commonwealth Heads of Government Meeting in Auckland in November 1995. While the Queen's advanced age is likely to preclude any further visits, some regard their infrequency as symptomatic of a larger problem, the gradual weakening of New Zealand's political, economic and cultural links with Britain. The decision to join the European Economic Community, as the European Union was once called, marked an important watershed in the British government's relations with the Commonwealth, including New Zealand. Although it continued to play a role as the symbolic head of the Commonwealth, from the time it joined the European body in 1973, Britain was first and foremost an integral part of Europe. When, in the 1980s, New Zealand had disagreements with France over atmospheric

---

* Previous visits by the monarch were 1953–54, 1963, 1970, 1974, 1977, 1981, 1986, 1990 and 1995.

nuclear testing in the South Pacific, and with the United States over the visit of nuclear-powered and -armed ships, the British government led by Margaret Thatcher took the side of the two major powers, not that of New Zealand. As well as striking a more independent stance both politically and strategically, New Zealand became significantly less dependent on its historic trading links with Britain. As we saw in chapter one, the country's major trading partner is now China, followed by Australia, the United States and Japan.

A second argument in support of a republic focuses on the *accountability* of the role of head of state. According to this argument, despite its reputation as one of the world's earliest and most stable democracies, New Zealand is represented by an institution in which the monarch is selected, not on the basis of personal aptitude or ability, nor by an elected government or vote of the people, but rather by virtue of being the first-born in a quaintly aristocratic family called the Royal House of Windsor. Given the absence of any tradition of retirement or, with the exception of Edward VIII, resignation, we can fairly safely assume that Princes Charles, William and George will occupy the throne for the remainder of the twenty-first century.

A further reason frequently advanced for the abolition of the monarchy is based on the argument that it lacks *legitimacy*. According to this argument, it is inappropriate for a sovereign state such as New Zealand to be governed by a foreign institution, especially one so remote both culturally and socially. Despite the present monarch's empathy with the needs of the country and its people, a sentiment best exemplified by her concern in the wake of the Christchurch earthquakes, the Queen is not a New Zealander and thus can hardly be expected to represent the values and aspirations of its people. In 2013, a former Deputy Secretary of Foreign Affairs and Trade, Peter Hamilton, claimed that having the Queen as head of state was holding the country back politically and economically: 'We little realise in New Zealand that we have a head of state who – no fault of hers – cannot represent and advocate for us in any meaningful manner internationally' (Hamilton, 2013: A1).

A final major argument made by advocates of a republic concerns the *ease* with which any transition might take place. As we will see in the next chapter, creating a separate branch of government with its own independent political functions and enhanced powers is likely to have a significant bearing on the form and substance of the constitution. So how might reform be achieved with minimal disruption to existing constitutional and political arrangements? One obvious solution would be simply to rename the position of Governor-General, giving it the title of 'President', a move that would satisfy the public's desire to retain the essential features of the vice-regal position, including its largely symbolic functions, whilst at the same time creating a distinctly independent and indigenous institution. Appointment to such a position could be the responsibility of the duly elected government or Parliament. Alternatively, although more costly, it could be decided by a vote of the people.

However persuasive the pro-republican arguments might appear, they are unlikely to persuade those in charge of the government, certainly in the near future. Commitment to the monarchy remains strong within the National Party, particularly among its elected MPs, and while a vast majority of Labour and Green MPs would like to see New Zealand become a republic, there is no great sense of urgency to their campaign, partly out of fear that it might result in an electoral backlash among older and more socially conservative voters. While it has been argued that the path taken by Australia might cause a review of this decision, republican sentiment in that country has faded in recent years, and the election of a Liberal coalition led by Tony Abbott is likely to further delay any serious reconsideration of Australia's commitment to the monarchy. And while some have predicted that the death of the longest-serving monarch will provide an opportunity for countries such as Australia and New Zealand to break existing ties with the monarchy, the popularity of the young royals means that such an outcome is by no means assured.

Conclusion

There are at least three schools of thought on the continuing relevance of the Westminster model: the first takes the view that the model continues to be an accurate depiction of the British archetype; the second argues that it has been so compromised as to have lost any real relevance; and the third adopts a moderate stance by arguing that the model's intrinsic flexibility gives it some remaining relevance, even in the face of reform (Dunleavy, 2006). When applied to New Zealand, the first of these three perspectives raises a number of issues. With regard to at least three of the elements listed in Table 2.1 – two-party system, simple plurality elections and one-party government – New Zealand no longer conforms to the Westminster model, although it can be argued that this is hardly surprising, given that a model is merely an idealised theoretical construct. Only on the measures of a unitary state, sovereign Parliament and dominant executive does New Zealand comply fully with the model.

Of particular significance to the debate over New Zealand's future as a Westminster democracy was a series of events culminating in the decision to replace the plurality electoral system with MMP. The gradual decline of National and Labour as mass-membership parties was followed by the proliferation of new breakaway movements, each representing a small group of disaffected voters. As a result, the seeds of a multi-party system were sown. The perceived unfairness of plurality voting for supporters of the new parties, together with growing public concern that single-party majority government had too much power, gave rise to yet another development, the decision by referendum to adopt the German system of proportional representation. This in turn resulted in a consolidation of the multi-party system and the replacement of majoritarian government with a succession of coalition and minority governments. Such an outcome would not have surprised the French political scientist Maurice Duverger, who once observed, 'in no country in the world has proportional representation given rise to a two-party system or kept one in existence' (Duverger, 1964: 245).

These quite radical effects of the new electoral system notwithstanding, a number of perceived departures from the Westminster model may not be as significant as appearances suggest. First, although the abolition of New Zealand's upper house, or Legislative Council, brought to an end a distinctive feature of the Westminster system, namely 'asymmetric bicameralism' (a two-house parliament in which the lower house plays the dominant role), the importance of this development should not be overstated. By the time the Legislative Council was abolished, its influence had diminished to a point where it no longer played any useful role within the decision-making process. Indeed, some have gone so far as to argue that its demise signalled a strengthening rather than a weakening of Westminster democracy, in so far as it resulted in a further concentration of power in the hands of a single chamber (Jackson, 1987: 113). Evidence of its irrelevance to the legislative process can be seen in the lack of any significant opposition to abolition, either on the part of the government or the wider public (Kumarasingham, 2010). When, almost four decades later, the National Party leader, Jim Bolger, suggested the reintroduction of an upper house, only 26 per cent of respondents to a national survey were in agreement (Herald–NBR survey of 2000 respondents, reported in *New Zealand Herald*, 27 July 1988: 2).

Secondly, while there has been a move from a purely representative system of democracy to one in which voters engage directly by way of petitions and plebiscites such as citizens'-initiated referenda, these are non-binding mechanisms that the politicians may and often do ignore. And thirdly, while the two-party system has been replaced, the new configuration continues to be dominated by two parties, at least electorally, with the contribution of the small parties creating more of a mirage-like effect than one based on genuine multipartism (Curtin and Miller, 2010). In short, while New Zealand has been described as 'no longer a good, let alone the best, example of the "true British system"' (Lijphart, 1999: 27), it is hardly a close fit with the alternative pluralist model of democracy, key features of which include constitutional supremacy and a decentralised and federal system of government.

Chapter Three

Constitution

Although New Zealand is one of only three countries without a written constitution,* constitutional issues are at the heart of our understanding of contemporary politics. More than a century and a half after the formation of the first elected Parliament, opinion remains divided on a range of constitutional issues, the most notable of which concerns the potential benefits and pitfalls of moving to a single, codified constitution. Given the complexity of the issue and its seemingly marginal importance to the lives of ordinary citizens, it is hardly surprising that the constitutional debate has been largely confined to members of the political and legal establishments. The decisions to abolish the upper house, enact a Bill of Rights and establish a local Supreme Court were made with minimal media scrutiny or attention to public opinion. When in 2000 a national conference was held with a view to stimulating discussion on the country's constitutional future, the proceedings were the object of media criticism for their 'hidden' agenda and focus on the views of a 'self-anointed elite' (James, 2000: 7).

At the heart of New Zealand's constitutional debate is the importance of the Treaty of Waitangi to the nation's distinctive identity, as well as to the settlement of historic claims against the Crown. At the last major constitutional review, that begun by the Māori and National parties in

---

* The other two countries are the United Kingdom and Israel.

2008 as part of their post-election government negotiations process, every effort was made to engage the public in a nationwide discussion. Taking its cue from the quasi-constitutional debate that preceded the 2011 mixed-member proportional (MMP) referendum, throughout 2013 a government-appointed advisory panel representing a combination of expert and lay opinion invited public feedback on various constitutional proposals, including the place of the Treaty of Waitangi in New Zealand's constitutional arrangements, the size of Parliament and the length of the parliamentary term, and whether to fix the date of each election. The panel's 'conversation' with New Zealanders included public meetings, media interviews, the dissemination of information via an official website and extensive use of social media.

Of course, no constitutional review is complete without attention to the question of individual and minority rights. The intimate nature of New Zealand society, together with its strong democratic tradition, help to reinforce an assumption that the rights and liberties of individual citizens are both self-evident and forever guaranteed. Matters upon which it is easy to become complacent include the time-honoured freedoms of thought and expression, as well as conscience and religion. While there is legal recourse to government statutes, notably the Bill of Rights Act 1990 and Human Rights Act 1993, none is entrenched, with the result that their provisions can be overridden by a simple parliamentary majority or taken for granted and ignored. The potential pitfalls of current constitutional arrangements also extend to indigenous and minority rights, including the provisions of the Treaty of Waitangi. While the Treaty's authority is recognised in a number of government statutes and court decisions, debate continues on whether it should enjoy the protection of supreme law.

What is a Constitution?

Constitutions are often the product of dramatic events, such as a war of independence (e.g., United States, 1787), civil war (Ireland, 1922), fall of an authoritarian regime (Germany, 1949) or the threat of nationalist separatism (Canada, 1982). On the other hand, they may also be a product of slow, intermittent and at times seemingly random reform, especially as young countries move from their colonial status towards full independence. Despite an early tendency to replicate the values of its colonial past, New Zealand's path to independence followed a very different trajectory from that of other former colonies. As a written constitution might have shown, this was not only reflected in the story of the nation's political and economic development, but also in the character and opinions of its people. As we saw in chapter one, as well as absorbing much of the culture and history of its indigenous population, New Zealand adopted a distinct set of values based on its remoteness and physical isolation, self-sufficiency, egalitarianism and social liberalism, together with its close ecological and working relationship with the land. In short, as one authoritative source has observed, 'Constitutions do not stand still – they develop over time' (Palmer and Palmer, 1997: 2).

A constitution serves two basic functions: first, as a *framework* for orderly and, for many democratic countries, limited government; and second, as a *map* that charts a nation's history, values and priorities. The first of these typically lays out the functions of the various political institutions, the relationship between them, and the distribution of power, such as that between the legislative, executive and judicial branches of government. The second, mapping function is concerned with an elaboration on the nature of the political culture and the rights and responsibilities of individual citizens, and may include a Bill of Rights. A primary concern of the framers of the United States Constitution was the protection of civil and political rights. In other constitutions, most notably the former Soviet constitution, the main focus may be on economic and welfare rights, perhaps including the right to a job, adequate housing, free education and health care, and state pensions for those in old age. It is sometimes argued that one of the benefits of written constitutions is that, in charting the nation's political and cultural development, they contribute to a more politically informed and engaged electorate.

For a classic example of a written constitution we need look no further than the United States. Unlike more detailed constitutions, such as that of India, with its 448 articles and 100 amendments, the United States Constitution is made up of just seven articles, together with some 27 amendments, the first ten of which were passed in 1791 and became known as the Bill of Rights. At the heart of the American constitution is the doctrine of limited government. According to one constitutional expert (McIlwain, 1939: 244), there can be no doubt as to the importance of this doctrine in any constitutional system:

> Constitutional government is and must be 'limited government' if it is constitutional at all. Whatever its form may be, whether monarchical, aristocratic or democratic, in any state that we may properly call constitutional, the supreme authority must be defined and defined by a law of some kind. That law may be unwritten and entirely customary, as it has been for the greater part of its history; or it may be set forth in a single official document as in our state and federal institutions, but in every case it is a law that puts bounds to arbitrary will.

For the United States, 'limited' government had its origins in the fear that, unless all precautions were taken, the new nation might suffer the same despotic rule that had caused many to migrate from Europe to the New World. The framers of the constitution believed that limited government could best be achieved through the separation of powers between the legislative, executive and judicial branches of government. The resulting lattice of checks and balances came to define relations between the branches, as well as between federal and state governments. Thus, for example, whereas the two houses of Congress were given the power to pass new laws, it was the role of the president to execute the laws and that of the judiciary to adjudicate, drawing on the overriding authority of the constitution and the convention of judicial review. Furthermore, rather than allowing the legislature to choose the president, the constitution specified that the president be elected by the people, and for a four-year term (later reduced to a maximum of two four-year terms). When it came to removing the president from office, the powers of impeachment for 'treason, bribery, or other high crimes and misdemeanors' (Article II, Section 3) were to be shared by the two houses of Congress, with the House of Representatives proposing the Articles of Impeachment and the Senate, presided over by the Supreme Court's Chief Justice, voting on whether or not the president should be removed from office. Despite the attention given to the Nixon and Clinton impeachment trials, no president has ever been removed from office in this way.*

As any constitutional history will show, simply declaring a commitment to the doctrine of limited government is not in itself sufficient to prevent a shift in the balance of power from one branch of government to another. With the postwar emergence of the United States as the dominant world power, the acquired powers of the modern president *vis-à-vis* Congress and the courts have become immense, especially in foreign affairs, national security and the use of military force. As President Woodrow Wilson once predicted, 'Our President must always, henceforth, be one of the greatest powers of the world, whether he act greatly and wisely or not' (Dahl, 1967: 98). As Commander in Chief of the armed forces, the modern president has successfully usurped any implied power to declare and conduct military action, although recourse to Congress has had to be sought where substantial funding is required, or where, as, for example, in the case of punitive action against Syria by the Obama Administration in 2013, the president needs to turn the tide of public opinion towards military engagement.

As well as checking the powers of one branch of government against the others, the framers of the constitution also sought to constrain the powers of government *vis-à-vis* the civil liberties and rights of individual citizens. Among the broadly defined guarantees made to citizens were: freedom of speech, assembly, religion and the press (First Amendment); the right to bear arms (Second); security against unreasonable searches and seizures, and the security of the home (Fourth); and the protection of the 'life, liberty and property' of citizens before the law (Fifth). In the Tenth Amendment the Bill reinforced the limited nature of the powers of government at the federal level. While this emphasis on personal liberty is partly explained by the influence of the French Revolution on eighteenth-century thought, more recently it has been used both to defend

---

* The Articles of Impeachment have been invoked on only three occasions, the most recent being in the case of Richard Nixon (1974) and Bill Clinton (1998). Nixon resigned of his own accord, and Clinton narrowly survived a vote in the Senate.

American laissez-faire capitalism and to justify the lack of attention to minority, economic and welfare rights.

New Zealand's Constitutional Arrangements

While it lacks a codified constitution, New Zealand does have a constitutional structure comprising four basic elements:

1. Treaty of Waitangi
2. Statutes
3. Common law
4. Conventions

Treaty of Waitangi

Regarded by some to be the core element in New Zealand's constitutional structure, the Treaty of Waitangi was signed between Māori chiefs and the Crown on 6 February 1840 and in subsequent months. Its brevity and the ambiguity of some of its language have no doubt contributed to the ongoing public debate over its meaning and importance. While it enjoys the undisputed status of being the founding document of New Zealand, legal scholars and elected officials are in disagreement over its place in the nation's constitutional arrangements, with some advocating that it should be the cornerstone of any written constitution, while others view it as an historic document of little relevance to contemporary debate.* In its endorsement of the United Nations Declaration on the Rights of Indigenous Peoples, the New Zealand government acknowledged the importance of the Treaty of Waitangi as 'a unique feature of indigenous rights in New Zealand' (Constitutional Advisory Panel, 2012: 35). Its importance has also been recognised by the courts, with a Court of Appeal judgment observing that 'the Treaty principles require the Pākehā and Māori Treaty partners to act towards each other reasonably and with

---

* For a discussion on the range of viewpoints with respect to the place of the Treaty in the constitution, see James, 2000.

utmost good faith. The duty is not a light one. It is infinitely more than a formality' (ibid.: 37). In contrast, a former leader of the National Party, Don Brash, observed that the Treaty should be viewed in the context of race relations in the 1840s. As for its relevance to new laws, 'we should do away with vague and undefined references to the principles of the Treaty of Waitangi in legislation and government documents' (Brash, 2005).

Because the English-language version was long accepted as the authoritative version of the Treaty, the potency of the claims made in the Māori version was almost totally overlooked. In the first article of the English version, the Māori signatories and, by implication, those chiefs who had yet to sign, were characterised as yielding unlimited and absolute sovereignty to Queen Victoria. The reference in the Māori version to 'kāwanatanga' (or governorship), on the other hand, suggests a considerably weaker and less subservient relationship with the Crown than that suggested in the English version, a view confirmed by the second article, which asserted Māori chieftainship (tino rangatiratanga) over the whenua (lands), kāinga (villages) and taonga (treasures). In the third article Māori were granted the full rights of English citizenship.

The subsequent confiscation of Māori land had the understandable effect of seriously damaging relations between Māori and the rapidly growing Pākehā population, as well as giving rise to ever more insistent calls for redress by the Crown. However, it was not until 1975 that the Waitangi Tribunal was established. As a semi-judicial body, its task was to hear claims based on alleged breaches of the Treaty and, where compensation was deemed appropriate, to make recommendations to the government. Having been confined to hearing complaints dating from the Tribunal's creation in 1975, in 1985 its brief was extended to the consideration of claims dating back to the signing of the Treaty in 1840. Of the many cases to come before the Tribunal, among the most controversial have been those involving the transfer of state-owned land and other resources into the care of state-owned enterprises (SOEs), as well, of course, as partial and full private ownership. One such case involved the Māori Council's 2012 claim to the Waitangi Tribunal following the government's decision to sell off up to 49 per cent of the shares in several state-owned power companies, including Mighty River Power.

The Tribunal subsequently requested that the government delay the sales process until Māori rights and interests with respect to the affected lakes, rivers and streams were fully assessed.*

Statutes

Most Acts of Parliament, even those of constitutional significance, are passed by a simple majority and hence are considered to be ordinary law. Of the many statutes that address matters of constitutional importance, a few stand out. While the Constitution Act 1986 has some of the features of a written constitution, it is much less expansive in its coverage, and hence more limited in its impact. One of the main purposes of this Act was to end the prerogative of Britain's Westminster Parliament to pass laws for New Zealand, a right that dated back to early colonial days. In a further effort to catch up with the times, the Act brought clarity to a dispute over the orderly transfer of power (Brookers, 2012: 256–68). Following the 1984 election, the outgoing and incoming governments were at odds over the question of succession, with the outgoing Prime Minister, Robert Muldoon, refusing to take instruction from the incoming government on devaluation of the currency. As well as making it clear that there was nothing to prevent elected MPs not yet sworn in from being appointed as ministers, the Constitution Act specified the precise maximum length of the parliamentary term, including when Parliament must meet following an election. Although those drafting the legislation could not have known it at the time, the coalition negotiations process had the potential to extend well beyond the prescribed final opening date for the new Parliament.

Although Geoffrey Palmer, the architect of the New Zealand Bill of Rights Act 1990, had intended that its provisions be entrenched, thereby requiring a three-quarters vote of MPs or a majority vote by referendum for amendment of any kind, the Bill's opponents ensured that this did not occur. Despite its lack of protection in law, over time the Bill of Rights has come to occupy an important place in the country's constitutional history and is seen as a standard against which other legislation is measured for its

---

* In February 2013 the Supreme Court reached the unanimous decision that the government could proceed with the sale of shares in Mighty River Power.

impact on civil and democratic rights. The substance of the Bill of Rights Act bears a strong resemblance to similar legislation introduced elsewhere, including Canada's Charter of Rights (Arseneau, 1990: 24–27). Its specific provisions range across a number of civil and democratic rights, including: freedom of thought, conscience and religion; freedom of expression; the right to peaceful assembly; and freedom of association and movement. Also incorporated in the Act are non-discrimination and minority rights, as well as the rights of those who have been searched or detained. Finally, the Act guarantees the right of citizens from the age of eighteen years to vote and be elected to the New Zealand Parliament (Brookers, 2012: 275–80).

A third example of a statute of constitutional significance is the Electoral Act 1993. The Bill was drafted prior to the second MMP referendum of 6 November 1993 and provided a detailed account of the rules that would be employed in the event that voters opted to change the voting system. It provided for the establishment of an electoral commission (the New Zealand Electoral Commission) to oversee the electoral rules on such matters as registering political parties, promoting voter education and participation, and conducting research on electoral matters. The Act was later amended to give the commission additional powers, including maintaining a register on party spending and allocating broadcasting time and funds. Among the other provisions of the Electoral Act were the rules around: eligibility to vote; setting electoral boundaries; candidate selection and the conduct of elections; the qualifications required of parliamentary candidates and MPs; and how to fill vacancies caused by the death, retirement or resignation of an electorate or list MP. While parts of the Electoral Act are entrenched, constitutional experts have warned that its legal status is by no means secure and could conceivably be overridden by a simple parliamentary majority (for example, Harris, 2004: 281).

Our final example is the Supreme Court Act 2003, which ended the right of appeal to the Privy Council and created a New Zealand Supreme Court as the country's highest appellate court. As well as questioning the independence and competence of senior members of the judiciary, opponents of the Supreme Court Act criticised the government's willingness to proceed on the basis of a simple parliamentary majority and without recourse to a national referendum (Harris, 2004: 284). Government ministers, on the other hand, argued that it was inappropriate for English judges, regardless of their undisputed legal acumen, to be acting as the final arbiters on New Zealand law. Moreover, they reasoned, the decision to create a New Zealand Supreme Court was established Labour policy that had been signalled several years in advance.

Common Law

A third major source of New Zealand's constitution is to be found in the judgments of the courts. Whereas Parliament makes the laws, the courts interpret them in a process that can be traced back to the English Magna Carta 1297 and Bill of Rights 1688. Because the interests of justice and fairness demand that the decisions of the court are consistent, great weight is given to precedent and to the accumulated wisdom of the judiciary. Passage of the New Zealand Bill of Rights Act 1993 provided the courts with an important set of civil liberties upon which to base their decisions. As well as specified individual and minority rights, the courts were given direction on the principles of natural justice, including the minimum standards to expect in the event that a person is subject to arrest and detention. Geoffrey Palmer has noted that, over a thirteen-year period, the New Zealand Court of Appeal considered some 577 appeals that were concerned with matters raised in the Bill of Rights (Palmer, 2008: 4).

The influence of common law is also seen in the way the courts interpret the importance of the Treaty of Waitangi under New Zealand law. In a number of landmark decisions, the courts have upheld the Treaty, including the principles of partnership and good faith that are at the heart of the relationship between Māori and the Crown. On no issue is this more graphically illustrated than the courts' treatment of Māori rights *vis-à-vis* the foreshore and seabed, beginning with the Māori Land Court's 1997 decision in favour of eight Māori iwi in their case against the Marlborough District Council and culminating in the Court of Appeal's decision upholding the right of the Māori Land Court to determine which parts of the foreshore and seabed were customary land. As Matthew Palmer (2006) has pointed out, the common law claims that informed the debate had a rich history dating back more than a century. The outcome of this particular case was direct intervention by the government in the form of the Foreshore and Seabed Act 2004, which declared the Crown to be the owner of the foreshore and seabed of New Zealand. As Matthew Palmer has argued, it proved to be a case study in the supremacy of Parliament over the courts. With greater flexibility and goodwill on the government's part, a more amicable solution might have been reached through the courts. Instead, the new legislation was widely viewed as a breach of trust between the Crown and Māori. In an agreement between the Māori and National parties following the 2008 election, the Foreshore and Seabed Act was replaced by the Marine and Coastal Area (Takutai Moana) Act 2011. This new Act restored the notion of customary interest and declared that the marine and coastal areas were 'incapable of ownership'.

Conventions

Constitutional conventions are the rules that regulate and control the democratic system, giving it legitimacy, order and structure. Because Parliament is sovereign, it can pass any laws. Power is shared between the three branches of government, with the monarch and her New Zealand representative playing a largely symbolic role within the political process. The executive adheres to a set of rules laid down in the *Cabinet Manual*, including the conventions of collective Cabinet responsibility and individual ministerial responsibility (New Zealand Government, 2008). Implementing the decisions of the executive and maintaining order from one administration to the next requires a public service that is independent, politically neutral, and capable of offering a range of services and advice to the incoming government.

Codified Constitution?

Debate over whether the existing constitutional provisions should be incorporated in a single, codified constitution can be reduced to a few arguments (see Constitutional Advisory Panel, 2013: 13–16; and James, 2000).

Argument Against

1. **It gives excessive power to unelected judges.** Elevating the constitution to supreme law will have the effect of replacing a sovereign

Parliament with an all-powerful judiciary. By increasing the powers of judicial review, a codified constitution would place considerable power in the hands of an unrepresentative and unelected body, as well as potentially compromising its political independence and neutrality. It is also likely that the courts will be tied up in complex and expensive litigation, a result that will advantage those with substantial personal resources.

2. **It locks in future generations.** One of the potential benefits of drafting a constitution early in a nation's political history is that it is easier to reach consensus over its core values, a goal that is less likely to be achieved as the political culture develops and becomes more fractured. Despite more than 150 years of accumulated wisdom, any attempt to produce a codified constitution will be largely defined by the experiences of the late twentieth and early twenty-first centuries. As one scholar has observed, 'I'm skeptical . . . that this group of people here today . . . know what is best for our children and grandchildren. It is paternalistic and presumptuous to write down rules binding generations to come. You had better not get it wrong' (Allen, 2000: 392).

3. **A constitution doesn't necessarily prevent an imbalance in the distribution of power.** As we have seen, even the American constitution, with its finely tuned commitment to checks and balances and the separation of powers, has been unable to prevent the growth of presidential power, or, on the other extreme, a paralysis of legislative decision-making, as one of the two houses of Congress or one branch of government checkmates the other. When in October 2013 an extreme faction of the Republican Party in the House of Representatives managed to orchestrate a shut-down of the United States federal government's non-essential services over the President's health-care reforms, Barack Obama opined that 'one faction of one party, in one house of Congress, in one branch of government' had been able to close down the entire government (Foster, 2013). As other examples would also confirm, the growth of factional politics and executive government are features of contemporary politics that no written constitution has been able to prevent. As one American constitutional expert has observed, 'What has preserved our political

stability is not a poetic piece of parchment, but entrenched institutions and habits of thought . . .' (Seidman, 2012).

4. **Where is the mandate?** One of the most striking features of any constitutional debate is the absence of public interest or pressure for change. Despite the fact that New Zealand has been a laboratory of social and political change, much of it elite-driven, but also some that was in response to public demand, the idea of a written constitution has failed to generate any discernible public interest. It is hardly surprising, therefore, that the attempt by the Constitutional Advisory Panel in 2012 and 2013 to conduct a 'conversation' with the New Zealand public on suggestions for constitutional reform was met with deafening silence.

5. **Problem of reaching a consensus.** A characteristic common to most parliaments, but especially those with a strong two-party tradition, is their dedication to partisan politics. Because of the potential importance of a written constitution for the entire political system, but especially for the balance of power between the three branches of government, reaching a sufficiently broad consensus across the party system is likely to prove difficult, if not impossible. On issues that would require significant constitutional change, such as replacing the monarchy and entrenching the provisions of the Bill of Rights, the conservative instincts of the National Party are likely to prevail, with the result that it would require a determined effort from a coalition on the centre-left of the political spectrum, supported by an overwhelming majority of voters, to provide a sufficiently broad consensus for change.

6. **'If it ain't broke, don't fix it'.** Despite the merits of some criticisms of current constitutional arrangements, making a plausible case for a state of constitutional *crisis* is much harder to sustain. One major strand of the constitutional debate of the 1980s and 1990s was the dominance of the executive over the legislature, giving rise to complaints that the executive was exercising 'unbridled power'. While some of that imbalance has been corrected under MMP, there is every prospect that a codified constitution will create further imbalances, such as those between elected politicians and an unelected judiciary.

Argument For
1. **Signpost to national sovereignty and identity.** One of the obvious benefits of a codified constitution is that it can help to bring clarity to a nation's identity, as well as define its political values and aspirations. Had New Zealand gone through this process early in its development, it would have been forced to confront the nature of its relationship with the United Kingdom, as well as think more seriously about the partnership between indigenous Māori, European settlers and the Crown. As Bruce Jesson has observed, 'New Zealand's colonial background is one of the defining features of this country, yet it is the subject of an embarrassed silence. The economic, political and social patterns that were established in the mid-nineteenth century are still pervasive, but their history and their continuing influence are not acknowledged' (Jesson, 2001: 7). Although Jesson was not suggesting that New Zealand adopt a codified constitution, his sentiments resonate with those of some advocates of constitutional reform.
2. **Makes for orderly and restrained government.** Because it defines and delineates the role, functions and powers of the legislature, executive and judiciary, a codified constitution offers the practitioners of politics a reliable framework or blueprint for orderly and democratic government. As well as dividing and limiting the powers of each branch of government, such a constitution might be able to resolve some of the uncertainty with respect to the following: the role of the Treaty; the independence and powers of Parliament *vis-à-vis* the executive; the role of the courts, especially in relation to judicial review; and the constitutional role to be played by local government.
3. **If accompanied by an entrenched Bill of Rights, a constitution protects individual and minority rights.** Not only was New Zealand very late in enacting a Bill of Rights, but when it did, it failed to offer the protection of entrenched law. This means that any rights can be amended or removed by the vote of a simple parliamentary majority. Although a responsible majority is unlikely to let that happen, the very possibility creates a sense of uncertainty and vulnerability. On the other hand, a constitutionally entrenched Bill of Rights recognises that '[p]rotecting the interests of "discrete and insular minorities"

is difficult and becomes increasingly so the more a society relies on majority rule' (Palmer and Palmer, 1997: 267). But it is not simply minorities but also individuals who require the protection of supreme law. Spying on individual citizens and residents by the Government Communications Security Bureau (GCSB) became a matter of public concern following the illegal surveillance, and later arrest, of the internet businessman Kim Dotcom. As the Dotcom saga began to unfold, it also became apparent that the GCSB had illegally spied on some 88 New Zealanders over the preceding decade (New Zealand Government, 2013).

4. **Educative value.** Constitutions are said to have a value seldom discussed in the academic debate, and that is to educate the public on the values of democratic government, the structure and functions of the political institutions, and the rights and liberties of individual citizens. One of the reasons often given for the lack of political engagement, especially among the young, is the absence of any formal education or training in civics. In this respect, New Zealand is often contrasted with the United States, a country that not only exalts its constitution, but also uses it as a basis for teaching young and new Americans in the rights and responsibilities of citizenship.

5. **Besides, almost all other countries have one.** At the risk of sounding trite, advocates of a written and codified constitution adopt the view that, since virtually every country has one, not to follow in their footsteps is something akin to an act of constitutional recklessness. Recent examples of countries producing their own codified constitutions and, in some cases, charters of rights, include a number of the new democracies of Eastern Europe, together with Africa and parts of Asia.

Conclusion

By commissioning an advisory panel to hold a conversation with the public and report back on the possibility of a codified constitution, the government was opening the door to at least two important questions: first, should New Zealand have such a constitution; and second, what should it include? For example, should a constitution incorporate the provisions of the Treaty of Waitangi and the New Zealand Bill of Rights? Even the most committed supporters of a codified constitution are prepared to concede that it will create uncertainties, especially with respect to the political role of the judiciary and its likely impact on the distribution of political power. Then there is the question of need. Clearly, the argument for a constitution would be easier to make in times of constitutional crisis, or perhaps social, economic or political dislocation. However, whenever a codified constitution has been proposed, it has been the government's wish to proceed with incremental rather than radical change, as exemplified by the passage of the Bill of Rights Act 1990 (as ordinary rather than supreme law) and the Citizens' Initiated Referendums Act 1993 (to be indicative rather than binding). Perhaps the most compelling explanation for the incremental nature of constitutional change has been the lack of a clear mandate to go any further. As a result, while there has been strong support for a codified constitution among constitutional groups and societies, and occasionally from Labour, no government has endorsed the suggestion, mainly, it would seem, through lack of public interest or support.

Given this lack of public interest, why did National agree to the idea of a constitutional review when it came into government in 2008? The reasons are straightforward and largely concerned with creating a public perception of openness, receptiveness to the concerns of the government's support parties and concern for the needs of Māori. The lead National minister, Bill English, would have known from the outset that a codified constitution was unlikely to win any significant public support. If that were to be the case, then there was no danger in considering other options that were dependent on the creation of a codified constitution, specifically the incorporation of the Treaty and an entrenched Bill of Rights. This left National with a few modest proposals that might well prove attractive, such as a longer parliamentary term and a possible reduction in the size of Parliament. Yet to be determined is the question of how any proposals for constitutional reform might be enacted. In the event that the advisory panel proposed minor reforms, should any resulting decisions be mandated by the government, a two-thirds or three-quarter majority in the nation's Parliament or, as with previous decisions on changing the electoral system, a majority vote in a binding or indicative referendum?

Chapter Four

Parliament

Although New Zealand's 160-year-old Parliament ranks ninth among the world's longest-serving parliaments, unlike many other legislative bodies, notably the British House of Lords, its importance has little to do with its longevity or arcane traditions. As the country's only nationally elected political institution, it is without rival in its ability to represent the interests of a diverse national community (hence the alternative title 'House of Representatives'), scrutinise the activities of the Prime Minister and Cabinet, and seek public endorsement by way of frequent, regular and free elections. Responsibilities such as these do have their limits, however. Despite the frequently expressed claim that a sovereign parliament can do pretty much as it likes, in reality the New Zealand Parliament is subordinate to the executive at all stages in the legislative process. While it is the responsibility of Parliament to consider, amend and approve all Bills, initiating new legislation is largely the preserve of Cabinet and the wider executive. As we will see, only the introduction of minority and coalition government has posed a challenge to the long-held assumption that the executive, not the elected Parliament, is the powerhouse of the political system.

Because Parliament is a chamber of deliberation and debate, much of it involving the cut-and-thrust of party politics, with up to seven or eight different parties participating at any one time, critics accuse it of being undisciplined, wasteful and excessively divisive. There are good reasons for this view, particularly given that the main focus of public attention tends to be on the adversarial nature of the contest rather than on the decidedly more constructive work of its less prominent committees. Whereas some regard any form of disagreement as distasteful, others appreciate the irony that pervades much of the political discourse, with MPs posturing as dramatic actors within a Parliament that is as much live theatre as a serious decision-making body. Despite the aptness of such imagery, however, it risks trivialising Parliament's role, as well as that of its elected representatives. Although most new legislation is introduced at the behest of the executive, Parliament retains some important powers, including responsibility for 'supply', which involves the approval of budgets and taxes, as well as 'confidence', in the event that the legitimacy of the government's parliamentary majority is questioned. Because losing a confidence motion will either bring the government down or force an early election, much effort during the government formation process is devoted to extracting pledges from the small support parties to back the government on any confidence and supply motions introduced by the opposition. But Parliament also has the important role of granting 'free' or 'personal' votes on a growing number of conscience issues. Recent examples of these have included the prostitution, anti-smacking, marriage equality and alcohol reform Bills.

As well as examining the role, functions and powers of the New Zealand Parliament, this chapter will address three unresolved issues. The first is concerned with the debate over the most appropriate size of the New Zealand Parliament, especially in light of the results of a citizens'-initiated referendum (CIR) (1997), which found that some 81.5 per cent of respondents supported a reduction in the number of MPs from 120 to 99. A second issue is whether the parliamentary term should remain at three years or be extended to four, as has been suggested by a number of politicians, including Prime Minister John Key. On the two previous occasions when a referendum was held on this issue, approximately two-thirds of voters opted to retain the three-year parliamentary term. A third consideration is whether, in light of the formidable powers of government, with Parliament being described as something of a 'plaything of the executive' (Waldron, 2008: 20), New Zealand should reinstate the upper house, albeit with greater powers and democratic accountability than those given to the former Legislative Council. Concerns about the present unicameral (single-house) legislature tend to focus on the alleged absence of effective checks on the pace and extent of legislative reform.

Physical Setting

While the physical structure of the New Zealand Parliament lies adjacent to that of the executive branch of government, there is considerable overlap between the two institutions. The present Parliament House was completed in 1928 and includes the debating chamber, the Legislative Council chamber (or former upper house), the ornately carved Māori Affairs Committee Room and the Speaker's quarters. It also contains office space for the bulk of the MPs and their staffs. Sitting alongside Parliament House is the Parliamentary Library, which was constructed in the late 1890s and provides a rich resource for party research units, public servants, and individual MPs and their advisers. On the opposite flank of Parliament House lies the Beehive, the executive building that accommodates the Prime Minister, senior ministers and their staffs, the Cabinet room, and the parliamentary catering service and restaurant, known as Bellamy's. On the opposite corner on Lambton Quay is the 22-storey Bowen House, a modern office block that accommodates a number of ministers and backbench MPs. Also located within the parliamentary complex are the Parliamentary Service (an administrative unit with a staff of over 400), the Office of the Clerk of the House and the 135-member Parliamentary Press Gallery.

As well as occupying common physical space, there is considerable overlap in the role and functions of ministers and MPs. Since ministers must also serve as elected MPs, approximately 20 per cent of parliamentarians at any given time will also have ministerial responsibilities. This distinctive feature of the Westminster system contrasts with the American separation of powers doctrine, which dictates that all members of Congress taking up a post in the executive branch of government must first resign their congressional seat. Quite apart from New Zealand's constitutional requirement that a minister must be a sitting MP, there are significant workload implications for those who combine the two roles (see chapter

Table 4.1: Composition of the 2014–2017 Parliament (as of March 2015)

	% Party Vote	Electorate Seats	List Seats	Total Seats
National	47.04	40*	19	59
Labour	25.13	27	5	32
Green	10.70	0	14	14
NZ First	8.66	1*	11	12
Māori	1.32	1	1	2
Act	0.69	1	0	1
United Future	0.22	1	0	1

Source: New Zealand Electoral Commission, 2015, http://www.electionresults.govt.nz/electionresults_2014/.

* Following the Northland by-election of March 2015 National went from 41 to 40 electorate seats and New Zealand First from zero to one.

five). Since the arrival of the mixed-member proportional (MMP) electoral system, ministers who have wanted to continue their executive work in Wellington during weekends and when Parliament is in recess have been able to do so more easily by nominating for the party list. Ministers with heavy portfolio responsibilities preferring to serve as list members have included Michael Cullen (Finance Minister, 1999–2008), Steven Joyce (Economic Development, 2008–) and Tim Groser (Overseas Trade 2008–).

The horseshoe layout of the parliamentary chamber, with government MPs on one side and opposition MPs on the other, gives physical shape to the adversarial nature of two-party politics that has long defined Westminster parliaments. Beginning with the formation of the National Party in 1936, the two major parties dominated Parliament to the exclusion of all competitors save for the Social Credit Political League, which had solitary wins in the seats of Hobson in 1966, Rangitikei in 1978, East Coast Bays in 1980 and Pakuranga in 1984. One of the features of MMP has been a repopulating of the crossbenches by small parties, notably the Alliance, New Zealand First, Act, Green, United Future and Māori parties. This reconfiguration into a multi-party chamber notwithstanding, the most telling verbal exchanges are those that take place between the two major parties, with the Prime Minister and senior frontbench government ministers lined up on one side of the House and the opposition leader and members of the ministry-in-waiting on the other. Because the junior MPs from both major parties are relegated to the backbenches, it is important that they catch the attention of their party leaders during question time and in contributions to debate. Although the seating arrangements make no distinction between the 71 electorate MPs and 50 list MPs, the former group dominates the senior ranks of each major party, largely on the grounds that the party list is a less secure option than a safe electorate seat (see Table 4.1).

Role and Functions

For a vast majority of MPs, the working week is divided between constituency responsibilities, which tend to occupy most of Monday and some of Friday, and those that bear on their duties as a parliamentarian. Apart from when it is in recess, the House sits on a Tuesday and Wednesday during the hours of 2 to 6 and 7.30 to 10 p.m., as well as on a Thursday from 2 to 6 p.m. Sitting hours may be extended to any other day except Sunday in the event that there is pressing legislative business to discuss. Each day the House sits, the Clerk prepares an Order Paper setting out the business for the day. Party caucuses meet on Tuesday morning and select committees (see following section) on Wednesday morning. Because Cabinet meets on a Monday, it is necessary for ministers to return to Wellington either during the weekend or first thing on Monday morning. Although most backbench MPs receive relatively little attention from the national media, government ministers and senior opposition MPs are kept busy issuing press releases and conducting media briefings and interviews.

The Standing Orders set out the rules and procedures that govern what Parliament does, including the circumstances under which business is conducted and points of order raised, the latter taking precedence over other business being discussed. Other matters covered in the Standing Orders 2011 include the rules of debate, how Bills become law, procedures for voting, the membership and role of select committees, and rules concerning the declaration by MPs of financial interests (see New Zealand Parliament, 2011). The Speaker, who is responsible for maintaining order and ensuring that the Standing Orders are observed, can impose a number of sanctions, including naming and suspending a member for a specified period ranging from 24 hours to 28 days. While the Speaker is normally a member of the governing party, this has not always been the case – in order to maintain its parliamentary majority, in 1993 the National government supported the appointment of a Labour member, Peter Tapsell, as Speaker. The Speaker is assisted by a Deputy Speaker and up to two Assistant Speakers.

The most important role of the House is to pass Bills into law. There are four categories of legislation:

1. **Government Bills:** The most common form of legislation, government Bills are introduced by ministers.
2. **Members' Bills:** These are proposed by MPs other than ministers. Unlike government Bills, they are drawn from a ballot, which is conducted at 12 noon on a sitting day. One of the most controversial such Bills in recent times was Labour MP Louisa Wall's Marriage (Definition of Marriage) Amendment Bill 2012.
3. **Local Bills** are introduced by a local authority and are usually specific to a locality and issue, such as rates or traffic in a particular municipality. An example of a local Bill is the Hutt City Council (Graffiti Removal) Bill 2012.
4. **Private Bills** are concerned with the interests of a particular individual or group of people, such as a church or sports body. Examples of private Bills include the Eden Park Trust Amendment Bill 2009, which proposed changes to the governance arrangements for Eden Park in light of the reconstruction work to be undertaken in preparation for the 2011 Rugby World Cup.

The passage of legislation normally follows five stages, with four involving the House as a whole. While an increasing number of government Bills are introduced under urgency, thereby avoiding the select committee stage in the process, most proceed through all five stages.

1. **First reading:** Following circulation of the Bill, it receives its first reading, during which time there is a debate and a vote to decide whether it should go to a select committee.
2. **Select committee stage:** At this important stage in the process, the nominated committee has the opportunity to discuss possible amendments to the Bill, as well as to consider any submissions from members of the public, some of which will be given in writing, while others will be delivered in person, either in the committee room of Parliament or by video. On occasions, select committees will receive submissions by travelling to different parts of the country.
3. **Second reading:** Having considered the purpose and implications of the Bill, MPs have the opportunity to debate the recommendations that have emerged as a result of the select committee's deliberations.
4. **Committee of the Whole House:** Unless Parliament's Business Committee decides that a Bill should bypass this fourth stage in the process, the Bill, along with any amendments recommended by the relevant select committee, will be considered by the House as a whole. At this stage, further amendments may be made, frequently on the recommendation of a minister.
5. **Third reading:** A final opportunity is provided to debate the Bill, after which a vote is taken, with all successful Bills then being prepared for Royal Assent. Given that almost no legislation, including the New Zealand Bill of Rights 1990, is entrenched, all that is required for a Bill to become law is a 50 per cent vote plus one. Although John Key's second government, that of 2011–14, commanded only 59 votes in a 121-member Parliament, the votes provided by the government's support parties, the Māori, Act and United Future parties, were sufficient to ensure passage of virtually all government-initiated legislation. Despite gaining an additional seat following the 2014 election, National remained short of an overall majority, a situation that required ongoing

negotiations with its three support parties and, in the unlikely event that their support was not forthcoming, with at least one other parliamentary party.

Select Committees

While the public face of Parliament is the debating chamber, select committees provide an opportunity for MPs to specialise in particular areas of public policy, as well as to work constructively across ideological and party divisions. Allocation of positions on the thirteen permanent subject committees (see Table 4.2) and the five specialist committees, together with any *ad hoc* committees, is decided by Parliament's Business Committee, which appoints each MP to one or two committees. While the Standing Orders do not preclude ministers from serving on select committees, most choose not to.* One of the anticipated reforms of the new multi-party Parliament under MMP was the prospect that committee chairs would be drawn from across the party spectrum. However, this has not been the case. Using its majority or near-majority vote on each of the select committees, the governing party is normally able to secure the position of chair on each and every committee. In 2013, for example, National MPs chaired twelve of the thirteen subject-specific committees, with the Government Administration Committee, chaired by Ruth Dyson, being the exception (see the New Zealand Parliament website). Select committees vary in size from five to twelve members, with an average of nine. Because membership tends to reflect the distribution of parties in the House, typically each select committee has two or three representatives from the small parties.

As well as receiving public submissions and considering and amending Bills, select committees hear petitions and review finances and estimates and, where relevant, treaties. They can also conduct inquiries, although they have neither the independence nor the inquisitorial ability of their

---

* Exceptions during the term of the 2011–14 National-led government included Todd McLay, Minister of Revenue, who served on the Finance and Expenditure Select Committee, and Michael Woodhouse, Minister of Immigration and Veterans' Affairs, who served on the Social Services Committee.

Table 4.2: Parliament's Select Committees, 2014–2017

	Chair	Membership
Commerce	National	9
Education and Science	National	11
Finance and Expenditure	National	11
Foreign Affairs, Defence and Trade	National	10
Government Administration	Labour	6
Health	National	9
Justice and Electoral	National	10
Law and Order	National	9
Local Government and Environment	National	11
Māori Affairs	National	8
Primary Production	National	9
Social Services	National	10
Transport and Industrial Relations	National	11

Source: New Zealand Parliament, http://www.parliament.nz/en-nz/.

counterparts in the United States Senate and House of Representatives. Despite the frequency with which individuals and groups make submissions, especially on matters of great public interest, it can be argued that insufficient weight is often given to their opinions, especially if they run contrary to the wishes of a determined government. In 2004, for example, the government created an *ad hoc* committee to consider the Foreshore and Seabed Bill, which sought to circumvent any decision by the Māori Land Court giving Māori freehold title to parts of the foreshore and seabed in the Marlborough Sounds. The government's chosen solution was to put the foreshore and seabed of New Zealand into public ownership. The committee received some 4200 submissions, 94 per cent of which expressed opposition to the Bill (Marsh and Miller, 2012: 276). Despite this clear expression of opinion, the recommendation of the committee was that the Bill be passed with only minor amendment.

As well as select and *ad hoc* committees, there are also a number of standing committees that have been assigned the task of ensuring that Parliament's business is conducted in an orderly and effective manner. These include the Business Committee, which is chaired by the Speaker, as well as the Standing Orders and Privileges Committees, the latter dealing with charges of unparliamentary behaviour against individual MPs.

Parties in Parliament

Unlike the weak party systems found in several Western legislatures, notably those of the United States, New Zealand's political parties have a long history of internal cohesion and discipline, much of it a product of a two-party system that tended to produce small governing majorities. When the MPs from a particular party gather for their weekly meeting, they are said to be in 'caucus'. In 2015, National had a caucus of 59 voting members (having lost one seat following the Northland by-election in March), although attendance may be boosted by the presence of non-parliamentarians, such as the party president and designated ministerial officials. Under the coalition arrangements of MMP, there is provision for joint caucus meetings (New Zealand Government, 2008: 7.53: 94). For the same 2014–17 parliamentary term, Labour had a much smaller caucus of 32 members (two fewer than between 2011 and 2014).

Writing at the peak of the two-party era, Austin Mitchell observed that 'Labour and National bind their members to silence and surround their caucus with a web of secrecy unattainable in larger parties' (Mitchell, 1966: 53). Despite the transition to a multi-party system, the new parliamentary parties are similarly obliged to maintain strong internal discipline over their elected members, partly because their organisational structures and *modus operandi* tend to be modelled on those of the major parties from which most have sprung, but also because the advent of minority and multi-party government obliges small support parties to keep the promises made during the government formation process. Not to be able to guarantee that every caucus member will observe the confidence and supply agreement struck with the incoming government would have the potential to make that party an unreliable partner in government.

To help ensure that internal party discipline is maintained, the parties appoint enforcers, known as party Whips, although in the case of the Greens their preferred title is party 'musterer'. While caucus is chaired by the party leader, the Whips are responsible for ensuring that its decisions are upheld by all MPs, both in the House and in the work of the select committees. Permission to be absent from Parliament is given by the Whips, whose responsibility also includes assigning speaking duties, providing guidance on parliamentary tactics, and making sure that all members vote according to the directions of caucus. That either abstaining or 'crossing the floor' and voting with the opposing party are such rare events, and tend to occur with the explicit permission of the party leadership, owes much to the cohesion and discipline maintained within each party caucus, especially those of the two major parties. As we will see in future chapters, whereas the National caucus is solely responsible for the election of the party leader, the vote for the Labour leader, which was once the sole responsibility of its caucus, is now split between the caucus (40 per cent), the party members (40 per cent) and the affiliated unions (20 per cent). The first Labour leaders to be elected under the new rules were David Cunliffe in 2013 and Andrew Little in late 2014. When Labour is in government, its caucus decides who will be in Cabinet, although the allocation of portfolios is the responsibility of the Prime Minister. An important function of caucus is to consider all new legislation. When a party is in government, draft legislation will be discussed, often after briefings from the relevant minister, before being introduced to the House (New Zealand Government, 2008: 7.54: 94).

Although it used to be said that the small parties held their weekly caucus meetings in a telephone box, all take the need for collective decision-making seriously, despite their relative inexperience as party political organisations. In the early years of MMP, a number of MPs abandoned one party for another, giving rise to the introduction of the Electoral Integrity Act 2001, an initiative taken by Labour with a view to stemming the flow of 'party hoppers' or 'waka jumpers', especially among the small parties. Temporary instability had been an anticipated feature of MMP, as new parties were formed and parliamentary candidates recruited, often at short notice, to fill the highly experimental party lists. What proved most damaging, however, was the low incidence of shared commitment to the party's ethos, ideology and agenda. Following the defection of eleven MPs from the major parties to an assortment of new parties in the months immediately preceding the first MMP election, party hopping became a feature of parliamentary life. In 1997 a list MP, Alamein Kopu, resigned from the Alliance to become an Independent shortly after entering Parliament for the first time. Within a matter of months, a second list MP, Frank Grover, resigned from the Alliance to join the Christian Heritage Party. With the dismissal of Winston Peters from the government in 1998, almost half of New Zealand First's seventeen MPs became Independents, although some later founded a new party, Mauri Pacific. Consistent with the government's view that these defections were a temporary phenomenon, the Electoral Integrity Act was given a sunset clause, which took effect at the 2005 election. While the flow of party hoppers has since slowed down, it has not been brought to a stop, as illustrated by the defection of Hone Harawira from the Māori Party in 2009 and the expulsion from the New Zealand First caucus of Brendan Horan in 2012.

Despite the recent decline in levels of internal party discipline and unity under MMP, maintaining an impression of internal unity remains an important priority, especially for the two main parties. By and large, both have been successful, although Maurice Williamson's suspension from the National caucus in 2002 following his criticism of the leader at the time, Bill English, and the disagreement between the Labour leader, Phil Goff, and his former Cabinet colleague, Chris Carter, have provided rare glimpses of the tensions that can easily build within both leadership groups. Where tensions can easily spill over into much more public disharmony and division is over questions of leadership. Don Brash's successful bid to replace the incumbent, Bill English, for the party leadership in 2002 divided the National caucus for some considerable time, as did David Cunliffe's challenge to David Shearer for the leadership of the Labour Party in 2011, and again in 2013.

A further threat to the traditional discipline of the party vote is the increasing use of 'free' votes on matters of personal conscience. There has been considerable speculation as to the reasons for the growing incidence of free votes in the New Zealand Parliament, with the decline of institutional religion and the reluctance of parties to be seen to be taking a stand on issues of private morality providing two possible explanations (Lindsey, 2005). These have extended well beyond the traditional issue of alcohol consumption to include matters such as abortion, adoption, pornography and gay rights. While MPs are granted a free vote by their party caucuses, pressure may be brought by their party colleagues to vote in a particular way. Whether as a result of shared values, force of habit or pressure from one's peers, on many conscience issues there appears to be a strong correlation between party affiliation and the exercising of a 'free' or 'personal' vote. When the final vote was taken on the Civil Unions Bill 2005,* for example, 88 per cent of Labour MPs and 100 per cent of Green MPs voted in favour, and 89 per cent of National MPs and 92 per cent of New Zealand First MPs voted against.

Despite the obvious link between party affiliation and the way many MPs cast their conscience votes, it would be misleading to focus exclusively on this one source of influence. As voting patterns for the Marriage (Definition of Marriage) Amendment Bill 2012 show, personal identity and values, together with shifting public attitudes, clearly had some bearing on the way MPs, especially younger and more recently elected members, cast their votes. When the final vote was taken, 77 of the 121 MPs (64 per cent) voted to support same-sex marriages and 44 (36 per cent) voted against. While Labour and Green MPs were heavily in support of liberalisation (88 per cent and 100 per cent respectively) and New Zealand First remained firmly opposed (100 per cent), the most significant change from the 2005 Civil Unions Bill was the shift in voting patterns among National MPs, with 46 per cent voting in favour of the 2012 Bill and 54 per cent against. Support for the Marriage Amendment Bill was particularly strong among parliamentary women (82 per cent, including 73 per cent of National's female MPs) and younger age groups, especially the cohorts of MPs first elected in 2008 and 2011. On the other hand, opponents of the Bill were more likely to be men (84 per cent), longer-serving MPs, and representatives of rural and provincial town electorates. With the exception of those MPs representing Māori electorates, ethnic minority MPs across the party spectrum were more likely to be against than in favour.

---

* This Bill sought to allow gay couples to legally formalise their union. However, it did not extend to gay marriage.

Size of Parliament

It is frequently alleged that the New Zealand Parliament has too many elected members relative to the country's small population of between 4.5 and 4.6 million, with countries such as the United States (435 lower house members in a population of 314 million), Canada (308 members and 35 million) and Australia (150 members and 23 million) cited as examples of countries with leaner and more efficient *per capita* ratios of elected legislators. Although the New Zealand Parliament grew in size from 74 seats in the late 1800s to 80 in 1966 and 95 in 1986, critics have focused on the sharp increase that accompanied the introduction of MMP in 1996 (New Zealand Parliament, 1999: 1). When the Royal Commission on the Electoral System first recommended MMP, it suggested a Parliament of 120 members, although its first preference had been a 140-member chamber (Wallace, 1986: 127). The commission further recommended that there be a 50/50 split between electorate and list seats, with list seats being distributed in proportion to each party's share of the vote (ibid.: 128). Moreover, it readily acknowledged that the 'overhang' provision might result in a temporary increase in the size of Parliament until the following election.*

In the late 1990s, public opposition to the enlarged Parliament intensified, especially after the collapse of the first MMP coalition and the implosion of National's coalition partner, New Zealand First. At the 1999 general election, a citizens'-initiated referendum (CIR) asked voters: 'Should the size of the House of Representatives be reduced from 120 members to 99 members?' Much of the 81.5 per cent 'Yes' vote could be attributed to intense feelings of public cynicism and distrust, ironically sentiments that had caused voters to turn to MMP in the first place. The new category of MP, the list member, came in for particular attention, with critics accusing them of being party 'hacks' and raising questions about what they did and who they were elected to represent. Following Parliament's rejection of the outcome of the referendum, one

---

* An overhang is created when a party receives more electorate MPs than its entitlement, based on its share of the party vote. For example, at the 2008 election the Māori Party won five seats while receiving only 2.4 per cent of the party vote. As a result, the size of the 2008–11 Parliament increased to 122 members.

of the New Zealand First MPs introduced a member's Bill recommending cuts in the number of list MPs and a Parliament of no more than 100 members.* Although it passed its first reading, the Bill was overwhelmingly defeated on the recommendation of the relevant select committee. This was not the end of the matter, however. Among the issues to be considered by the 2010 government review of constitutional arrangements, public feedback for which was being sought as recently as 2013, was the size of the New Zealand Parliament. Although it failed to provide a comprehensive list of arguments in support of a possible reduction in the size of the House, one that was mentioned was the financial burden on taxpayers of maintaining a larger Parliament (Constitutional Advisory Panel, 2012: 14).

Table 4.3: Number of Seats and Population per Seat, 1896–2014

Year	Seats	Population	Population per seat
1896	74	0.74 m	10,043
1906	80	0.94 m	11,704
1916	80	1.15 m	14,365
1926	80	1.4 m	17,602
1936	80	1.6 m	19,673
1956	80	2.2 m	27,176
1966	80	2.7 m	33,461
1976	87	3.1 m	35,970
1986	95	3.3 m	34,811
1993	99	3.6 m	36,161
1996	120	3.7 m	30,680
2014	121	4.5 m	37,272

Source: Data drawn from Statistics New Zealand, 1998; and 2015.

As the data in Table 4.3 clearly show, while MMP was responsible for a surge in the number of MPs, comparing numbers of MPs over time on the basis of population per seat reveals a remarkably consistent pattern: indeed, had the former first-past-the-post (FPP) electoral system remained, the natural increase in national population statistics over the

---

* Known as the Electoral (Reduction in Number of Members of Parliament) Amendment Bill 2006.

past two decades would have resulted in incremental increases in the size of the House, bringing it close in size to the present 120-member Parliament. By expanding the analysis further to include the entire twentieth century we can see that, on a *per capita* basis, the current New Zealand Parliament is proportionately smaller than at any other time.

But how does the size of the New Zealand Parliament compare internationally? By limiting our analysis to countries of similar size it is possible to avoid a number of the pitfalls found when comparing New Zealand with the United States, Canada or Australia: as well as differences of scale, these countries are distinguished by their complex federal structures. With the exception of Costa Rica (57 elected members for a population of 4.8 million) and Singapore (99 and 5.4 million respectively), the New Zealand Parliament is of similar size to unicameral or lower house legislatures in the other small nation-states listed in Table 4.4. Perhaps the most useful comparison is that to be made between New Zealand and the legislatures of Norway, Denmark and Finland (neither Scotland nor Wales is a sovereign state). Serving a population of 37,272 constituents per seat, the New Zealand Parliament is somewhat smaller than the parliaments of the three Scandinavian countries, leading to the conclusion that, for sovereign and developed democracies of approximately four to five million people, a parliament of 120 (121 between 2014 and 2017) members is close to the optimum size for meeting the most basic requirements of fair and equal representation, as well as effective and accountable government.

Opposition to a smaller Parliament is based on three main arguments: first, it would compromise the quality of representation, both locally and nationally; secondly, it would risk weakening the effectiveness of the House, especially in holding the government of the day to account; and thirdly, it would reduce the pool of talent available for appointment to Cabinet and the wider executive (Wallace, 1986: 117–29). As we saw in chapter one, one of the acknowledged benefits of living in a small democracy is the close and intimate relationship that exists between the voting public and their elected representatives. The relatively small size of each electorate has made it possible for voters to engage with their politicians in ways not possible in much larger democracies, obvious examples of which include Germany, France, Britain and the United States. As well as

Table 4.4: New Zealand Parliament in Comparative Perspective

	Lower House seats	Upper House seats	Other (e.g., EU, Westminster)	National population (2014)	Population per MP
Costa Rica	57	0	0	4.8 m	84,210
Denmark	175	0	13	5.5 m	28,645
Finland	200	0	13	5.4 m	25,352
Ireland	166	60	12	4.6 m	18,930
New Zealand	121	0	0	4.5 m	37,272
Norway	169	0	0	4.7 m	27,810
Scotland	129	0	58	5.3 m	27,748
Singapore	99	0	0	5.4 m	54,545
Uruguay	99	31	0	3.4 m	26,153
Wales	60	0	34	3.1 m	32,978

affording the elected representatives the opportunity to become closely informed on local issues, as we will see in the next chapter there is a much greater chance that these local concerns will be represented on the national stage.

Of at least equal importance to the future of New Zealand democracy has been the need to increase Parliament's influence relative to that of the executive. One of the potential dangers of a small Parliament is the dominance enjoyed by an executive of 20 to 25 members in a party caucus that may number as few as 50 (as occurred as recently as the governing Labour caucus of 2005–8). By reducing the size of the Parliament to 99 or 100 members, it is argued, the opportunities to hold the Cabinet and wider executive to account and to control the flow of legislation emanating from Cabinet will become that much more difficult. However, the implications for the workings of Parliament are much more extensive than the numbers in caucus might suggest. In a smaller Parliament, MPs were required to sit on as many as three or four select committees at the same time. Today, it is much more likely that members will sit on no more than two committees, a workload that both allows for greater specialisation and strengthens the ability of the select committees to scrutinise the work of the executive.

A final argument against a smaller Parliament relates to the pool of potential talent available for promotion to the executive. While it is not unknown for first-term MPs to be promoted to the executive, they are more the exception than the rule, with Margaret Wilson, a former Labour Party president, Steven Joyce, National's campaign director, and Tim Groser, a former senior diplomat, serving as notable examples. But, as we will see in chapter six, there are also geographical, sectional, gender and ethnic considerations to bear in mind when appointing an executive, not to mention the obvious criterion of competence. As the number of replacements among the lowest ranked ministers would suggest, every prime minister (or Cabinet, in the case of Labour) has to make a number of compromises when appointing the members of a Cabinet, not least the need to balance certain quota considerations against the basic requirements of the job. It therefore stands to reason that the smaller the caucus the harder it is to come up with a sufficiently broad array of talent to fill all the required portfolios.

Term of Parliament

A proposal that has won support among senior politicians in both major parties is to increase the parliamentary term from the present three years to four years. When the New Zealand Parliament was first convened in the 1850s, the parliamentary term was set at five years. By the 1870s it had been reduced to three years, largely on the grounds that the public needed a more effective curb on the powers of government. Since then, the three-year term has been exceeded on only three occasions, all during times of national crisis.* In 1956 the three-year limit was entrenched in electoral law (Wallace, 1986: 156). More recently, it was incorporated in the Constitution Act of 1986, with the important proviso that a 'snap'

---

* One- to two-year extensions occurred during the First World War, the Great Depression and the Second World War.

election could be called at any time within the three-year cycle.* Two government-initiated referenda in 1967 and 1990 sought public approval for a four-year term. Although both were defeated by margins of over 68 per cent, lobbying in support of the longer term has continued, especially among the major parties, members of the business community and some media organisations, as well as right-wing bloggers and the decidedly pro-business think tank, the Maxim Institute. Given the strength of their arguments, it came as no surprise when the Constitutional Advisory Panel appointed by the National and Māori parties selected the four-year term as a potentially important area of constitutional reform, a step that will require either a 75 per cent vote of MPs or a simple majority in a national referendum (ibid.: 156).

Although New Zealand shares the three-year term with its closest neighbour, Australia, a vast majority of Western countries have either four- or five-year parliamentary terms. Countries with four-year terms include the nations of Scandinavia, as well as Germany, which gave New Zealand its MMP electoral system. Importantly, several of these countries have much in common with New Zealand: as well as enjoying a long democratic tradition, each has an enviable record of economic stability and prosperity. Those countries with a five-year term include the United Kingdom, Canada and France, although the election cycle rarely lasts a full five years. Whereas the United States House of Representatives faces re-election every two years, Senators are elected for six years, with one-third of the Senate being re-elected every two years.

Unlike the absence of a persuasive set of arguments in support of a smaller Parliament, the arguments for a four-year term are deserving of close consideration; indeed, they managed to convince the members of the Royal Commission on the Electoral System (Wallace, 1986: 164–65). They can be summarised thus: first, they allow for a longer-term legislative agenda than that available in the three-year cycle; secondly, four years provide the opportunity for better economic planning and management;

---

* Early elections were called in 1951, 1984 and 2002. Whereas the latter two took place in the same year as the scheduled election, the 1951 'snap' election occurred within two years of the previous (1949) election.

thirdly, they give voters greater opportunity to be informed and to judge the effectiveness of the incumbent government, as well as the claims of the opposition; and fourthly, triennial elections are not only more costly, they also prove to be unnecessarily disruptive to the way of life of the citizens. Of these arguments in support of a four-year cycle, perhaps the most telling has to do with the time constraints on any government to implement its full agenda, especially its economic agenda, before the next scheduled election. As a number of commentators have observed, a three-year term encourages short-term thinking on the part of the governing and bureaucratic elites, with the result that the more substantive, and sometimes necessary, reforms are too often avoided in favour of more pragmatic quick-fix solutions. One all-too-frequent observation of government ministers is that: in their first year, ministers attempt to come to grips with their new portfolios and government action is constrained by the economic problems inherited from the previous government; in the second year, attempts are made to rush through the government's legislative agenda, often with insufficient scrutiny by Parliament and members of the public; and the third year is dominated by the forthcoming election, notably the need to woo voters in sufficient numbers to form the next government.

Balanced against these arguments are at least four notes of caution: first, extending the parliamentary term to four years reduces the level of democratic accountability, an important loss in a country with no second chamber or federal system of government; secondly, four years gives increased powers to the executive, a potentially retrograde development in a country with no written constitution and few checks and balances on the power of the executive; thirdly, while an extra year may extend the life of a good government, it also increases the risk of bad government; and finally, while the focus of attention has been on the dangers of a single three-year governing cycle, in reality the New Zealand voting public is predisposed to give governments of modest achievement at least two, and often three, three-year terms. As the life cycle of New Zealand governments since 1935 shows (see Table 4.5), on average governments can expect to be re-elected and serve in office for close to nine years. By anyone's reckoning, this is a generous amount of time to plan and implement a legislative agenda of quite major importance, as illustrated by the radical policy agendas passed by the Fourth Labour Government between 1984 and 1990, as well as by National between 1990 and 1996.

Table 4.5: Number of Three-year Parliamentary Terms, 1935–2017

1 Term	2 Terms	3 Terms	4+ Terms
		National 2008–17	
		Labour 1999–2008*	
		National 1990–99†	
	Labour 1984–90		
		National 1975–84	
Labour 1972–75			
			National 1960–72
Labour 1957–60			
		National 1949–57	
			Labour 1935–49

* Labour–Alliance 1999–2002; Labour Progressives 2002–2008
† National–NZ First 1996–98.

Reinstating the Upper House

As we saw in chapter two, one of the most serious criticisms of the New Zealand Parliament concerns the lack of checks on the speed of legislative reform, causing one legal scholar, Jeremy Waldron, to observe that 'New Zealand has procedures for fast-track legislation which are quite disgraceful by world standards and which are utterly at odds with what Walter Bagehot called "the slow and steady forms necessary for good consideration"' (Waldron, 2008: 21). Because it is in the executive's interest to pass potentially controversial legislation with minimal scrutiny and deliberation, especially from the opposition parties, there is an increasing trend to pass Bills under 'urgency', thereby avoiding the select committee stage, including the opportunity for public submissions. As Waldron points out, such cavalier behaviour would not be possible in countries with a strong upper house, or in legislatures that respect the influence of their committees. While it was thought that, under MMP, the executive's ability to dictate the terms of the legislative process would be greatly reduced, this has not been the case, mainly due to the continuing dominance of the two major parties over their small support parties.

One obvious solution is to reinstate the upper house, although with significantly greater powers than those given to the former Legislative Council. Its role could be similar to that of the United States Senate, whose powers are equal to those of the House of Representatives and include the right to initiate legislation. Alternatively, its role could be restricted to the review of all legislation passed in the lower house. As the examples of the Irish, Canadian and Australian senates show, while upper houses can provide important checks on the legislative process, they also have a propensity to frustrate that process to a point where little gets done. Given their arcane traditions and close ties with the social and political establishment, upper houses are also remarkably resistant to reform, especially, as in the case of the United Kingdom's House of Lords, where long-held privileges are under theat.

Conclusion

The recent history of the New Zealand Parliament is best described as one of only modest reform. While the advent of MMP required that changes be made to parliamentary procedures, especially to accommodate the needs of a multi-party chamber and new category of MPs, the list members, the re-distribution of political power within the parliamentary chamber proved to be much less extensive than had been anticipated. The executive continued to dominate the legislative process, party caucuses exercised the same strong discipline over their members, and there were echoes of the former two-party system in the manipulation and control that continued to be exercised by the executive over Parliament's select committees. And while it was possible for the small support parties to frustrate the collective will of the governing party, this proved to be much less common than expected, mainly because of the pressure they were under to prove that small parties were as capable as the large parties of providing stable and constructive government (Miller and Curtin, 2011). Indeed, the only real suggestion that the parties' grip on their MPs might conceivably be weakening came from the increase in the incidence of free or conscience votes, as illustrated by the very different perspectives adopted by National MPs over the Marriage (Definition of Marriage) Amendment Bill 2012.

This leads to the question of whether Parliament is ripe for further and more extensive reform. Despite the public's wish for a smaller Parliament, there is little prospect of that occurring; indeed, pressure for a somewhat larger chamber is likely to grow in response to a combination of population growth and concern among MPs over increased workloads. Where public and elite attitudes are likely to coincide is in response to any suggestion that New Zealand should reinstate its upper house. Creating a further tier of politicians offends the populist instincts of many voters, many of whom are likely to assume that having a multi-party Parliament and government offers protection enough against hasty and ill-considered legislation. Of the reforms discussed in this chapter, the one most likely to be implemented is the four-year term, partly because the arguments for reform are widely accepted, but crucially because it enjoys support among senior figures in both major parties, as well as some of the small parties. However, increasing the term limit involves a process that any government will find difficult to navigate, especially given its vulnerability to claims that it is acting out of self-interest. As a result, it is likely to avoid the option of a 75 per cent vote in Parliament, preferring to take the alternative route of a simple majority in a government-initiated referendum.

In the absence of significant public or elite support for an upper house, one final reform that is relatively straightforward to implement, as well as being long overdue, is the strengthening of Parliament's select committees. The dual purpose of this initiative would be to increase the independence of parliamentary committees *vis-à-vis* the executive and to raise the level of public participation in the decision-making process (Marsh and Miller, 2012). If presented with the opportunity to play a more substantive role in the parliamentary system, select committees might conceivably: conduct their own investigations or enquiries including, where appropriate, the appointment of independent commissions (ibid.: 336); develop and shape public policy; foster public education, engagement and debate; hold the relevant ministries and their public servants to account; and provide a counterpoint to the current dominance of Cabinet. To achieve these goals, appointment to select committees, including the choice of chairs, should be the prerogative of Parliament rather than the executive. As a result, appointments of committee chairs may well be based as much on seniority and ability as party affiliation. Without having to create new political institutions or incur significant additional costs, strengthening the role of select committees might offer an opportunity to invigorate the democratic process and give genuine weight to the claim that the House of Representatives is, indeed, the 'People's Parliament'.

Chapter Five

Electoral System

The advent of the mixed-member proportional (MMP) system had a greater impact on New Zealand's political institutions and system of representation than any other innovation of the previous one hundred years. As we saw in earlier chapters, within the space of a single three-year parliamentary term a number of quite fundamental changes took place. Parliament was both enlarged and transformed from a two-party chamber to one consisting of up to seven or eight separate political parties. With the winning party no longer assured of its absolute majority, coalition and minority government became the order of the day. As for its influence on the way people vote, with two votes replacing the traditional one, there was now the opportunity for voters to give their party vote to one party and their electorate vote to another. With the introduction of a new category of MP, the list member, parties began to explore new forms of representation, including defining constituency not simply in terms of geographical location, but rather by gender, ethnicity, and other groups and interests.

Any major change is bound to attract its fair share of critics, especially among those who feel a sense of nostalgia for what they perceive to be an earlier golden age. As well as providing an assessment of how MMP works, this chapter will weigh up its perceived weaknesses and strengths. Whereas supporters tend to highlight its success in providing more diverse and effective representation, as well as reducing the power of government, detractors are of the view that it leads to less stable and effective government, gives too much influence to small parties, fails to bring clarity to the role of list MPs, and threatens the harmony and sense of common purpose that have long been features of New Zealand's democratic system. Drawing on data from the New Zealand Election Study, we will consider the extent to which attitudes to MMP are a reflection of party affiliation and age. Given that young voters have had no direct experience of voting in the former first-past-the-post (FPP) electoral system, for example, it seems reasonable to assume that they will be less attached to FPP than older voters.

A good way into understanding the contemporary electoral system's strengths and weaknesses, as well as the debates around its reform or replacement, is through the 2011 referendum. Although a parliamentary committee conducted a review of the MMP experiment following the 1999 election (a requirement of the 1993 Electoral Act), critics complained that any such review should have been the subject of a national referendum. In 2008, the incoming National government promised a referendum on MMP and its alternatives, with the referendum to be held in conjunction with the 2011 general election. In the event that a majority of voters supported the retention of MMP, a review would be conducted on how it might be improved. This chapter will provide an analysis of the reasons for the referendum, the structure and nature of the public debate, the recommendations of the review process, and why the government decided against their implementation.

Origins of Reform

The transition from one electoral system to another provides a powerful case study in the dynamics of democratic change: on the one hand, the ability of individual leaders to direct the political agenda, and on the other, the power of mass opinion to either endorse or reject that decision. As with other reforms of constitutional significance, the initial decision to look into the way the country conducted its elections was taken by the governing elite, primarily at the behest of the Minister of Justice and Deputy Prime Minister, Geoffrey Palmer. A major reason for his concern was

Labour's defeat at consecutive elections. Despite having received more votes than the incumbent National government at the 1978 and 1981 elections, National won a majority of the seats.

Although the Royal Commission's recommendation that New Zealand adopt the German MMP system was a cause for lively debate among politicians, party activists and electoral reformers, for the next five years public opinion barely registered any interest. When the Prime Minister, David Lange, was asked on the eve of the 1987 general election how his government might respond to the Royal Commission's report, he promised to make it the subject of a referendum. Immediately after the election he admitted somewhat bizarrely that what he should have said was that the government would *not* hold such a referendum.

While National had shown no interest in electoral reform up to that time, the issue of broken promises provided National with an opportunity to exploit the growing public mood of cynicism and betrayal that accompanied Labour's free market reform agenda, particularly over its decision to privatise a number of state assets. In what appeared to be a reasonably safe commitment given the lack of public interest in electoral systems, National pledged to give voters the referendum that had been promised, then denied, by Lange. It could hardly have foreseen the public backlash that was about to follow. Within months of taking office as the party that would restore people's trust in politicians and the two main parties, National was accused of the same policy U-turns and broken promises as Labour. The nub of the public's anger was directed at those free market reforms that were seen to represent a continuation, indeed an intensification, of those begun under Labour.

An unexpected consequence of this 'plague on both your houses' was a dramatic surge in the level of public interest in the MMP debate. While a vast majority of voters lacked any understanding of how MMP might actually work, or even what its adoption might mean for the future of the political system, they did have an expectation that it would curb the powers of the two major parties and provide fair representation to the growing array of parties formed in protest at the policies of successive Labour and National governments. That both major parties urged voters to reject MMP was hardly a deterrent; indeed, most viewed it as an incentive. At the first electoral referendum, some 85 per cent of voters supported change, with 71 per cent preferring the MMP option. At the run-off referendum held in tandem with the 1993 election, MMP was the preferred system of 54 per cent of voters.

How MMP Works

Proportional System
The first distinguishing feature of MMP is its proportionality. Unlike the vagaries of disproportional electoral systems, notably FPP, under MMP parties receive an allocation of parliamentary seats roughly equivalent to their share of the party vote. This means that, in the event that a minor party receives 21 per cent of the vote, as the Democrats (formerly Social Credit) did in 1981, it would receive approximately 21 per cent of the available seats. This would be a very different result from the 2 per cent of the seats the Democrats actually received at that particular election. A party's proportional share of the seats is determined by the national outcome of the first of the two votes (that is, the 'party vote'). Because small parties find it difficult to win electorate seats, their vote tending to be widely spread rather than concentrated in particular electorates, small parties may have all their MPs drawn from the party lists (as occurred with the Greens' fourteen seats and New Zealand First's initial allocation of eleven seats in the 2014–17 Parliament).

To qualify for their proportional share of the parliamentary seats, parties must be registered with the New Zealand Electoral Commission and meet one of two thresholds. The concept of a threshold was introduced in Germany in the aftermath of the Second World War. Its purpose was to exclude from election to the Bundestag small, ideologically extremist parties that might conceivably be in the potentially dominant position of holding the balance of power. Today, many countries with proportional systems have thresholds, with Israel's Knesset having a threshold as low as 2 per cent and the Turkish parliament one of 10 per cent. The first of New Zealand's two thresholds is set at 5 per cent of the party vote (or approximately 120,000 votes). Since it first contested an MMP election as a separate party organisation, the Green Party has managed to reach the 5 per cent threshold on each and every occasion – although it fell a few votes short on polling night in 1999, it picked up the necessary additional votes once the 'Specials' were counted. Two examples of parties that narrowly failed to reach the threshold, and thus missed out on parliamentary representation, were the Christian Coalition (4.3 per cent) in 1996 and New Zealand First (4.1 per cent) in 2008. Votes cast for any parties that fail to reach this threshold are disregarded, and therefore deemed to be 'wasted' votes.

Although the Royal Commission on the Electoral System made only passing reference to a second threshold (Wallace, 1986: 45 and 66), a one-seat threshold was provided for in the electoral legislation. This means that a party that wins an electorate seat is entitled to its proportional share of list seats, regardless of whether it reached the 5 per cent threshold. In 2008, for example, the Act Party received four list seats despite receiving a mere 3.7 per cent of the vote. It did so on the grounds that one of its candidates, Rodney Hide, managed to win the electorate seat of Epsom. Other parties to have benefited from the one-seat threshold include Jim Anderton's Progressive Coalition in 2002, when its 1.7 per cent of the vote gave it two seats – Anderton's own electorate seat of Wigram, together with one list seat; and United Future in 2005, when 2.7 per cent of the vote nationwide gave it a total of three seats – Peter Dunne's Ohariu-Belmont, together with two list seats. Critics of this second threshold argue that it results in too many small parties exercising too much power. Such criticisms are particularly dismissive of the 'coat-tails' provision that rewards list candidates with seats on the basis of a single success in an electorate seat, especially if, as occurred in Epsom, that seat was effectively gifted to the small party by one of the two major parties.

Mixed-member System

As the term 'mixed-member proportional' implies, a second feature of MMP revolves around the sorts of MP it creates. In fact, it legitimises two distinctive categories of MP: those who represent the geographical electorates, and those who are elected from the party lists. This second party list allocation gives each party its proportional share of the seats.

Electorate seats. Although MMP has little in common with FPP, both systems follow the FPP or plurality method for determining the outcomes of the electorate contests. Regardless of how many candidates contest an electorate seat, or how low the highest vote might be, the candidate who wins the greatest number of votes is declared the victor. In the Auckland seat of Waitakere in 2011, for example, Paula Bennett (National) and Carmel Sepuloni (Labour) each received 43.8 per cent of the vote. Because Bennett had nine more votes than Sepuloni, she was declared the winner. Although the margin between United Future's Peter Dunne and his Labour challenger, Charles Chauvel, was considerably wider in the Wellington seat of Ōhariu, Dunne's winning share of the vote was a mere 38.2 per cent.

To ensure that the electorate seats are adjusted in line with any movement in the population, an independent body, the Representation Commission,* meets after each five-yearly census, the most recent being in 2013. It begins its calculations by dividing the South Island population into sixteen electorates of approximately equal size (in 2013 there were 59,679 per electorate) (Representation Commission, 2013). The number of seats in the North Island (48) is based on the South Island quotient, a process that tends to result in the addition of one or two seats following each redistribution, especially in those parts of the country where population growth is greatest, such as in the upper North Island. To ensure that the size of Parliament remains the same, any growth in the number of electorate seats results in a corresponding reduction in the total number of list seats. In making their decisions about where the boundaries will be drawn, members of the commission take into account such considerations as where the existing boundaries lie, the effect boundaries may have on existing communications networks, the topography of the electoral districts concerned and the need to give due recognition to any characteristics communities might have in common (Electoral Act 1993, 35:3: 25). These may include the urban/rural split, tribal interests and the development over time of a shared identity.

---

* Members of the Representation Commission include the Government Statistician, Surveyor-General, Chief Electoral Officer, and representatives of the government and opposition.

Currently there are 64 General seats and seven Māori seats, making a total of 71 electorate seats (compared with 65 in 1996). From the time of the creation of separate Māori seats in 1867, the total number of designated Māori seats was held at four. Beginning in 1993, the number of seats has reflected the size of the Māori population enrolled on the separate Māori roll. Over a period of four months, Māori who self-identify as being of Māori descent may choose to go on either the Māori roll or the General roll. Once they have made their decision, they cannot move to the other roll until the time of the next Māori option some five years later. At the 1996 election, the number of Māori seats increased to five, and by 2002 it had reached the present number of seven. The electorate covering Northland is Te Tai Tokerau. Although much of Auckland is in the Tāmaki Makaurau electorate, parts of the city are also served by the Te Tai Tokerau and Hauraki-Waikato electorates. The two Māori seats covering the eastern part of the North Island from the Waikato south are Waiariki and Ikaroa-Rāwhiti, and on the western part of the North Island lies Te Tai Hauāuru. Finally, the Te Tai Tonga seat covers the entire South Island, together with a large part of Wellington. With the exception of the Auckland seat of Tāmaki Makaurau, a characteristic shared by all the Māori seats is their immense physical size.

List seats. Although the total number of list seats (49)[*] is in decline (down from 55 in 1996), it has not dropped to a point where the proportion of seats to party votes is in any way compromised. Following the allocation of electorate seats, most of which are won by the two major parties,[†] parties are allocated seats from the party list broadly equivalent to their share of the party vote. At the 2014 general election, for example, National won 41 of the 71 available electorate seats. Because its party vote was 47.04 per cent, a further nineteen list seats had to be added, bringing the party's total number of seats to 60 (or 49.59 per cent of all seats). This meant that the first nineteen candidates on National's party list who had not won

---

[*] Due to a one-seat overhang, the number of list seats in the 2014–17 Parliament increased to 50.
[†] Exceptions following the 2011 election were the seats of Epsom (Act), Ōhariu (United Future), and four of the seven Māori seats (Mana and Māori parties).

an electorate seat were automatically elected as list MPs (see Table 5.1, overleaf).

Many list members have been chosen because they represent a constituency not easily defined within the boundaries of a geographical electorate. In particular, these constituencies include the Asian and Pasifika communities, each of which makes up approximately 6 per cent of all voters. With up to 300 associations operating at regional or national levels, the Asian community poses a particular challenge for legislators and government agencies. Both major parties have Asian, and specifically Chinese, list MPs, whose task it is to represent the diverse needs of the Asian communities living in New Zealand. At the level of individual voters, enquiries are likely to cover a wide range of policy areas, such as immigration, health, education and commerce. Chinese MPs are also called upon to assist Chinese delegations visiting New Zealand and Foreign and Trade Ministers on their frequent visits to China.

A number of list MPs have been chosen, not to represent an otherwise neglected ethnic or special interest group, but rather to 'shadow' an electorate MP, usually from a rival party. In the seat of Epsom, for example, National's Paul Goldsmith plays a similar role to that of the electorate member, Act's David Seymour. This is likely to involve maintaining an electorate office, holding electorate clinics, attending local community events and generally flying the party flag in the electorate. However, because the list member's constituency responsibilities tend to be less onerous than those of the electorate member, there may be greater opportunity to become involved in policy development, as well as party and select committee activities. In Auckland Central, the Labour list MP Jacinda Ardern has cast a physical shadow over the electorate MP, Nikki Kaye, until recently her electorate office having been a mere two or three doors away from that of the National MP.

The party list system is frequently criticised for its lack of democratic accountability. The Electoral Act 1993 states that: 'Every political party . . . shall ensure that provision is made for participation in the selection of candidates representing the party for election as members of Parliament' (Section 71: 46). It goes on to state that selection can be made either by party members or by elected delegates. In fact, with the exception of the Greens, party lists tend to be compiled and ranked by small national committees, often at the behest of the party leader. This gives rise to public concern that the successful list candidates have been selected not necessarily on the basis of competence or ability to represent significant parts of the electorate, but rather for their loyalty to the party hierarchy. When Labour was in government between 1999 and 2008, it was criticised for using its party list as a safety net to protect incumbent MPs who were about to lose their electorate seats. One of the most controversial results was that involving a government minister, Jim Sutton, in the South Island seat of Aoraki. Having held the seat comfortably at the previous election, in 2005 Sutton attracted only 11,315 votes, almost 7000 votes fewer than the winner, National's Jo Goodhew. Having been emphatically defeated in his electorate, Sutton's eleventh ranking on Labour's list ensured that he would be returned to Parliament and Cabinet after the election.

A further criticism of party lists is that they are 'closed' in so far as voters are not able to change the predetermined rankings of the party. Some countries have an 'open' list system, which gives voters the opportunity to re-order the list rankings if they so desire. Of course, since most voters will be unfamiliar with a vast majority of the names appearing on party lists, any attempt to re-order the party's rankings is likely to be random at best. Compounding the possible confusion still further is the practice of presenting the list as an honours board of the party's most prominent politicians (see Tables 5.1 and 5.2, overleaf). Because many of those ranked high on the list are likely to win electorate seats, the honours board system makes it difficult for ordinary voters to distinguish between genuine list candidates and those chosen to add lustre to the party's image as a credible electoral force. An alternative approach adopted in some countries is to prevent dual candidacy by requiring that all candidates choose whether to stand as electorate candidates or as candidates on the party list. While such a requirement would have minimal impact on the major parties, small parties would be seriously disadvantaged, on the grounds that they lack the personnel to run two credible candidate lists – indeed, small list parties are inclined to incentivise list candidates by requiring that they campaign in targeted electorates.

Table 5.1: National Party List, 2014

1.	John Key	27.	Louise Upston
2.	Bill English (L) (EL)	28.	Tim Macindoe
3.	David Carter (L) (EL)	29.	Jami-Lee Ross
4.	Gerry Brownlee	30.	Paul Goldsmith (EL)
5.	Steven Joyce (L) (EL)	31.	Melissa Lee (EL)
6.	Judith Collins	32.	Kanwaljit Bakshi (L) (EL)
7.	Hekia Parata (EL)	33.	Jian Yang (L) (EL)
8.	Chris Finlayson (EL)	34.	Alfred Ngaro (EL)
9.	Paula Bennett	35.	Maurice Williamson
10.	Jonathan Coleman	36.	Jacqui Dean
11.	Murray McCully	37.	David Bennett
12.	Anne Tolley	38.	Jonathan Young
13.	Nick Smith	39.	Brett Hudson (EL)
14.	Tim Groser (EL)	40.	Maggie Barry
15.	Amy Adams	41.	Ian McKelvie
16.	Nathan Guy	42.	Mark Mitchell
17.	Craig Foss	43.	Simon O'Connor
18.	Simon Bridges	44.	Mike Sabin
19.	Nikki Kaye	45.	Scott Simpson
20.	Michael Woodhouse (EL)	46.	Paul Foster-Bell (EL)
21.	Jo Goodhew	47.	Joanne Hayes (EL)
22.	Chester Borrows	48.	Parmjeet Parma (EL)
23.	Todd McClay	49.	Chris Bishop (EL)
24.	Peseta Sam Lotu-liga	50.	Nuk Korako (EL)
25.	Nicky Wagner	51.	Jonathan Naylor (EL)
26.	Lindsay Tisch		

L= List-only candidate   EL= Elected list MP

One of the anticipated benefits of MMP is the use of party lists to advance the representation of women and minority groups. Under the previous electoral system, Māori were largely relegated to the four designated Māori seats, as were women to unwinnable and barely marginal seats. When party organisers were challenged to select more women candidates, they frequently cited total numbers of female candidates, few of whom were likely to win their seats. Of the 40 women who contested seats at the 1981 general election, for example, only eight (8.7 per cent)

Table 5.2: Labour Party List, 2014

1.	David Cunliffe	26.	David Clark
2.	David Parker (L) (EL)	27.	Carol Beaumont
3.	Grant Robertson	28.	Poto Williams
4.	Annette King	29.	Carmel Sepuloni
5.	Jacinda Ardern (EL)	30.	Tamati Coffey
6.	Nanaia Mahuta	31.	Jenny Salesa
7.	Phil Twyford	32.	Liz Craig
8.	Clayton Cosgrove (EL)	33.	Deborah Russell
9.	Chris Hipkins	34.	Willow-Jean Prime
10.	Sue Moroney (EL)	35.	Jerome Mika
11.	Andrew Little (EL)	36.	Tony Milne
12.	Louisa Wall	37.	Virginia Andersen
13.	David Shearer	38.	Claire Szabo
14.	Sua'a William Sio	39.	Michael Wood
15.	Maryan Street	40.	Arena Williams
16.	Phil Goff	41.	Hamish McDouall
17.	Moana Mackey	42.	Anjum Rahman (L)
18.	Kelvin Davis	43.	Sunny Kaushal (L)
19.	Meka Whaitiri	44.	Christine Greer
20.	Megan Woods	45.	Penny Gaylor
21.	Raymond Huo (L)	46.	Janette Walker
22.	Damien O'Connor	47.	Richard Hills
23.	Priyanca Radhakrishnan (L)	48.	Shanan Halbert (L)
24.	Iain Lees-Galloway	49.	Anahila Suisuiki (L)
25.	Rachel Jones	50.	Clare Wilson

L= List-only candidate   EL= Elected list MP

went on to be elected. While the number of female candidates at the following election rose to 81, only twelve succeeded in winning their seats (New Zealand Electoral Commission, 2002: 176). With the introduction of ranked party lists, each party's commitment to female and ethnic representation would become more transparent, especially since the full list would be made available to voters before polling day.

While the increase in the number of designated Māori electorate seats had some effect on the rise in Māori representation (see Figure 5.1), by far the most important reason was the introduction of list MPs. In 1996, for

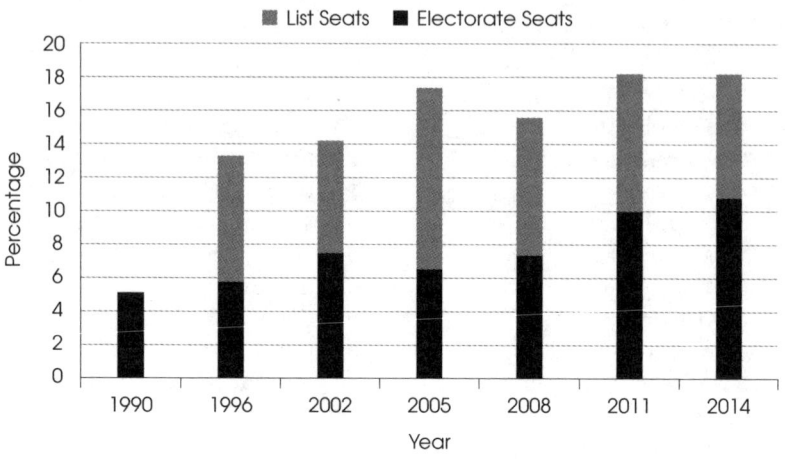

Figure 5.1: Māori Representation in the New Zealand Parliament

example, whereas six Māori were elected in electorate seats (five Māori seats plus the General seat of Tauranga), eleven were elected on the party lists. Over the next few elections the number of Māori successfully winning General seats increased to four in 2011 and six in 2014. Between a third and a half of all Māori MPs are elected on the party lists.

Although the impact of MMP on the proportion of women MPs was less spectacular (see Figure 5.2), with the growing numbers of women entering the workforce from the 1980s contributing to the initial spike, the advent of party lists in 1996 did make a substantial difference to the proportion of women MPs, with over two-thirds being elected from the party lists. Since then, the ratio of electorate to list women members has steadily increased, partly as a result of the commitment of National to the nomination of women candidates in winnable electorate seats. However, despite the early progress in the overall proportion of women MPs to 30.8 per cent in 1999, further progress towards gender parity has been stalled. Much of this is due to a growing sense of complacency that, early progress having been achieved, little more needs to be done to advance the representation of women. When parliamentary candidates were asked after the 2011 election whether it was important to balance a parliamentary

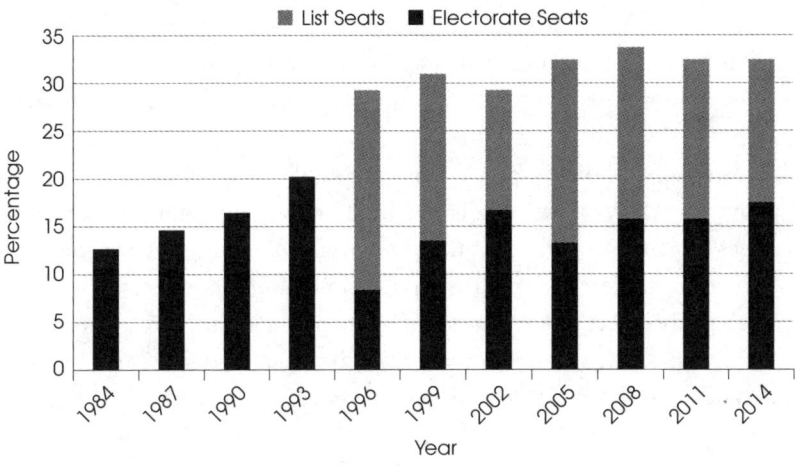

Figure 5.2: Women's Representation in the New Zealand Parliament

caucus by gender, only 17 per cent of National candidates and 25 per cent of New Zealand First candidates agreed (New Zealand Election Study, 2011). While support for gender equality was stronger among centre-left parties, the proportions who agreed were surprisingly low, at 67 per cent for Labour and 65 per cent for the Greens. It is hardly surprising, therefore, to find that New Zealand has slipped to twenty-fifth place in world rankings of women in national parliaments, still significantly ahead of the United Kingdom, Australia, Canada and the United States, but well behind Scandinavia, South Africa and parts of Latin America (see Interparliamentary Union website).

2011 Referendum*

The decision to hold a referendum on the future of the MMP system was announced by Prime Minister John Key at the opening of the new Parliament

---

* For a more detailed analysis of the 2011 electoral referendum and subsequent review, see Lundberg and Miller, 2014.

in December 2008. No doubt influenced by his own party members, as well as influential members of the business community, many of whom had been longtime critics of MMP on the grounds that it led to unstable and indecisive government, the Prime Minister initially expressed a preference for one of the proposed alternatives, the supplementary-member system,* on the grounds that it provided limited opportunities for small parties to gain seats whilst at the same time enhancing the prospects of a return to single-party majority government. The danger for National was that any direct attempt to manipulate public opinion might provoke a public backlash similar to that which had accompanied the electoral referenda of 1992 and 1993. Instead, the government's preferred strategy was to spoil the public with choice (see Figure 5.3). By posing five alternative systems, it was increasing the odds that a non-proportional or semi-proportional system might somehow be preferred to one of the two proportional systems, namely the single-transferable vote (STV) and MMP.

Although the level of public interest in the referendum debate remained low, those supporting the retention of MMP tended to focus on four main arguments: first, that proportional elections resulted in a fairer distribution of seats across the party system; second, that Parliament under MMP was a more representative body, with greater numbers of women and ethnic minorities than under FPP; third, that the advent of coalition and minority government had placed important checks on the powers of the executive; and finally, through a combination of the 5 per cent and one-seat thresholds, small parties now received their share of the seats, with the result that many fewer votes were wasted than under FPP. Opponents, on the other hand, took the view that, as well as resulting in weak and unstable government, MMP was fundamentally undemocratic. Whereas elections were once about choosing governments, they now involved a series of post-election tradeoffs, a process that disproportionately rewarded the

---

* Unlike MMP, which assigns the seats as a proportion of the total vote, under the supplementary-member system only a small share of the total number of seats is divided up proportionately. Had the 2011 election been conducted under the supplementary-member system, for example, 90 electorate seats would have been decided by the rules of FPP, with a further 30 list seats being divided up in proportion to each party's share of the party vote. Under such an arrangement, the Green Party would have received a total of three seats, not the fourteen it achieved under MMP.

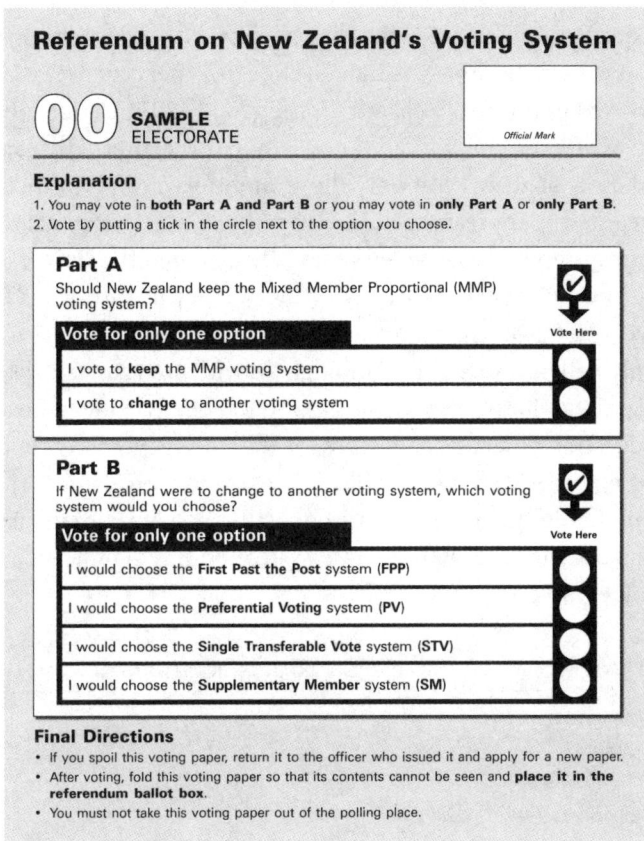

Figure 5.3: Referendum Ballot Paper, 2011

Source: Electoral Referendum Bill 2010.

small parties – the 'tail wagging the dog' – and took place away from the public view. Further undermining the democratic process, in the opinion of MMP's critics, were the 51* list MPs. Not only were list members deemed to be unelected and unaccountable, they were chosen for the purpose of representing the interests of the parties, not the voting public.

---

* The number of list seats was reduced from 51 to 49 in 2014.

As expected, knowledge of the various electoral options among young voters was extremely limited. Although close to 40 per cent of 18–26-year-olds surveyed in the New Zealand Election Study 2011 claimed to know how the MMP system worked, knowledge of the alternative systems dropped away sharply, with only the straightforward plurality or FPP system registering any reasonable level of recognition. Given that no voters in this age group had ever voted in an FPP election, the lack of understanding by over 70 per cent of respondents was hardly surprising. For the 26–36-year-old group, some knowledge of MMP and FPP was claimed by roughly half of respondents although, as with the younger age group, ignorance of the alternative systems raised questions as to the success of the public education campaign and, more generally, the government's purpose in providing voters with such a wide range of choice (see Figure 5.4). MMP was the preferred system of all age groups, although opposition increased incrementally with age, with the FPP system finding significant support among older age groups.

Table 5.3: Results of the 2011 Referendum (Percentage of Total Votes)

Retain MMP	56.2
Replace MMP	41.1
First-past-the-post (FPP)	31.2
Preferential voting (PV)	8.3
Single-transferable vote (STV)	11.2
Supplementary member (SM)	16.1
Informal votes	33.1

Source: http://www.electionresults.govt.nz/electionresults_2011/referendum.html.

Perhaps the most significant feature of Figure 5.6 (overleaf) is the extent to which the centre-right and centre-left polarise on the question of MMP. As successive surveys since 1996 have shown, National voters express a strong preference for FPP and Labour voters for MMP. What is most interesting about the 2011 result, however, is the level of opposition to MMP among National voters at a time when their party was in such a dominant position electorally, so much so that it was able to implement its full economic agenda. More remarkable still, however, is

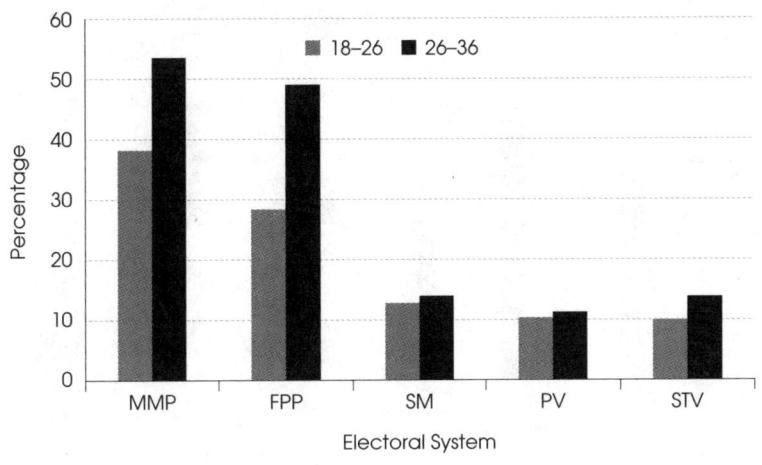

Figure 5.4: Knowledge of Electoral Systems by Age
Source: New Zealand Election Study, 2011.

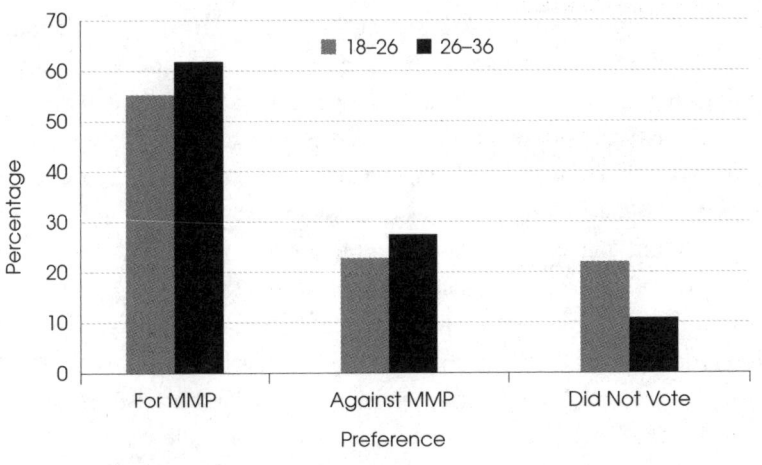

Figure 5.5: Support for MMP by Age
Source: New Zealand Election Study, 2011.

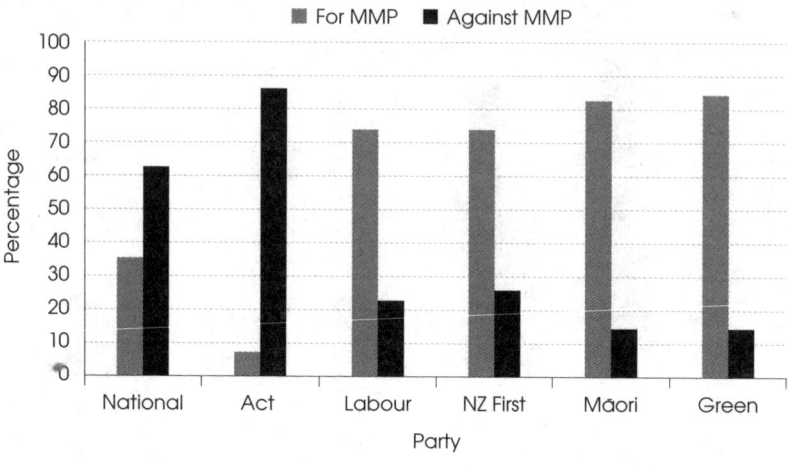

Figure 5.6: MMP Vote by Party
Source: New Zealand Election Study, 2011.

the level of opposition to MMP among Act voters. Given Act's influence on government policy between 2008 and 2011 and its high level of parliamentary representation (five seats) relative to its modest share of the vote (3.7 per cent), the opposition of Act voters towards MMP is seemingly counter-intuitive and can only be explained by examining the nature of the party's vote. Most are National voters who cast a strategic vote for Act in Epsom, and perhaps even a party vote for Act nationally, with a view to providing National with a compatible support party in government. Clearly, many would feel more comfortable with a voting system that allows them to cast their vote expressively. The levels of support for MMP among Green and Māori Party voters in particular, but also those who support New Zealand First, are more readily explainable.

The Review

A majority of the public having chosen to retain MMP, the next step was for the New Zealand Electoral Commission to conduct a review of the new system's most problematic features, including the two thresholds, the previously discussed dual candidacy and open versus closed party lists, and whether list MPs should be allowed to stand in by-elections (Lundberg and Miller, 2014). Specifically excluded from the review was the future of the designated Māori seats, as well as the size of Parliament. As part of the review, members of the public would be given an opportunity to make oral and written submissions. It was expected that any recommendations could be implemented in time for the 2014 general election.

Some 4700 submissions were made during the first phase of the review process. The issue that raised the greatest concern was that of the two thresholds, with many respondents expressing the view that the one-seat threshold was unfair to parties that narrowly failed to meet the 5 per cent threshold, as well as resulting in a proliferation of very small but potentially influential parties. The event that appeared to arouse greatest public concern was the so-called 'Teapot Tape' affair involving the Prime Minister and Act's electorate candidate, John Banks, in the seat of Epsom in 2011. The intention of the prearranged media event was to inform National voters that the major party was happy for them to cast a strategic vote for Act in Epsom, in the hope that Banks would be able to bring a further two or three list MPs into Parliament on the back of his success. Although it did have the desired effect on National's Epsom voters, the meeting was viewed by many as an abuse of the democratic process and yet another example of the deal-making *modus operandi* of the Prime Minister (prior to entering politics, John Key was a currency trader with Merrill Lynch). As a result, some 77 per cent of those who made submissions called for the abolition of the one-seat threshold (Lundberg and Miller, 2014). This became the most significant recommendation of the review.

But removing one threshold raised questions about the level at which the second should take effect. In its report recommending the introduction of MMP, the Royal Commission had suggested a threshold of 4 per cent, reasoning that it would 'provide small parties with a reasonable chance of gaining seats while discouraging the proliferation of minor and/or extremist groups in the House' (Wallace, 1986: 66). A threshold of 5 per cent, on the other hand, was deemed to be too demanding. While a substantial minority of submitters supported retention of the 5 per cent threshold,

55 per cent wanted it lowered to 4 per cent (Lundberg and Miller, 2014). The review's recommendation on lowering the threshold reflected the wish of the majority.

On the issue of dual candidacy, by the time of the review much of the public resentment that followed the 2005 election had died away – on that occasion, twelve MPs who had lost their electorate seats were returned to Parliament on the party lists. Unlike electoral thresholds, the consequences of any attempt to abolish dual candidacy were far from clear-cut. For example, what impact would it have on the quality of electorate candidates, given that a significant number of quality candidates might prefer the safer option of a high place on the party list? And what impact would abolition have on the competitiveness of list parties such as the Greens and New Zealand First, especially since they would have little incentive to contest the electorate seats? Although a mere 27 per cent of voters were in support of dual candidacy (Lundberg and Miller, 2014), the review failed to recommend abolition.

A similar level of uncertainty surrounded the issue of closed versus open lists. Clearly, it was not in the interests of the political parties to forfeit the right to rank-order their lists. Retaining the right to recruit and promote candidates is an important source of influence and power. Moreover, there is always the fear that open lists will encourage competition between candidates of the same party, which in turn can lead to internal party disunity. A further concern, however, is whether members of the public will know enough about the candidates to be able to make informed judgements as to their relative merits. While the idea of open lists clearly appeals to the populist instincts of many voters, it did not win the support of those conducting the review.

Conclusion

Despite having initiated the electoral referendum and subsequent MMP review, in May 2013 the government announced that it would not be implementing any of the New Zealand Electoral Commission's recommendations, including the abolition of the one-seat threshold and the lowering of the 5 per cent threshold to 4 per cent. One of the claims of this chapter has been that individual leaders play an instrumental role in shaping and directing the political agenda. At the risk of overstating the argument, New Zealand might never have adopted MMP were it not for the intervention of several key political actors, notably the Minister of Justice, Geoffrey Palmer, who in 1985 appointed a Royal Commission to investigate New Zealand's electoral system. At the time of Palmer's decision, there was little or no public or elite interest in electoral reform; indeed, it took a crisis of public confidence in the behaviour of successive governments to ignite the MMP debate. When, nearly two decades later, voters were asked if they still supported MMP, it was yet another progressive and reforming government minister, the Justice Minister Simon Power, who both initiated and defined the terms of the review. Following Power's decision to retire from politics at the 2011 election, responsibility for the review was passed on to his decidedly more risk-averse and pragmatic successor.

It is hard to argue with the political motives behind the decision of the incoming Justice Minister, Judith Collins, to reject the recommendations of the review. There was a sense within National that the submission process had been subject to capture by its political adversaries. Much had changed between the time the review was announced in 2010 and the release of the New Zealand Electoral Commission's report. Act's representation in Parliament had dropped from five seats to one and the Māori Party's from five to three, leaving the government in the potentially parlous state of being the most popular party, yet without any support parties with which to form a government. Amid growing speculation that Act and United Future were unlikely to survive beyond the 2014 election, any prospect that National might remove the lifeline keeping its support parties afloat all but disappeared. Critics would inevitably allege betrayal, but it was political self-interest that dictated the final outcome.

Chapter Six

Cabinet Government

As well as being the most powerful of New Zealand's political institutions, Cabinet has the distinction of being the most dynamic. Whereas the overall structure of Parliament has remained relatively stable under the mixed-member proportional (MMP) system,* the same cannot be said for Cabinet and the wider executive. According to the *Cabinet Manual* (New Zealand Government, 2008), each new prime minister not only determines the composition of Cabinet, but also what it actually does. This includes its size, how ministers are ranked and the allocation of portfolio responsibilities. Most important, however, is the decision about whether it will be a majority or a minority government. On some occasions all the seats in Cabinet have gone to the major party, while on others there has been a *pro rata* allocation to the small parties, either involving seats around the Cabinet table or, more commonly, ministerial portfolios outside of Cabinet. At any time during the life of a government, it is the Prime Minister's prerogative to remove ministers and appoint others.

The potential power of the prime minister notwithstanding, the sort of government the country ends up with is as much a product of electoral circumstance as it is prime ministerial initiative. Because a significant

---

* The overall distribution of parliamentary seats as between the major and small parties has remained constant at a ratio of approximately 80:20. Of the seven parties represented in the 2014–17 Parliament, all but one (Māori Party) were formed before the first MMP election.

proportion of the voting public supported New Zealand First at the 1996 election, Winston Peters was allowed to dictate the terms of the new government. Having been left with the balance of power, he was able to decide whether New Zealand had a centre-left or centre-right government. As to the overall composition of the government, more often than not the final decision has been left to the Prime Minister. On three successive occasions, for example, Helen Clark chose to exclude the Greens from her government. And who could have anticipated the outcome of the 2008 election, when John Key, having secured National's majority through separate negotiations with the Act and United Future parties, entered into a separate governing arrangement with the Māori Party, as well as a memorandum of understanding with the left-wing Green Party?

Despite its obvious versatility, Cabinet is not an institution that operates in isolation. Rather, its most outstanding feature is its interlocking and interdependent relationship with other parts of the political system. As we saw in chapters two and four, whereas Parliament debates, amends and passes new Bills, Cabinet and its sundry committees play a pre-eminent role in setting the budget and formulating and executing the legislative agenda. As well as overseeing the government departments and ministries associated with their particular portfolios, ministers engage with the public, attending to the needs of constituents, party activists and relevant interest groups, and dealing with enquiries from the media. This interconnected function of the political system can be compared with the inner workings of a wheel, with Parliament as the rim, the public service, parties and interest groups as the radiating spokes, and Cabinet as the hub.

Of particular relevance to this chapter is the process of government formation under MMP. When multi-party government was first contemplated, it was widely anticipated that the dominant model would be majority coalitions, partly because majority government was the outcome best known to New Zealand voters, but also because no one party was expected to achieve a majority of the seats under proportional representation. However, as we now know, the only majority coalition during the MMP era has been that between National and New Zealand First, an arrangement that lasted a mere twenty months. Since then, minority government has been the order of the day, with small parties occupying positions at arm's length from the government. Why this has occurred, and with what implications for the aspirations of stable and effective government, will be the major focus of this chapter.

Forming a Government*

Before discussing governing arrangements under MMP, it is important to be reminded of New Zealand's long history of single-party majority government. During the six decades of two-party dominance, the winning party was able to assure voters of its ability to deliver stable and decisive government. Of the two parties, National was far and away the more successful. Over a 35-year period from 1949, when it defeated Peter Fraser's war-time government, National was out of office a mere six years. As we have seen, its successes were mostly based on slender majorities; indeed, at successive elections in 1978 and 1981, National was re-elected despite winning fewer votes than Labour. With the rise of small parties, the winning party's electoral base shrank still further, leaving National with a mere 35 per cent of the vote and 50 per cent of the seats at the final election under the first-past-the-post (FPP) system.

Although multi-party government was widely anticipated to be an inevitable outcome of MMP, the diverse range of governing options received little attention at the time the new electoral system was first introduced. In 1996, either National (44 out of 120 seats) or Labour (37 seats) could have formed a minority government, had one or more of the small parties been willing to enter into a confidence and supply agreement with the major party concerned. However, this was not the preferred option of New Zealand First. After conducting parallel negotiations with both major parties, Winston Peters opted for a formal coalition with National (61 seats). It soon became clear that the coalition agreement was primarily the product of a party with few ideas as to how coalition government

---

* For a more detailed analysis of the role of the small parties in government formation, see Miller and Curtin, 2011.

might actually work. Amid claims that the 'tail was wagging the dog', irreconcilable tensions began to develop in the two parties' relationship, culminating in the coalition's collapse in August 1998.

Table 6.1: Alternative Governing Options under MMP

Single-party majority government	61-plus seats
Single-party minority government	Under 61 seats
Multi-party majority coalition	61-plus seats
Multi-party minority coalition	Under 61 seats

Following the failure of the first majority coalition, successive prime ministers began to experiment with alternative models (see Table 6.1). In 1999, although Helen Clark's Labour Party (49 seats) had the opportunity to appoint a majority government with the Alliance (10 seats) and Greens (7 seats), it was Clark's preference, as well as that of the Alliance, to form a minority government that excluded the Greens. By early 2002, the second coalition under MMP also began to unravel, on this occasion over a range of government policies, but especially the government's decision to support the United States invasion of Afghanistan in the wake of the 9/11 terrorist attacks. When the Greens staged a walkout in Parliament over the release of genetically modified organisms, Clark called a snap election and encouraged voters to give Labour an absolute majority, although she undertook to include the former Alliance leader, Jim Anderton, and his new breakaway party, the Progressives, in any future government (see Table 6.2, overleaf).

The composition of the 2002–5 government provided an early insight into the future shape of New Zealand governments. With a combined total of only 54 seats, Labour and the Progressives needed to sign a support agreement with a small party, one that offered the government confidence and supply over the following three years. Since the Greens had made it clear that any support would be highly conditional, Clark turned her attention to the centre ground, forging a confidence agreement with the moderate United Future (eight seats), a party that had enjoyed a brief surge in support in the final weeks of the 2002 campaign. Given the political inexperience of all but one of his MPs, United Future's leader, Peter

Table 6.2: Types of MMP Government

Election	Majority coalition	Minority government	Ministries outside Cabinet	Support agreement
1996	National NZ First*			
		National (1998–99)		Act
1999		Labour Alliance		Greens
2002		Labour Progressives		United Future Greens
2005		Labour	NZ First United Future	Greens
2008		National	Act Māori Party United Future	Greens†
2011		National	Māori Party Act United Future	
2014		National	Māori Party Act United Future	

* Coalition terminated in 1998.
† Greens signed a memorandum of understanding with National.

Dunne, had little interest in ministerial positions. Instead, he negotiated a confidence and supply agreement in exchange for a number of policy concessions, including the creation of a Families Commission.

By 2005, Helen Clark had devised a structure of government that was subsequently adopted, with modifications, by John Key in 2008, 2011 and 2014. The Clark/Key model has three main elements:

1. minority government;
2. close proximity to the ideological centre ground;
3. keeping support parties at arm's length.

Minority Government

Whereas earlier coalitions had been short-lived, under the Clark/Key model they proved to be much more stable and constructive. As well as satisfying the ambitions of their own parties' MPs by reserving for them the full complement of Cabinet seats, Labour and National were able to enact the bulk of their policy agendas with minimal disagreement or rancour. In 2005, Labour (50 seats) might have formed a government with the Greens. Instead, it chose to go it alone.* Three years later, National (58 seats) followed suit, a decision it repeated in 2011 (59 seats) and 2014 (60 seats).† Public attitudes towards minority government are evident in the results of Figure 6.1. While majority government remained the preferred form of government, by 2011 the gap in support between majority and minority government had virtually disappeared. Part of this growing support for minority government can be attributed to a desire to limit the ability of small parties to over-play their hand, especially by adopting the role of spoiler in their negotiations with National and Labour.

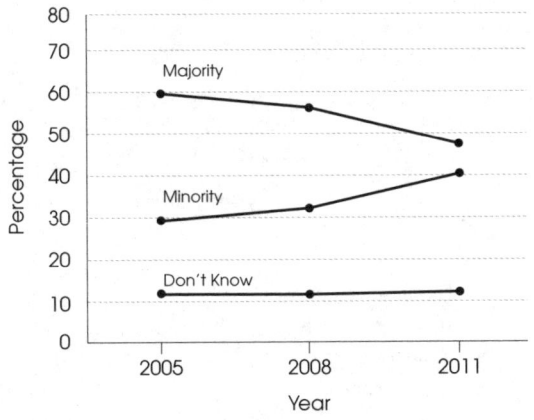

Figure 6.1: Preferred Majority or Minority Government

Source: New Zealand Election Study, 2005–2011.

---

* Although Jim Anderton, a former president of the Labour Party, was the leader of the Progressives, from 2002–8 he was a Labour minister in all but name.
† Reduced to 59 seats following defeat in the Northland by-election in March 2015.

Ideological Proximity

Clark's decision in 2005 to rebuff the Greens and instead look to the ideological centre ground was partly due to her personal difficulties with the left-wing party over a number of years, but also the unwillingness of other parties to lend support to any government of which it was a part. Clearly, Clark understood the electoral risks of being pulled to the left by the Greens. However, she was also reassured by the fact that the small environmental party offered no threat of one day being wooed by National. An altogether more attractive alternative was to reinforce Labour's credentials as a centre party by forging a support agreement with New Zealand First (seven seats) and United Future (three), parties that would provide Labour with its legislative majority while remaining out of government (see Table 6.3). When Key decided to adopt the same arrangement in 2008, he sought to counterbalance the free market economics of Act with the economic interventionism of the Māori Party. Whereas Act offered ballast on the right for National's economic agenda, the Māori Party could be relied upon to support National's liberal social objectives.

Table 6.3: Potential Governing Blocs under MMP

Centre–Left Bloc		Centre–Right Bloc
Labour		National
Alliance (–2002)		Act
Progressives (2002–11)		Conservatives
Greens		
Mana Party (2011)		
	Floaters	
	NZ First	
	United Future	
	Māori Party	

Keeping Support Parties at Arm's Length

A third and related feature of the Clark/Key model is its ability to keep the powers of small parties in check throughout the three years of each electoral cycle. Of course, small parties are well placed to make important gains from such an arrangement. From their perspective, not being in Cabinet provides the opportunity to create distance from government policy and performance, especially in the months leading up to the next election, when small support parties are most at risk of an electoral backlash. Astute leaders will negotiate the terms of their agreement with an eye to these potential electoral costs. Any personal satisfaction derived from holding ministerial office must be balanced against the demands of the party rank-and-file, especially with respect to party policy. To this end, 'careful planning, good faith, and a "no surprises" approach are key to making the arrangements work effectively' (New Zealand Government, 2008: 65).

Nature of Cabinet

Before proceeding further, it is clear that the terms 'cabinet' and 'executive' require some explanation, as do the powers of appointment adopted by the Prime Minister and endorsed by the two main parties. Prior to the appointment of non-Cabinet ministers, it was not uncommon for the terms 'cabinet' and 'executive' to be used interchangeably, although the latter was not restricted to those sitting around the Cabinet table, since it also included the Executive Council (ministers advising the Governor-General), sundry government departments, and the 85,000 or so members who then made up the public service. Even within the media, Cabinet is sometimes used more broadly, and incorrectly, to include the wider executive, including the ministers outside of Cabinet. When referred to in its broadest sense, 'executive' and 'government' tend to be regarded as one and the same. For Māori, the government is frequently referred to as the 'Crown'.

Put simply, Cabinet is a committee of ministers formally appointed by the Governor-General on the advice of the Prime Minister. Although the size of Cabinet has grown to twenty, it has been known to have as few as seven members (Mitchell, 1966: 22). The gradual increase in its size during the postwar period had much to do with the growing scale and complexity of modern government. On the few occasions when a Cabinet minister was deemed to require additional support, the Prime Minister would appoint one or more under-secretaries, a position once occupied by

Robert Muldoon during his time as under-study to the Minister of Finance. Although under-secretaries were seen as ministers in waiting, there was no expectation that they would regularly attend Cabinet meetings or enjoy the full status of a Cabinet minister. Several senior politicians, including Helen Clark, have advocated a return to a smaller Cabinet, mainly on the grounds that the optimum size for an effective executive committee is deemed to be more in the order of twelve to fourteen. Implementing such a proposal is never easy, however, as Clark found following her elevation from Labour leader to Prime Minister. Quite apart from any resulting increase in workload responsibilities, with approximately fifty portfolios to be distributed (see Table 6.4), reducing the size of Cabinet inevitably would have had a harmful effect on the career paths of backbench MPs.

A starkly different approach adopted for the first time in 1987 was to follow the example of the United Kingdom and several other Western democracies in making ministerial appointments outside of Cabinet. The main reason for this expansion in the size of the executive was to satisfy the ambitions of able backbench members (Holland and Boston, 1990: 65), although it could hardly have escaped the notice of Prime Minister David Lange that adding four non-Cabinet ministers increased the executive's size – and potential influence – within its 57-member caucus.* Although the new ministers enjoyed a similar status to that of a Cabinet member, including the same salary and expenses and use of the title 'Honourable', their portfolio responsibilities tended to be more modest than those of their Cabinet colleagues, with several taking on the role of associate minister (either with or without designated portfolios). Despite playing an active role in Cabinet committees, non-Cabinet ministers do not attend plenary sessions of Cabinet unless invited. With the advent of MMP, the appointment of such ministers has become a convenient method for both rewarding the small support parties with portfolio responsibilities and compensating members of the Prime Minister's own party who miss out on seats in Cabinet, especially in circumstances in which seats have

---

* Together with the 24 ministers, Speaker and Deputy Speaker, and senior and junior Whip, the ratio of officeholders to backbenchers in the second Lange government was 28:29.

Table 6.4: John Key Ministry, 2014–

Rank	Minister	Major Portfolios
1.	John Key	Prime Minister; Tourism; National Security and Intelligence
2.	Bill English	Deputy Prime Minister; Finance
3.	Gerry Brownlee	Canterbury Recovery; Defence
4.	Steven Joyce	Economic Development; Science; Tertiary Education; Regulatory Reform
5.	Paula Bennett	Local Government; Social Housing; State Services
6.	Jonathan Coleman	Health; Sport and Recreation
7.	Amy Adams	Justice; Courts; Broadcasting; Communications
8.	Christopher Finlayson	Attorney-General; Treaty Negotiations
9.	Simon Bridges	Energy and Resources; Transport
10.	Hekia Parata	Education
11.	Anne Tolley	Social Development
12.	Nick Smith	Environment; Building and Housing
13.	Murray McCully	Foreign Affairs
14.	Nathan Guy	Primary Industries; Racing
15.	Nikki Kaye	ACC; Civil Defence; Youth
16.	Tim Groser	Trade; Climate Change
17.	Michael Woodhouse	Immigration; Police
18.	Todd McClay	Revenue; State Owned Enterprises
19.	Peseta Sam Lotu-liga	Corrections; Ethnic Communities; Pacific Peoples
20.	Maggie Barry	Arts, Culture and Heritage; Conservation; Senior Citizens
	Ministers Outside Cabinet	
21.	Craig Foss	Small Business; Statistics; Veterans' Affairs
22.	Jo Goodhew	Voluntary Sector; Food Safety
23.	Nicky Wagner	Customs; Disability Issues
24.	Louise Upston	Land Information; Women
25.	Paul Goldsmith	Commerce and Consumer Affairs
	Support Party Ministers	
26.	Peter Dunne	Internal Affairs
27.	Te Ururoa Flavell	Māori Development; Whānau Ora
	Under-Secretaries	
	David Seymour	Under-Secretary to the Ministers for Education and Regulatory Reform

Source: http://www.dpmc.govt.nz/cabinet/ministers/ministerial-list.

to be reserved for the coalition partner – in the National–New Zealand First Cabinet of 1996–98, for example, New Zealand First received five seats inside Cabinet, together with four ministerial positions in the wider executive. After several years of disuse, the position of under-secretary was reintroduced in 2014 for the purpose of giving the Act leader and novice MP, David Seymour, a role in the executive, but at a lower level than minister or associate minister.

Most new policy is formulated in the Cabinet's standing committees, examples of which include the Strategy, Economic Growth and Social Policy committees (see Table 6.5). Whereas Cabinet once had up to 36 different committees (Holland and Boston, 1990: 66), the committee structure was refined over several governments, bringing the number of committees down to the present ten, although the Prime Minister has the power to create *ad hoc* committees. Standing committees have a membership of up to seventeen or eighteen, all chosen by the Prime Minister (New Zealand Government, 2008: 18), who is an *ex officio* member of all

Table 6.5: Key Government Cabinet Committees, 2014–

Committee Type	Membership	Chair	Frequency
Strategy	11	John Key	Monthly
Economic Growth and Infrastructure	20 (2)*	Bill English	Weekly
Social Policy	19 (2)*	Paula Bennett	Weekly
Treaty of Waitangi Negotiations	10 (1)*	John Key	Fortnightly
External Relations and Defence	9	Murray McCully	Fortnightly
National Security	7	John Key	As required
State Sector Reform/ Expenditure Control	11 (1)*	Bill English	Weekly
Cabinet Legislation	10	Gerry Brownlee	Weekly
Appointments and Honours	16 (3)*	John Key	Weekly
Cabinet Business	10	John Key	As required

Source: http://www.dpmc.govt.nz/cabinet/committees.

* Number of ministers from support parties.

committees. Membership includes senior ministers, many of whom sit on several committees, ministers responsible for any relevant portfolios and ministers outside of Cabinet. Public officials and advisers may be asked to attend Cabinet committees, and National's senior Whip, who is not a minister, is an *ex officio* member of the Cabinet Legislation Committee (see Cabinet Committees, Department of the Prime Minister and Cabinet website). Because these committees are largely composed of members of the same party, it is much easier to conduct business and reach a consensus than it is in the multi-party parliamentary committees.

Cabinet has been described as 'the apex committee of that pyramid which constitutes the framework of government by committee' (Mitchell, 1966: 22). Although the Prime Minister plays a dominant role in setting and controlling the Cabinet agenda, even the most autocratic of New Zealand's postwar prime ministers, Robert Muldoon, was prepared to acknowledge the collective nature of Cabinet decision-making (Muldoon, 1977). However, whereas Muldoon was prepared to fully exploit the dual role of Prime Minister and Finance Minister, several of his successors have adopted a more consultative style of leadership, on the basis that they were simply the 'first among equals'. Lange, for example, observed that he 'did not treat the Cabinet like an echo chamber; I valued its collective judgment and I willingly accepted the responsibility as prime minister of acting on it' (Lange, 2005: 188). This consultative approach was shared by one of Lange's successors, Jim Bolger, who once stated: 'In Cabinet I allowed ministers to contribute to all decisions. My approach was if they had the opportunity to put forward their views even if they were not accepted, they at least had had their say' (Bolger, 1998: 200). Whereas Helen Clark had a reputation for being a firm, hands-on manager of her government, John Key's leadership style is more akin to that of a chairman of the board (see chapter seven).

Because votes are rarely called for or taken, it is the Prime Minister's prerogative, as the chair of Cabinet, to summarise the mood of the discussion and announce any decisions that might follow. It would take the will of a substantial majority of ministers to challenge this authority. One such exception occurred in 1988, when Lange was one of only two ministers (the other was Michael Cullen) to oppose the introduction of a flat tax rate of 23 cents in the dollar. Although Cabinet formally passed the motion to adopt a flat tax rate, Lange later announced that the government would not be proceeding, a decision that marked the end of his effectiveness as Prime Minister (Lange, 2005: 249). As a number of studies have shown, prime ministerial power should not be overstated – while the Prime Minister enjoys a wide range of responsibilities, in the end political power comes from an ability to persuade.

Prior to the weekly meeting of Cabinet, ministers receive briefing papers on the various topics to be discussed. Proposals that involve financial expenditure will include a separate report from Treasury. Ministers who want to make their mark on the government will have spent the preceding weekend perusing these papers and deciding whether to support or oppose their recommendations. Either before or after any decisions have been made, Cabinet is likely to consult with the party caucus, as well as the leaders of any of the government's small support parties. Although some of the matters coming before Cabinet must be treated with the utmost confidentiality, especially where there are implications for the business and financial sectors, keeping the governing party and small support parties in the loop is crucial to the stability and effectiveness of the government. It is for this reason that both Clark and Key have maintained a 'no surprises' policy that includes regular meetings with the leaders of their various support parties. Cabinet meetings, which take place on the tenth floor of the Beehive, begin mid-morning each Monday and normally last until some time in the afternoon. When the Prime Minister is absent on overseas business, they tend to be chaired by the Deputy Prime Minister. Following each meeting the Prime Minister briefs members of the Press Gallery on any important decisions and new initiatives, leaving the ministers responsible for their implementation very much in the shadow.

Appointment, Resignation and Dismissal

On first appearance, the two main parties follow quite different approaches to the appointment of ministers. Whereas National gives its Prime Minister the power to appoint the members of Cabinet, Labour places that authority in the hands of its caucus, although the Prime Minister determines the actual size of Cabinet and whether or not seats will be allocated to support parties (in consultation with the leaders of those parties). While involving the Labour caucus in the election process has a number of obvious benefits, such as fostering a sense of involvement and collective responsibility, it can easily result in bitter in-fighting, as illustrated by the increasingly dysfunctional nature of the Labour Cabinet prior to Lange's resignation in 1989. Having been forced to work with Cabinet colleagues for whom he had lost all respect, Lange became increasingly disenchanted with his role as Prime Minister. 'Cohesion was gone for good, and any kind of philosophical unity. It was a place of contest. We could turn our collective mind only to inconsequential issues; anything of moment was subject to dispute and settled by shifting alignments of support' (Lange, 2005: 252).

Despite these differences in the way National and Labour appoint their Cabinets, there are some obvious similarities. In both parties, the Prime Minister allocates portfolios, a power that can be used to reward loyalty and talent, as well as to marginalise any ministers who might either lack experience or have the potential to create problems. A feature of Helen Clark's style of leadership was the extent to which the allocation of portfolios reflected her dependence on her most senior ministers, notably her Deputy Prime Minister, Michael Cullen, whose responsibilities included the most demanding of all portfolios, Finance, together with Tertiary Education, Attorney-General and Leader of the House. Similarly, John Key's distribution of portfolios has reflected the trust placed in his most senior ministers, specifically Bill English, Steven Joyce and Gerry Brownlee (see Table 6.4).

Regardless of the method of appointment, both parties must remain mindful of the need to choose a Cabinet that is both experienced and representative of a range of interests. In the case of the incoming National administration in 2008, for example, the Prime Minister had to bear in mind the need for experience, gender and ethnic representation, and fairness in terms of regional distribution, especially as between the South and North Islands, but also metropolitan, provincial and rural New Zealand. Of the 58 National MPs elected at the 2008 election, fifteen were entering Parliament for the first time. Although Prime Ministers no longer hold to the position of Muldoon and other earlier prime ministers of not appointing ministers with less than three to six years of parliamentary experience, there is still a reluctance to do so, as illustrated by the fact that only Steven Joyce of all the new MPs made it straight into Cabinet in 2008. Then, of course, there are those who are deemed to be inappropriate appointments, regardless of how long they might have been in Parliament. By excluding all but one of the new members, together with those not worthy of appointment, Key was left with a group of approximately 35 MPs from which to appoint a twenty-member Cabinet, together with three ministers outside of Cabinet. In addition, of course, the Prime Minister needed to appoint a Speaker, Deputy Speaker and two Whips. By 2014, seven of the 'Class of 2008' (those first elected to Parliament in that year) had been appointed to the Key ministry, with five having won seats in Cabinet.*

Table 6.6: Clark and Key Ministries Compared

	Clark Ministry 2008		Key Ministry 2014–	
	Inside Cabinet	Total (incl. non-Cabinet)	Inside Cabinet	Total (incl. non-Cabinet)
Women	5	7	6	9
Māori	2	5	3	4
Pasifika	0	1	1	1
South Island	6	7	4	6
Auckland	4	5	7	7
List Member	3	5	6	7

As figures for the last Clark ministry and the 2014 Key ministry show (see Table 6.6), every effort is made to ensure that women, Māori and the regions are represented in the ministry, if not in Cabinet. Unlike the caucus election process for Cabinet, appointment to non-Cabinet positions is the responsibility of the Prime Minister. As a result, when Clark was in

---

* Those appointed to Cabinet were Amy Adams, Simon Bridges, Nikki Kaye, Hekia Parata and Michael Woodhouse.

government she was able to make use of non-Cabinet positions to increase the numbers of women, Māori and Pasifika. In the same way, Key increased the proportions of South Island ministers by making targeted appointments to his wider executive.

Both major parties give the Prime Minister the power to make periodic changes to the composition of the ministry by either re-assigning portfolios or removing ministers. When several changes are made at the same time, it is referred to as a Cabinet 'reshuffle' or 'spill'. One such occasion was in early 2013, when Key made several dismissals and appointments, bringing new talent into his ministry and redeploying several existing ministers to new portfolios. Although Cabinet reshuffles are common in the United Kingdom and some other Westminster democracies, they are relatively rare in New Zealand, and tend to be used to reinvigorate a government close to an election.

Individual and Collective Responsibility

Despite its unquestioned importance, competence is not the only measure of the success of a minister. Every new minister is made aware of two important doctrines that are expected to both guide and constrain their behaviour as ministers: individual ministerial responsibility and collective Cabinet responsibility (New Zealand Government, 2008). The first of these principles makes individual ministers responsible for the actions of the public servants, government departments and ministries under their care, with the qualification that it would be unfair to assign blame where there is no proof that the minister bore either personal or direct responsibility. Attributing blame is not always as straightforward as it might appear, however, as illustrated by the introduction of the 'Novopay' payroll system for the Ministry of Education in 2012 and 2013. Opposition parties accused the minister and her associate ministers of being directly responsible for problems with the scheme's implementation and demanded their resignation. Although the Ministry of Education apologised for the ongoing flaws, including incorrect wage and salary payments to teachers and others employed in the education sector, none of the ministers resigned; indeed, the Prime Minister went so far as to publicly blame the Australian provider rather than the associate minister who had been assigned to oversee the scheme's introduction.

Clearly, there are times when ministerial responsibility is more difficult to deny, especially where the circumstances involve personal tragedy. The death in 2010 of 29 miners in an explosion at Pike River on the South Island's West Coast resulted in claims that the Department of Labour had failed to adequately monitor safety in the mine. A Royal Commission report into the disaster confirmed that there had been negligence on the part of the department in not taking action against the employer: 'The Department of Labour did not have the focus, capacity or strategies to ensure that Pike was meeting its legal responsibilities under health and safety laws.... The department should have prohibited Pike from operating the mine until its health and safety systems were adequate' (Panckhurst, 2012). The report recommended that sweeping changes be made to the way the department carried out its responsibilities. The Minister of Labour, Kate Wilkinson, subsequently resigned her portfolio and, in the Cabinet reshuffle of 2013, lost her warrant as a minister.

In addition to the requirement that ministers take responsibility for the actions of others, individual responsibility also applies to the personal life and behaviour of the ministers themselves. In 2012, the minister responsible for the Accident Compensation Corporation (ACC), Nick Smith, wrote a letter on ACC letterhead in support of a friend who was making a claim against the corporation. When the complainant, Bronwyn Pullar, revealed the contents of the letter to the media, Smith was forced to resign on the grounds that he had abused his power as a minister. In 2013, the United Future MP, Peter Dunne, resigned following claims that he had leaked a report on the spy agency, the Government Communications Security Bureau, to a member of the Parliamentary Press Gallery. Although he continued to insist that he was not the source of the leak, Dunne declined to cooperate with a government-initiated inquiry into the leak, thereby forcing the Prime Minister's hand. A third high-profile resignation involved the leader of the Act Party and former Auckland mayoral candidate, John Banks. Following his unsuccessful campaign for mayor in 2010, Banks allegedly filed a false election expenses return under the Local

Electoral Act 2001. The police decided not to prosecute Banks for his failure to declare the sources of two substantial donations, both of which, although received by Banks, were signed off as anonymous, one from internet entrepreneur Kim Dotcom, the other from the SkyCity casino. When a retired Wellington accountant, Graham McCready, launched a private prosecution against Banks, the New Zealand High Court ordered that he stand trial. In October 2013, Banks resigned as a minister.

A final example of an alleged breach of ministerial responsibility concerns a former Police and Justice Minister, Judith Collins, who was accused by Nicky Hager in his book *Dirty Politics* (2014) of being implicated in a campaign by right-wing blogger Cameron Slater to smear the character of the chief executive of the Serious Fraud Office, Adam Feeley. When an email appearing to incriminate Collins was passed on to the Prime Minister, Collins resigned as a minister. Had the allegations not been made during the final weeks of the 2014 election, Collins may well have survived as a minister. However, having been forced to defend her behaviour earlier in the year when, during an official visit to China, she allegedly met with representatives of Oravida, a company in which her husband was a director, the Prime Minister was not prepared to risk a public backlash, especially with the dirty politics scandal swirling around him. Although a government inquiry found no evidence that Collins had behaved inappropriately with respect to the former chief executive of the Serious Fraud Office, she was not immediately reappointed to the executive.

The convention of collective responsibility is at the heart of New Zealand's system of Cabinet government. According to the *Cabinet Manual*, once a decision has been reached all members of Cabinet must speak with a single voice, thereby ensuring that the government is viewed by Parliament as a 'collective whole' (New Zealand Government, 2008: 65). For the most individualistic and opinionated ministers, this principle is not always easy to uphold, especially when the minister is called upon to represent the interests of particular government ministries and departments, or when the nation's financial resources are being carved up and allocated to favoured projects. Debate may be robust, but once decisions have been reached, ministers are called upon to manage their implementation, even those with which they are in fundamental disagreement. To do otherwise would be to undermine the unity and purpose of government. In 1991 the Minister of Māori Affairs, Winston Peters, publicly criticised his National government over its failure to adopt his Ka Awatea report on Māori development. When this began to spread into a more general attack on the direction of government policy, Prime Minister Jim Bolger dismissed him from Cabinet. In another such case, in 2004 a Labour minister, Tariana Turia, took issue with her Prime Minister, Helen Clark, over the government's proposed Foreshore and Seabed legislation. The purpose of this legislation was to place disputed parts of the country's foreshore and seabed for which customary title was being claimed into public ownership (M. Palmer, 106; Marsh and Miller, 2012: 275–78). When Turia announced her intention to oppose the legislation, Clark dismissed her from her ministry. Turia then resigned from the Labour Party, forced a by-election in her seat of Te Tai Hauāuru, and formed a new political vehicle, which became known as the Māori Party.

The advent of coalition government created a previously unforeseen set of problems. Whereas collective responsibility was relatively easy to uphold in a Cabinet comprising members of the same party, what might happen where the interests of the junior coalition partner were in conflict with those of a majority of ministers? The first serious effort to address this issue occurred in 1998, when Winston Peters walked out of the weekly meeting of Cabinet in protest at its decision to sell the government's shares in Wellington Airport. Prime Minister Jenny Shipley promptly dismissed him from Cabinet, which caused the coalition to collapse. As a consequence of this experience, the rules around collective responsibility were amended with a view to providing the junior coalition partner in any government the freedom to adopt different policy positions from those of the senior partner. This involved introducing an 'agree to disagree' clause in any coalition agreement, although it was agreed that, '[A]ny public disassociation from Cabinet decisions by individual ministers outside the agreed processes is unacceptable' (New Zealand Government, 2008: 66).

For small support parties whose ministers remain outside of Cabinet, an even more flexible collective agreement has been struck. As we will see, while ministers are required to adhere to government policy on matters that lie within their portfolios, on all other policies they are free to represent the views of their party, regardless of whether they are in fundamental disagreement with those of the government. When Peters was Foreign Affairs Minister in the Clark government of 2005–8, for example, while he spoke for the government on foreign policy, he was free to oppose Cabinet on a range of domestic issues. This included his party's opposition to a free trade agreement with China, the negotiations for which were led, not by the Foreign Affairs Minister, but rather by the Trade Minister, Phil Goff.*

Conclusion

This chapter has identified three factors that largely define the New Zealand system of Cabinet government under MMP: minority government; a preference for forging governing arrangements with parties in the ideological centre ground (or by a counter-balancing process, as exemplified by National's agreement with Act, on the one hand, and the Māori Party, on the other, from 2008 onwards); and preserving the dominance of the two major parties by keeping small parties at arm's length from the governing process. Despite frequent lapses by journalists and others into describing the Key government as a coalition, it is in fact a minority National administration, with the Māori, Act and United Future parties having guaranteed support only in the policy areas covered by their portfolios. While they may choose to support the government on other matters, unlike their Cabinet colleagues, they are not bound by the convention of collective Cabinet responsibility. While the Key government is not unlike minority governments elsewhere, including the Scandinavian countries of Norway and Denmark, it is different in the special status given to small support parties

---

* The New Zealand–China Free Trade Agreement 2008 was passed with the support of National.

of essentially being *of* the government, but not *in* it. To help ensure that they continue to enjoy something approaching the dominance previously exercised under FPP, the major parties have reduced the opportunities for ideological blackmail by either making deals with small centre parties or, in the case of Key's National government, forming compensatory agreements with parties of the right and left, thereby allowing the government to play one against the other. The third and final piece in the Clark/Key governing jigsaw has been the decision to establish distance between small support parties and the business of Cabinet government. While such an arrangement may appear to benefit the governing party disproportionately, small parties have welcomed the opportunity it provides to reconcile their office-seeking and policy-making goals with the need to retain or increase their share of the vote at the next election.

In any finely balanced parliament even a one-seat adjustment in the distribution of seats can have consequences for the balance of power, as illustrated by the potentially delicate negotiating process facing National following its shock loss to New Zealand First in the Northland by-election of March 2015. Before then, Key was assured of maintaining his 61-seat majority by virtue of the largely unconditional support of David Seymour (Act), especially in advancing the government's economic agenda. With the loss of Northland, the government's other two support parties, United Future and the Māori Party, suddenly found themselves in the position of being able to leverage further influence in exchange for preserving the government's majority.

As we have seen, there are at least three possible explanations for the power of Cabinet within New Zealand's governmental system: its smallness and *esprit de corps*; the support of an institutional structure featuring the public service, including a wide range of government ministries and departments, together with an elaborate advisory network; and a legislative process that, for a variety of reasons, has been subject to the dominating influence of the executive. Because this third factor was discussed in previous chapters, this conclusion will focus on the first two of these explanations. Studies of group management have identified size as a significant factor in the effectiveness of the decision-making process. Although a group of twenty Cabinet ministers is considered to be close to the maximum number for executive governance, the dynamics of decision-making in the combined meetings of Cabinet need to be balanced against maintaining a network of Cabinet committees, as well managing a broad range of subject portfolios. To ensure that the highest levels of trust and confidentiality are maintained, every prime minister has supplemented the full Cabinet with an inner or 'kitchen' Cabinet, usually comprising five or six of the most senior ministers.* As well as acting as a sounding board for the Prime Minister, inner Cabinets can provide high-level advice on electoral and political strategy. In January 2014, for example, John Key convened his inner Cabinet in Auckland, reportedly with a view to discussing how his party might approach any post-election governing arrangements involving Winston Peters and New Zealand First (Young, 2014).

Along with smallness and intimacy comes an *esprit de corps* that has its roots in a shared ideology and social identity. Although no two people believe exactly the same, ministers of the same party subscribe to a common ethos, as well as the conventions of collective responsibility. In a country the size of New Zealand, it is not uncommon for ministers to have: received a similar education; been indoctrinated into the party by shared membership of a union, professional body or the youth wing of the party; attended party conferences, social events and other party functions prior to standing for Parliament; and spent several years together in the party caucus before finally being selected as a minister. While this process of political socialisation is not guaranteed to result in a constructive and harmonious work environment, relations within successive Cabinets would suggest that it certainly helps. Indeed, one of the potential dangers associated with New Zealand's experience of Cabinet government is that of a 'fortress Cabinet' that is dominated less by healthy disputation and debate than a form of psychological interdependence and conformity that has been described as 'group-think' (Janis, 1982).

Finally, whereas early postwar Cabinets were largely devoid of institutional support beyond the advice being offered by career public servants

---

* Key's inner Cabinet in the period 2008–14 consisted of Bill English, Gerry Brownlee, Steven Joyce, Judith Collins and Murray McCully.

employed in government ministries and departments, recent administrations have had the benefit of independent advice from a variety of sources, most notably the Department of the Prime Minister and Cabinet, Treasury and the State Services Commission, the last of which is responsible for making appointments and reviewing the performances of ministries and departments. The Department of the Prime Minister and Cabinet consists of seven business units, including the Cabinet Office and Policy Advisory Group. The latter body, which currently has twelve policy advisers and a director (see Cabinet Committees, Department of the Prime Minister and Cabinet website), is responsible for offering independent and often competing advice to that provided by members of the public service, whose independence is often questioned by incoming governments because of their close association with the previous administration. Unlike the Prime Minister's Office, which has a more directly political role, the Department of the Prime Minister and Cabinet focuses on policy advice, often presented as an attachment to the weekly briefing papers. Together they provide the Cabinet with a powerful tool with which to dominate the policy-making process.

Chapter Seven

Leaders and Leadership

In the increasingly personal world of politics, prime ministers and party leaders play a major role in framing the public's understanding of politics, conveying a vision of the good society and inspiring popular support. While leaders are often judged by the decisiveness, even ruthlessness, with which they wield power, leadership has been described as a two-way relationship between leaders and followers, with 'leaders inducing followers to act for certain goals that represent the values and the motivations ... of both leaders and followers' (MacGregor Burns, 2010: 19). When viewed in this way, leadership is less about the personal use of power than an ability to apply the skills of human interaction and persuasion, including intelligence, empathy and effective communication. With the decline of traditional voting allegiances and corresponding rise in the influence of the media, especially television, closer attention is being paid to the qualities that distinguish successful leaders from those who merely aspire to such a role. Adding a further layer of complexity to the media–leader relationship is the pervasiveness of today's celebrity culture, which scrutinises the personal lives of the most prominent politicians as never before.

Although opinion is divided on the influence of personality on the way people vote, with some scholars claiming it is important and others that it is not (Karvonen, 2010: 65–84), what is less open to dispute is the extent to which New Zealand now mirrors the presidential style of politics practised in the United States, particularly the media-driven leadership approaches we have come to associate with the election campaigns of recent candidates, notably Hillary Clinton and Barack Obama. In a number of respects, leadership contests in the two countries follow similar paths, with traditional methods, such as locally managed and conducted campaigns, having been replaced by the techniques of mass marketing, including centralised planning, televised interviews and debates, and a focus on the personal qualities and influence of the leader. When taken to extreme, personality politics is elevated above more traditional motivations, including the values and policies of the parties these candidates are offering to represent (Langer, 2011: 15).

On the other hand, generalisations about the impact of a more personal and presidential style of leadership should not be overstated. Unlike their counterparts in the United States, New Zealand voters do not directly elect their own Prime Minister, nor do they exempt their leaders from the expectation that their lifestyles broadly resemble those of ordinary voters. Little tolerance is likely to be shown to the prime minister who travels in a private jet or adopts the pomp and ceremony common among leaders in other countries. There are good reasons why this is the case. New Zealand continues to hold to an egalitarian ethos, the Prime Minister is the political leader, not the head of state, and while the Prime Minister chairs Cabinet and is the go-to person when the media require definitive comment on government action, final authority rests, not with the Prime Minister, but with the collective will of Cabinet.

A recurring theme in leadership studies has been the impact of the mixed-member proportional system (MMP) on the qualities of a successful leader (for example, Henderson, 2003; Hayward, 2010). Archetypal prime ministers, such as William Massey (1912–25) and Robert Muldoon (see Table 7.1), have tended to be known for their dynamic and populist style of leadership. In articulating the fears, frustrations and anxieties of particular segments of society, charismatic populists have been able to mobilise large-scale support. A less attractive feature of populist leadership, however, is the tendency to divide and rule. As one study of populism has pointed out, it fails to 'respect the core features of politics – the search for compromise between different interests, the need to understand another's position and the complexities of implementation' (Stoker, 2006: 139). As we have seen in previous chapters, these are precisely the skills required of successful leaders in the consultative and cooperative environment of MMP.

Table 7.1: Postwar New Zealand Prime Ministers

Prime Minister	Party	Years
Peter Fraser	Labour	1940–49
Sidney Holland	National	1949–57
Keith Holyoake	National	1957
Walter Nash	Labour	1957–60
Keith Holyoake	National	1960–72
John Marshall	National	1972
Norman Kirk	Labour	1972–74
Wallace Rowling	Labour	1974–75
Robert Muldoon	National	1975–84
David Lange	Labour	1984–89
Geoffrey Palmer	Labour	1989–90
Michael Moore	Labour	1990
Jim Bolger	National	1990–98
Jenny Shipley	National	1998–99
Helen Clark	Labour	1999–2008
John Key	National	2008–

This chapter will explore the personal qualities that characterise New Zealand's more presidential style of politics by focusing on three political contexts: prime ministerial leadership, the role of the Leader of the Opposition and leadership among the small parties. It will consider the distinctive requirements of each role and whether success in one sphere guarantees success in another. But first, the discussion will consider different approaches to the study of leadership and their relevance to the multi-party nature of governmental decision-making under MMP.

Studying Political Leadership

In assessing the qualities that distinguish leadership success from failure, it is only natural to ask whether a leader is born or made. We know, for example, that Helen Clark and John Key aspired to political leadership from an early age and, indeed, held leadership positions in academia and business respectively, long before each was first mentioned as a future prime minister. Does this suggest that the skills of a leader are apparent from their earliest years or, rather, are they developed and refined over the course of a career? One of the most astute observers of political leadership, and someone who was a personal friend of several American presidents, once asked whether leadership stemmed from an ability to innovate, mobilise or inspire. While the conclusion reached by James MacGregor Burns (2010) that leaders are neither born nor made may appear somewhat cynical, it reflects the view that power is fundamentally a two-way relationship between the aspirations of leaders and the expectations of their followers.

One way of studying political leadership is through the pages of political biographies. Typically, they provide the reader with a narrative on the life and times of the subject, including early life experiences and their impact on the acquisition of political knowledge and understanding. From Michael Bassett's study of the lives of some of New Zealand's best-known prime ministers, including Gordon Coates (1995) and Peter Fraser (with Michael King, 2000), and Barry Gustafson's biographies on Michael Joseph Savage (1986), Robert Muldoon (2000) and Keith Holyoake (2007), it is possible to learn much about each leader's political ambitions and skills, as well as the nature of the relationship they enjoyed with their followers. From the biography of Holyoake, for example, we learn that he was a pragmatic, hard-working and likeable politician, with an approachability that has drawn frequent comparisons with a more recent National Prime Minister, John Key. It has been said of Holyoake's pragmatism and powers of persuasion that, 'when a consensus was achieved it almost invariably gave him what he wanted personally' (Gustafson, 2007: 121). Turning to more recent prime ministers, Jon Johansson's study of Muldoon and David Lange compares the strengths and weaknesses of two of the country's most controversial prime ministers, both of whom struggled to adjust to the demands of leading a government at a time of profound economic and social change (Johansson, 2005). There is much to be said for the value of single-actor narratives in deepening our understanding of the history of political leadership in New Zealand.

A second, *relational* approach to the study of leadership focuses on the interdependence that exists between leaders and followers. *Transforming* leaders are described as the great visionaries who exemplify a style of leadership that not only motivates, but also inspires (MacGregor Burns, 2010). *Transactional* leaders, on the other hand, are known for their pragmatism and inclination towards a bargaining or deal-making brand of politics involving the exchange of goods and services. Whereas transformational leadership has a moral and ideological dimension that is said to lift the human spirit and mobilise its followers towards collective action, transactional leadership is concerned with the values of 'honesty, responsibility, fairness [and] the honoring of commitments' (ibid.: 426). Transformational change goes to the heart of the relationship between leaders and followers. Transactional change, in contrast, is more versatile, practical and stylistic.

For a similar set of distinctions, we turn to the work of Denis Kavanagh and Peter Morris, whose study of Britain's Margaret Thatcher contrasts the *mobilising* with the *reconciling* style of leadership (see Kavanagh and Morris, 1994). Reflecting their views that leadership is a matter of choosing 'horses for courses', Kavanagh and Morris regard mobilising leadership to be appropriate in times of national crisis, be it social, political or economic, when conditions call for change, and reconciling leadership to be a necessary antidote when there is a need for social cohesion and consensus. Unlike MacGregor Burns, Kavanagh and Morris see the relationship between these contrasting styles of leadership as cyclical in nature, with a period of turbulent reform (for example, the Thatcher period in the 1980s) creating a corresponding need for a period of relative stability and calm – hence the reconciling style of leadership of John Major, Thatcher's successor as Prime Minister.

While the mobilising model works well in single-party majority governments, it creates obvious problems when applied to the multi-party governing arrangements of MMP. Because such arrangements are said to require a style of leadership based on cooperation between political parties leading to compromise and decisions that are often based on consensus, there are solid grounds for the view that MMP works better under the more transactional and reconciling styles of leadership of a Clark or Key than the mobilising and potentially divisive leadership of a Muldoon or Brash, or indeed Jenny Shipley, who was chosen by her fellow MPs precisely because they believed she would resist the demands of National's coalition partner, New Zealand First. Within months of her taking office, the coalition broke apart.*

A third, *functional* approach to leadership is concerned with what a political leader actually does. Although New Zealand politicians are required to display a wide range of abilities, the functional approach calls for an overall judgement on the characteristic that most distinguishes their style of leadership (Miller, 2005). *Communicators* are the public performers who use their eloquence and fluency, especially during election campaigns, to inspire popular support. *Legislators*, on the other hand, are concerned less with personal popularity than designing and implementing public policy. Whereas David Lange was a great public performer, his deputy, Geoffrey Palmer, was the quintessential legislator, who introduced a raft of constitutional, monetary and social reforms that changed the face of New Zealand politics. Unlike the dynamic leadership of the communicators and the more principled approach of the legislators, the *managers* are the pragmatic deal-makers, whose ability to compromise and collaborate, even with political opponents, fits well with the requirements of MMP. Leading exponents of the managerial approach to leadership include Jim Bolger, Clark and Key.

Developing a Political Career

Leaders are of two types: career politicians, and those who either begin their time in politics late or choose to leave early to pursue another vocation. The changing nature of political representation is reflected in the growing trend towards the short-term political career, as exemplified by the early departure from politics of two potential prime ministers, Steve Maharey (Labour), to become a university vice-chancellor, and

---

* For a discussion on the application of the transformational and transactional styles of leadership to New Zealand, see Hayward, 2010.

Simon Power (National), for a career in banking. Rather than remain in Parliament following election defeat, Shipley and Clark both announced their retirement from elective politics and went on to pursue new careers, Shipley in business and Clark with the United Nations. Even before his third election victory, Key was the subject of growing speculation that he might retire from politics before the 2017 election. Embarking on post-prime ministerial careers was uncommon prior to the 1990s and is likely to have coincided with the advent of a younger, more highly educated and professionally trained generation of political leaders.

Although Clark and Key have contrasting backgrounds and abilities, both are ranked among New Zealand's most successful and popular prime ministers. Clark's early career followed a classic route for an aspiring Labour politician, especially one coming from the party's intellectual wing: university-educated, steeped in the culture and values of the party, and with extensive prior experience as a party official and parliamentary candidate. What gave her a point of difference, however, was the farming and National Party background of her family. Clark's intellectual ability, ambition and single-minded determination were apparent from her earliest years at university. Having been mentored by the professor of politics at the University of Auckland, Robert Chapman, she completed a postgraduate thesis under his supervision on political attitudes in the New Zealand countryside before enrolling in a PhD comparing farmers in politics in New Zealand and Scandinavia. This led to an appointment as a lecturer in public administration and comparative politics, a position that offered insight into the inner workings of the Wellington bureaucracy, as well as developing her skills as a public speaker and debater.

In tandem with her academic career, Clark embarked on an apprenticeship in party politics, with appointments to a variety of positions within the student, youth and women's divisions of the party, together with the party's national executive. As a result of Clark's growing interest in foreign policy, especially her opposition to apartheid and the Vietnam War, she developed an undeserved reputation for radicalism that remained with her throughout her time in Parliament. She first expressed an interest in elective politics during her student days, unsuccessfully contesting the Labour nomination for the seat of Auckland Central (it went to Richard

Prebble). In 1975 she was selected as Labour's candidate in the National stronghold of Piako. These were necessary first steps for an ambitious but still relatively young political activist. In Clark's 2009 valedictory speech, as she reflected on her long parliamentary career, the advice she offered to politically ambitious young people was to 'be prepared to run first for their party in electorates which are highly unlikely to be won, but where one will learn a lot and have more to offer when a winnable seat comes along. Success is seldom instant in politics, and, where it does come quickly, it can equally quickly fizzle out' (Clark, 2009). Long before the retirement of the incumbent MP, Warren Freer, Clark was being touted as a future candidate for the safe Auckland electorate of Mt Albert. After winning the seat in 1981, she turned her attention to securing a Cabinet position in a future Labour government. Although disappointed at being left out of the 1984 Lange Cabinet, three years later she was appointed to the portfolios of Housing and Conservation, followed by Health. At the age of 39 she became New Zealand's first female Deputy Prime Minister. In 1993, the Labour caucus elected her to replace Mike Moore as Leader of the Opposition.

Compared with Clark, Key's preparation for the role of prime minister was brief and somewhat unconventional. A career in business, principally as a foreign exchange dealer with Merrill Lynch, might seem to be a natural preparation for any aspiring National Party politician, were it not for the fact that much of it was based overseas, hence away from any direct involvement in domestic politics. While Key's interest in a political career had become known to senior National Party officials by the late 1990s, it took the direct intervention of the party president, Michelle Boag, to secure his nomination for the new West Auckland seat of Helensville, which he narrowly won in 2002, despite his party's landslide loss to Labour. Little was known about Key at that time, apart from his substantial wealth and residency in the affluent city suburb of Parnell. Offsetting these potentially negative biographical facts was a backstory that included being brought up in a state house by a solo mother who had escaped the Nazi invasion of Vienna (Key, 2002). Subsequent attempts by Labour to pry into Key's currency trading background and personal wealth were widely condemned as mean spirited and had the unintended consequence of drawing attention to his perceived strengths, especially an ability to understand and speak the language of ordinary New Zealanders.

Although it is usual for prime ministers to gain experience in Cabinet before reaching for the top job,* Key's rise to prominence in National's smallest-ever caucus of some 26 members can only be regarded as spectacular.† At a two-day conference convened by a group of political scientists at the University of Otago shortly after the 2002 election, Key was the only MP in attendance. As a newly elected politician, he expressed the desire to understand the reasons for his party's poorest performance in over six decades of electoral competition. A year later, Don Brash challenged Bill English for the party leadership. Having backed the much older contender – at 62 years of age, Brash was widely regarded as a short-term leader – Key was rewarded with the plum position of shadow Minister of Finance. When Brash offered his resignation following the party's defeat at the 2005 election, Key was well placed to replace him as Leader of the Opposition. While his congeniality and acute sense of timing tended to mask his undoubted ambition, rising from newly elected MP to opposition leader in a mere three-and-a-half years was, at that time, without precedent in the modern era (the exception being Brash, who became opposition leader after having been elected to Parliament a mere fifteen months earlier).

Qualities of a Leader

Despite their contrasting political backgrounds, Clark and Key share a number of the characteristics of a successful prime minister. Few would question their emotional intelligence, personal authority and ability to inspire, but can either be described as a charismatic leader? The almost messianic way in which 'charisma' is applied hardly sits well with a voting public that values empathy and modesty above most other traits, as befits the aura surrounding the life of New Zealand's most iconic

---

* Other postwar prime ministers lacking in previous ministerial experience were Sidney Holland, Norman Kirk and David Lange.
† Although 27 National MPs were elected, the MP for Pakuranga, Maurice Williamson, was suspended from caucus in July 2003 following public criticism of his leader, Bill English.

role model, Sir Edmund Hillary. So ambiguous has the term 'charisma' become that it is now more often applied to the sports stars and television personalities of celebrity culture than to political leaders. Among New Zealand's most admired politicians are Michael Joseph Savage and Norman Kirk, both of whom died while in office. Despite their unquestioned competence, Clark and Key have yet to reach similar levels of public esteem.

For a comprehensive list of the qualities expected of a political leader we turn to the coding frame produced by Ana Inés Langer in her study of British prime ministers (Langer, 2006; 2011). It is clear from this list (see Table 7.2) that the qualities of a political leader reflect a mixture of inherited capabilities and those acquired during the course of a career. While some characteristics, notably intelligence and psychological predisposition, are at least partially determined at birth, others, such as integrity, competence, judgement and an ability to communicate are products of a person's upbringing and career. It is largely because of this life-long opportunity to develop personal strengths and correct weaknesses that future leaders are not always easy to identify, especially if their rise to the top extends over a long career. A further danger is to focus on just one element, when successful leadership requires competence in a range of qualities. One of the criticisms of the psychoanalytic approach to the study of leadership, for example, is that excessive attention is given to the psychological dimension at the expense of other traits. Typically, such studies focus on the psychological make-up of their subjects by delving back into early childhood experiences, dangerous territory given that the methodology is unlikely to include interviews with the politicians themselves. Examples of psycho-biographical studies include those on President Richard Nixon and a former Australian leader, Prime Minister Bob Hawke (Mazlish, 1972; Anson, 1991).

In judging the relative merits of our two most recent prime ministers, it is important to acknowledge the influence of gender on public perceptions of leadership (see Curtin, 2008). Strong leadership, which generally is seen in a positive light, is often viewed negatively when it is identified in women. During the course of her career, Clark's leadership was frequently characterised as 'ruthless' and 'bossy', and her behaviour

Table 7.2: Langer's Personality Traits of a Leader

1. Integrity: qualities include honesty, decency and trustworthiness.
2. Strength: courage, power, determination.
3. Charisma: public appeal or popularity grounded on unspecific leadership qualities.
4. Competence: leadership skills for performing as prime minister, including ability as statesman and past political experiences/performance.
5. Intelligence: 'brain power' to understand or solve issues, to come up with fresh solutions, etc.
6. Communication and rhetorical skills: quality of performances in Parliament, the media, and/or other public realms.
7. Psychological: psychological characteristics of the prime minister's personality that are clearly linked to leadership qualities (e.g., control freak).
8. Political/personal: leadership qualities that touch upon personal life or the 'image' of it.*
9. Timing: ability to pick the right moment to contest the leadership, call an election, introduce new policies and ideas, etc. (Stern, 1993).

Sources: Langer, 2006; 2011.
* Cited in and adapted from Karvonen, 2010: 90.

towards her colleagues as that of a 'control freak'. On the other hand, few questioned her ability to understand and reflect the public mood. Although Clark's sensitivity to the shifting tides of opinion began to diminish as her government approached its third term, her astute understanding of the motivations of voters and her essential pragmatism ensured that Labour continued to dominate the centre ground of politics for the best part of nine years. Such was her importance to the party that her resignation as Leader of the Opposition in November 2008 marked the beginning of Labour's leadership and electoral decline.

Unlike the more measured Clark, Key is a visceral politician whose understanding of the needs of ordinary voters is more a matter of instinct than intellect or training. Although comparatively few voters have had a personal encounter with Key, his approachability, informality and lack of 'airs and graces', indeed, his very ordinariness, appear to connect him with the New Zealand public in a way not seen since the days of Holyoake and Kirk. According to one international study on leadership (Garzia, 2011), it is 'the constant struggle of contemporary political leaders to appear... as much as possible... as an *ordinary Joe*'. Quoting another study, this account goes on to observe that '"[we] want to trust competent leaders, but we also want to like them personally, and this is easier when they are perceived as essentially similar to us"'. One of the perceived strengths of Key's leadership on becoming Leader of the Opposition was its novelty. For example, unlike most politicians, including Clark, Key adopted a bipartisan stance on a number of issues, even supporting the passage of the deeply unpopular anti-smacking legislation and New Zealand's free trade agreement with China. To some observers, this willingness to seek accommodation with other parties made him appear refreshingly non-political. Ironically, although Key has gone on to become a highly partisan Prime Minister, launching bitter attack after bitter attack on the credibility of Labour and the Greens, his reputation as a largely non-ideological deal-making politician has persisted.

One way to judge the success of a leader is through the lens of public approval or empathy. As we see in Figure 7.1, although Clark's popularity was at its peak in the 1999 and 2002 elections, it remained consistent throughout her nine years as Prime Minister, in 2008 even exceeding that of Key, despite her party's loss to National. Since the survey from which these figures were drawn was conducted in the immediate aftermath of that election, respondents were aware of Clark's retirement, a decision that may well have strengthened their feelings of affection and regret. Key was a relatively unknown quantity in 2008, which may help explain why one in five respondents were either neutral or did not express an opinion on his leadership. In contrast, Clark's other National Party opponents during her nine years as Prime Minister, especially Brash and Shipley, were strongly disliked by many voters. Both were among New Zealand's most ideological politicians, and hence were deeply polarising figures (note the intensity of the feelings towards the major party leaders shown in Figure 7.2). Brash, of course, was also widely criticised for denying in the lead-up to the 2005 election that he had prior knowledge of secret campaign donations from the Exclusive Brethren. He later apologised for misleading his party and the voting public. On the other hand, the low support for English and Phil Goff is reflective of the poor performances of their parties at the

Leaders and Leadership

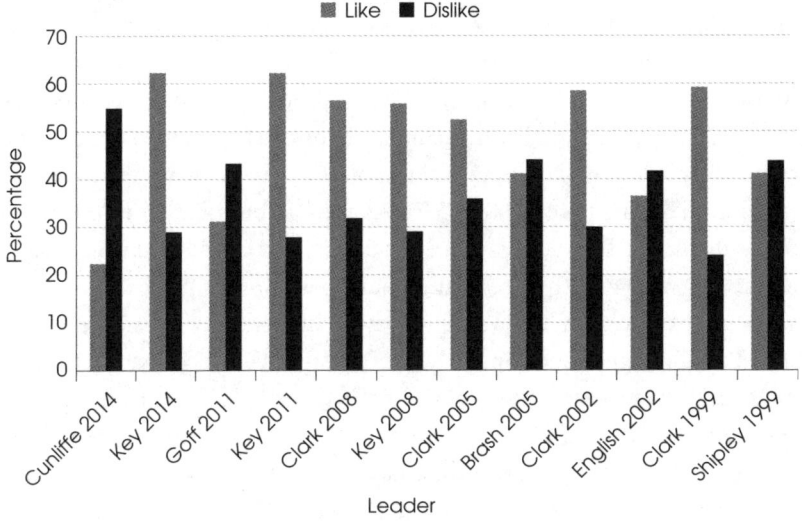

Figure 7.1: Feelings Towards Major Party Leaders
Source: New Zealand Election Study Surveys, 1999–2014.

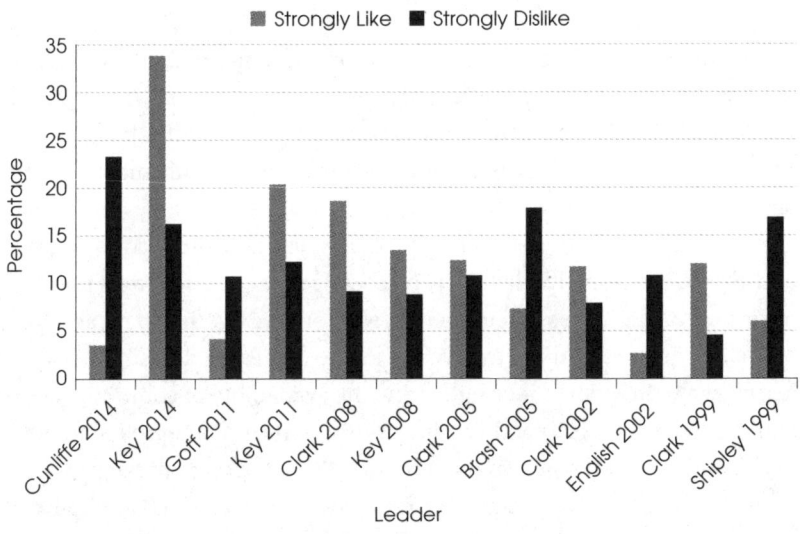

Figure 7.2: Intensity of Feelings Towards Major Party Leaders
Source: New Zealand Election Study Surveys, 1999–2014.

2002 and 2011 elections. In both cases their leadership was deemed to be a significant factor in the loss.

Since character is at the heart of the relationship between leaders and followers, any perceived breach of integrity or trust is likely to undermine public respect. Jenny Shipley's admission that she made up the figure of six million dollars in relation to TVNZ's contractual salary commitments to the dismissed broadcaster John Hawkesby, and Clark's decision to sign a painting that was then sold at a charity auction as her own original work, are examples of how a simple lapse of judgement can easily escalate into a much larger issue. Similarly, Key's insistence that he had not heard of Kim Dotcom before the police invaded the internet entrepreneur's residence in 2012, and David Cunliffe's efforts to conceal the sources of donations to his campaign for the leadership of the Labour Party, despite having accused National of adopting precisely the same method of concealment, raised questions about the integrity of both leaders.

Role of Prime Minister

Although the Prime Minister remains the first among equals, the transition to a more personal and presidential style of leadership has resulted in a gradual increase in the role of prime minister *vis-à-vis* that of Cabinet and the wider executive. Two main reasons have been advanced for this development: first, the gradual replacement of collective values and affiliations with a more individualistic approach to politics; and second, the rise of the media, especially television and social media, as a source of political information, discourse and influence (Karvonen, 2010: 4). In recognition of the importance of these trends, the Prime Minister's advisory network has grown with a view to strengthening the availability of communication and media expertise. Together with a more centralised approach to political campaigning by the two main parties, this development has provided the Prime Minister with unparalleled access to professional advice from a variety of sources, including press secretaries, polling and advertising agencies, public relations and human resources consultants, and personal groomers and speechwriters. Whereas Walter Nash (1957–60) had no more than a small secretarial staff, today's prime minister can draw on the support of a small army of public servants, consultants and advisers. At the hub of this network are the Department of the Prime Minister and Cabinet and the Private Office of the Prime Minister, the latter body having a more direct role in advising the Prime Minister on the political developments of the day. In addition to its staff of four press secretaries, the Office of the Prime Minister employs somewhere between fifteen and twenty staff, all of whom are directly responsible to the Prime Minister.

The role of the modern prime minister can be summarised under three main headings: the executive function, the communication function and the party leader function.

Executive Function

Unlike the heads of state in the United States and other constitutional democracies, the role of the prime minister in New Zealand is not spelled out in law. However, the *Cabinet Manual* (New Zealand Government, 2008: 18) does list a number of constitutional conventions. These include the Prime Minister's role as: head of the executive; adviser to the Governor-General on the appointment and dismissal of ministers; allocator of ministerial portfolios; overseer of the government's policy agenda; and, by tradition, minister responsible for the two intelligence services, the Security Intelligence Service (SIS) and the Government Communications Security Bureau (GCSB) – following the 2014 election Key handed over day-to-day responsibility for intelligence services to his Attorney-General, Christopher Finlayson. Perhaps most importantly, the Prime Minister is the chair of Cabinet, a role that includes setting the agenda, controlling any discussion, and determining Cabinet procedures and outcomes. Beyond these core functions, the Prime Minister is responsible for 'maintaining and coordinating' the government (ibid.). By implication, this includes overall responsibility for conveying the government's decisions to the public, a task that gives the Prime Minister ultimate responsibility for any and all portfolios.

As these responsibilities suggest, prime ministers have both a macro- and a micro-management function. At the macro-management level, their responsibilities extend to the public service, state-owned enterprises and Crown entities, Cabinet committees, and, under MMP, the formation and management of a minority and/or multi-party government. Whereas some prime ministers have adopted a relatively distant role more akin to that of the chair of a public company, others, like Key and especially Clark, are better described as chief executives, immersing themselves in the day-to-day running of the government and taking overall responsibility for its actions. Even in the extreme case of Lange, a prime minister who adopted a relatively hands-off approach to leadership, there were occasions when he chose to exercise executive power, including the decision to override the collective will of Cabinet by announcing that the government would not be proceeding with its flat tax proposal (Lange, 2005: 249). Perhaps the most potent, if seldom used, power of the Prime Minister is the ability to advise the Governor-General to dissolve Parliament and call an early election. Although it was widely predicted that this power would be used more frequently under the less stable multi-party conditions of MMP, it has happened only once, in 2002, at the behest of Clark, who feared that the implosion of her coalition partner, the Alliance, was destabilising the government and jeopardising Labour's chances of re-election.

As well as assuming responsibility for the macro-management of the government, the Prime Minister is required to be something of a micro-manager. It may seem almost inconceivable to the modern observer, but there was a time when New Zealand prime ministers were absent on overseas trips for several months at a time. During his term as Prime Minister, for example, Savage spent a total of four months on a visit to the United Kingdom to attend the coronation of the new monarch, King George VI (Gustafson, 1986: 206–10). Today, an absence of more than a few days would raise serious questions about the Prime Minister's ability to micro-manage the government. Even a prime minister with as detailed a grasp of her executive as Clark was unable to prevent ten ministerial dismissals or forced resignations, a pattern that continued under Key. Unlike Muldoon, who held the two most powerful positions of Prime Minister and Finance Minister, recent prime ministers have reduced their overall workload with a view to exercising closer control over the day-to-day management of government. For strong and independent leaders, there may be value in overseeing the appointment of advisers, including those prepared to challenge the decisions of the Prime Minister. As a number of political leaders have found, being surrounded by compliant advisers has its costs, not least the tendency to become isolated and lose touch with the needs of voters. On the other hand, good leadership requires access to a highly competent workforce, including a trusted chief of staff, a role both Heather Simpson and Wayne Eagleson executed with distinction during the prime ministerships of Clark and Key.

Communication Function
Public performances were once largely confined to the debating chamber and formal campaign meetings. Holyoake was uncomfortable with television and tried to avoid it, believing that an affectation in his voice became even more pronounced on the new medium of television. According to his biographer, when forced to make a television appearance, Holyoake would try to exercise control, advising on the placement of cameras and even insisting that he receive the interviewer's questions in advance (Gustafson, 2007: 157). While debating remains an important skill, other more traditional forms of communication have been largely superseded by television. The new focus on live studio interviews and news sound bites has not been an easy transition for some leaders. Despite his manifest ability as a debater and orator, Palmer struggled with television. In the intimate surroundings of a studio, his performances appeared wooden, declaratory and tense. And while Phil Goff debated well on television and radio, his loquacious answers to journalists' questions rarely fitted within the requirements of the five- or ten-second sound bite.

But leaders must also understand the art of storytelling. As the BBC broadcaster Gavin Esler has pointed out, to be truly successful a leader must have an ability to tell a great story. 'With more than half a billion people worldwide telling stories about themselves on Facebook, and millions more trying to communicate on other social media, with President Obama and Prime Minister Cameron using Twitter to keep in touch with followers, we can all learn from these masters of communications how to present ourselves, how to tell stories and how to avoid serious errors' (Esler, 2012: 15).

For examples of highly accomplished communicators in all media it is impossible to go past Lange, Clark and Key. The legally trained Lange had an irrepressible way with words, regardless of whether he was representing a client in the District (then Magistrates') Court, engaging in debate with Muldoon, delivering an extemporised speech or responding to questions in a television studio. As well as being an entertaining raconteur, he had an ability to speak with great force and conviction, as illustrated by his exchanges with the American pastor, Jerry Falwell, in the Oxford Union debate in 1985. While Clark lacked the rhetorical flair and repartee of Lange, she excelled in the use of television, especially as a forum for simplifying the complexities of government policy. On the other hand, one of her most costly mistakes was to under-estimate the debating ability of Key during the 2008 campaign. Despite occasional awkwardness with pronunciation and an informal, even casual, demeanor, Key proved to be a well-briefed and effective performer. With the help of 'talking points' provided by his press secretaries, Key is well prepared to respond to the issues that concern journalists, either within the precincts of Parliament or on his numerous trips around the country and overseas. As with Clark, Key is selective in his choice of radio stations, generally preferring to be interviewed by the more ideologically sympathetic broadcasters on commercial radio than their counterparts in the publicly owned Radio New Zealand.

Party Leader Function

One of the most important functions of any prime minister is the ability to represent the values and beliefs of the party. As well as being the flag-bearer for the party during an election campaign, the Prime Minister personifies the party within Parliament and the executive. This multi-faceted role is not without risk, particularly the danger of becoming isolated from party members and activists, many of whom see themselves as guardians of the party's ideology. However, it is the role of the prime minister to balance the demands of the party's grassroots support against alternative sources of advice, including career civil servants, political advisers and the many interest groups that regularly visit the Prime Minister's ninth-floor Beehive office. During visits to the party's regional and national conferences, the Prime Minister is likely to provide assurances that the policies set by Cabinet and its committees are compatible with those of the party. In extreme cases where these assurances are not believed, the credibility of the Prime Minister may be seriously compromised, as happened when breaches occurred between party members and Lange, Palmer, Moore and Bolger at the height of the free market reforms of the 1980s and early 1990s.

Leader of the Opposition

One of the most under-studied aspects of political leadership is the role of the Leader of the Opposition. There has long been a tendency to view the requirements and skills of leadership in opposition as complementary to those of the Prime Minister, so much so that they are regarded to be essentially one and the same. However, as a major analysis of opposition leaders in the United Kingdom has revealed, the skill-set required of an opposition leader is not necessarily transferable to that of prime minister. As a result, it is possible to succeed in one role but not the other, as illustrated by Winston Churchill, who clearly did not enjoy being in opposition, finding it difficult to adjust to his new role after five years as wartime prime minister (Theakston, 2012: 7). The same study also noted the importance of context in judging the effectiveness of an opposition leader, especially the performance of the government at the time and the political and electoral circumstances under which the opposition leader assumes the role (Heppell, 2012: 245).

Because relatively few New Zealand prime ministers remain in politics after losing an election, this discussion will focus on the functions of new opposition leaders as they rebuild the party in preparation for the next election.

Renew the Party Organisation
With most defeated prime ministers now choosing to retire with immediate effect, the likely first step for any outgoing government is the selection of a new leader, followed by a review of the party organisation. Until Labour changed its rules, the choice of leader in both major parties was

in the hands of the party caucus. Whereas most Western parties had long since expanded the selection process to include the participation of the party membership (Cross and Blais, 2012), New Zealand and Australia resisted reform until 2012 when, as part of an attempt to democratise the party organisation with a view to attracting new members, Labour introduced a 40 per cent caucus, 40 per cent party membership and 20 per cent trade-union leadership selection process. While the old system was still in place when David Shearer became leader in December 2011 following the resignation of Goff, the new rules were implemented in time for the election of Shearer's replacement, David Cunliffe, in September 2013. Crucially, while Cunliffe proved popular with party members and some union affiliates, he failed to win the support of the party caucus, a situation that undermined and eventually destroyed his credibility as leader. In a potentially ominous sequel, his successor, Andrew Little, won the support of only 15 per cent of his caucus colleagues on the first count of voting. He also remained less popular than his main rival, Grant Robertson, among party members, even after the preferences of the bottom two candidates had been re-allocated.* However, unlike the frosty reception given to Cunliffe, when the final results were announced the members of caucus quickly rallied in support of the new leader.

Restore Unity and Self-belief

One of the most important tasks of the opposition leader is to rebuild internal morale, never an easy task, but made more difficult when the party is recovering from an election defeat and transitioning to a new leader. It took National three elections and four leaders to recover from election defeat in 1999, and there was never any expectation that Labour would quickly bounce back from defeat and the loss of its long-term leader. Among the shortcomings Goff inherited on becoming leader were a demoralised party organisation, a caucus in urgent need of fresh blood and

---

* In Round 1, Little won 15 per cent support among caucus members and 25 per cent among party members. By Round 3, the percentages had risen to 43.8 and 44.8 per cent respectively. In contrast, union support in Round 3 was 75.6 per cent. The combined final figures were Little 50.5 per cent and Robertson 49.5 per cent. Source: M. Coatsworth, President, New Zealand Labour Party, 18 November 2014.

a failure on Clark's part to groom Goff as her successor. At 55 years, Goff's age should not have been an issue, especially in the context of the vast ministerial experience he had gained since his first appointment as a minister at the age of 31. Yet from the time of his selection he was looked upon as an interim leader whose time in office was unlikely to last beyond the 2011 election. Contributing to his subsequent failure to reignite the party were an under-performing caucus, an effective National-led government and a global economic crisis, all of which were exploited by Key and helped to reinforce his dominance. Under such adverse circumstances, restoring unity and self-belief proved an impossible task. Whereas Cunliffe's age was never an issue, opinion within the party was divided on his personal qualities and ability to unite the party organisation and parliamentary caucus, especially in light of allegations of disloyalty to the previous two leaders. Personal self-belief was never an issue with Cunliffe, and, indeed, he was frequently accused of over-confidence, but what he seemed to lack were sound judgement, empathy and an ability to inspire public confidence in his leadership.

Instil Confidence that S/he is Prime Minister in Waiting

An essential function of the opposition party is to begin to rebuild public confidence in its credibility as an alternative government. As well as appointing a shadow Cabinet and perhaps even presenting a shadow budget, the opposition leader must project the image of a prime minister in waiting. With opinion polls regularly asking voters to rank their preferred prime minister, being placed in competition with the incumbent prime minister can be a major challenge, especially early in the life of a government. In her valedictory speech, Clark recalled that in 1996, a Colmar Brunton/One News poll put her on a mere 2 per cent as preferred prime minister (Labour was on 14 per cent) (Clark, 2009). From her perspective, the tables were turned in 2002, when the opposition leader, Bill English, suffered a similar fate during her first term as Prime Minister.

Oppose the Government in Parliament

In the gladiatorial environment of Parliament's debating chamber it is up to the opposition leader to hold the government to account. While

Shearer might well have become a competent prime minister, he appeared to be temperamentally unsuited for the 'rough-and-tumble' of opposition politics. Unlike Muldoon and Lange, who were two of the most ruthlessly effective opposition leaders of postwar New Zealand, Shearer proved to be a mild-mannered politician who found it difficult to strike a balance between destructive and constructive opposition. As Muldoon so ably demonstrated, implicit in any criticism of the government's performance is a confidence that there is a clear and credible alternative, something that has not been immediately apparent in the parliamentary performance of less successful opposition leaders.

Sharpen Communication Skills

The sheer intensity of the media attention that comes with the role of opposition leader is something that is almost impossible to anticipate. Given the media's narrow focus on the party leaders, there are likely to have been relatively few opportunities for backbench MPs in particular to develop expertise in the art of the live studio interview and news sound bite. While this is best exemplified by the experience of Shearer, who was elected as a backbench MP less than three years before becoming party leader, it also has relevance to the experiences of Brash and Key, neither of whom had previously been a minister. As the aforementioned study has observed, the opposition leader is under immense pressure to at least equal the performance of the Prime Minister in Parliament and on television, and to do so in a way that 'enables [the public] to gain an image of competence that will ultimately aid their chances of electoral success' (Heppell, 2012: 4). In advertising for a new press secretary following his election as Leader of the Opposition, Little indicated that he was looking for someone 'who can make sure Mr Little appears in a positive story on the 6 pm news at least twice a week, and increase his Facebook likes to 40,000' (TV3, 3 News, 15 January 2015).

Prepare for the Next Election

It has been said that opposition parties don't win elections, governments lose them. This is only partially the case, however; indeed, as a number of opposition leaders have been able to demonstrate (see chapter ten), election campaigns provide an opportunity for the main opposition party to gain all-too-rare media exposure for its leader, motivate party activists, who in turn will mobilise voters, and offer an alternative policy agenda and vision to those provided by the government. Despite the seemingly unbalanced nature of the contest, especially in the event that the government is able to exploit its superior resources, three years well spent in opposition can have beneficial effects on party organisation, commitment and morale.

Leadership of Small Parties

Unlike the major parties, whose identities transcend those of a single leader, most of New Zealand's new parties are defined by the personal beliefs and ambitions of their founding leaders. Perhaps the most prominent example of this type of small party is New Zealand First, which, from its beginnings in the 1990s, was widely referred to as the 'Peters' Party. The strong association between the Internet/Mana Party and Kim Dotcom and Hone Harawira, and the explicit reference in the Progressive Party's registered name to 'Jim Anderton's Progressive Coalition', are further examples of the importance of personality to the formation and survival of small parties. When Anderton chose to retire from politics in 2008, his Progressive Coalition retired with him, a not uncommon outcome among movements of the personality-based sort.

Given the importance of leadership to a small party's *raison d'etre* and aspirations for success, there is considerable pressure on the leader to fulfil a variety of roles, including those of agitator, organiser, campaigner, and, in the event that the party becomes a support party or partner in government, legislator and minister.

Agitator
Because they are in competition with at least seven or eight party leaders in a media environment traditionally dominated by National and Labour, the small party leaders are under constant pressure to provoke, excite and disrupt with a view to attracting public attention and influencing the

course of the political debate. For a leading exponent of the art of agitation, it is hard to go past Peters, whose ability to exploit weaknesses in others and give voice to the anger and frustration of many older voters has made him one of the most influential politicians of the modern era. His decision to contest the National-held seat of Northland in a by-election in March 2015 is but one example of Peters' ability to get under the skin of the government. While their appeal has been less concerned with personality than the power of ideas, the leaders of the Green Party have been successful at keeping the environment and social justice issues, including child poverty, at the forefront of attention, especially through the use of new media, along with more traditional forms of action, including public protest.

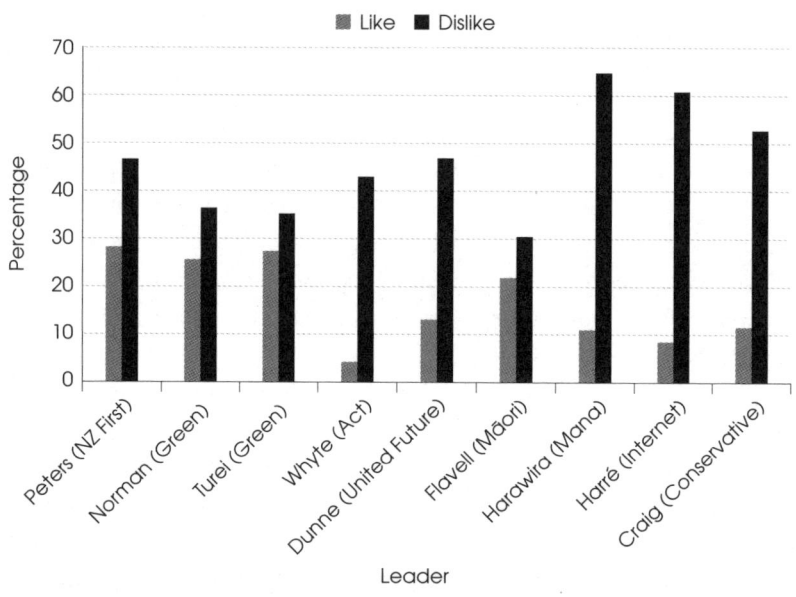

Figure 7.3: Feelings Towards the Small Party Leaders

Source: New Zealand Election Study, 2014.

Although by definition their appeal is limited to a niche market, the leaders of small parties tend to be viewed by the voting public with suspicion, even distrust, as illustrated by the results of Figure 7.3, with strongest feelings being directed towards those agitators who have attracted the greatest notoriety, namely Hone Harawira (Mana), Laila Harré (Internet) and, to a lesser extent, Act's Jamie Whyte. More than anything the low levels of esteem shown in Figure 7.3 may well reflect widespread concern that the leaders adopting the most extreme ideological positions are the least likely to contribute to stable and effective government. In contrast, the Green Party leaders, who had not previously experienced the curse of government, failed to generate strong feelings in either direction.

Organiser

A common characteristic among new parties is the absence of a pool of organisers, especially those with experience in creating a structure capable of mounting a nation-wide campaign. As a result, the leader of a new party is often called upon to fulfil a number of important tasks – elected representative, motivator, manager and administrator – in short, something of a Jack of all trades. Much of the responsibility for the early development of the Alliance, New Zealand First, United Future and Māori parties fell to the party leaders who, by virtue of being elected politicians, were able to fall back on the parliamentary resources provided for party leaders, including staffing and administration. While the examples of Colin Craig and the Conservatives, as well as Kim Dotcom, demonstrate that a benefactor with deep pockets can be a welcome resource, equally the Green Party has been able to compensate for its more limited finances by drawing on the enthusiasm and commitment of its grassroots members to build and consolidate its support.

Campaigner

Whereas the leaders of small parties are often ignored in the three years between elections, the election campaign provides the opportunity to re-establish their relevance, either as an alternative source of opinion, or as a potential partner in government. One of the most impressive campaign performances was that of United Future's Peter Dunne in 2002. His party's dramatic rise in the polls in the final days of the campaign was largely attributed to his performances in the televised leaders' debates, especially reassurances that, unlike the other small party leaders, he would be a stable and reliable influence on the next government. As a result, not only did his party's poll ratings rise from 1 per cent to nearly 9 per cent in the space of a week, its parliamentary representation also experienced a corresponding increase, going from one seat at the previous election to seven seats in 2002.

Legislator

It is frequently alleged that the uncompromising views of personality-based parties, especially breakaway movements from a major party, might preclude any form of cooperation, even under the multi-party arrangements of MMP. Despite presenting a comprehensive list of proposals, including policies deemed 'non-negotiable', it would be unrealistic for the leader of a small party to expect to negotiate acceptance of more than a handful of proposals, either as a coalition partner or under a confidence and supply arrangement. However, as Jeanette Fitzsimons, the former co-leader of the Green Party, found during her time in Parliament, in any finely balanced parliament, even those small parties that have been relegated to the ranks of the opposition are able to negotiate trade-offs as part of the legislative bargaining process. This situation was used to advantage by Russel Norman and Metiria Turei when, in 2008, they were able to negotiate a home insulation agreement with the incoming National-led government.

Conclusion

This chapter has focused on two main themes: the personal qualities that distinguish successful political leaders from those of more modest achievement, and the structural factors that help determine the style of leadership most appropriate to any given role. Unlike the 'lattice of leadership' found in Australia's federal system of government (Uhr, 2005), with the exception of local government, political leadership in New Zealand operates on a single dimension, that of its unitary system of government. Within that dimension, the skills required of one role are not necessarily transferable to those of another. This means that a successful Leader of the Opposition does not necessarily possess the skill-set required of a successful Prime Minister. Similarly, simply combining the qualities of the leader of a small party with those of a government minister is no guarantee of success, especially for populist leaders, whose careers tend to be built on an instinctive and unremitting opposition to whoever happens to be in government.

As we have discovered, the personal style of politics now found in New Zealand is a product of at least three major developments: first, the increasing influence of a more 'presidential' style of electoral politics; second, the gradual de-alignment of voters from traditional party loyalties and affiliations; and third, the changing environment of MMP. While these developments will be discussed more fully in chapters eight and ten, it is important to establish their relevance to the subject of leadership. Although New Zealand lacks a presidential system of government, it has been influenced by trends established in the United States and now widely practised in each and every Westminster democracy. They include: the development of more professional party organisations and campaigns; central planning, with most of the day-to-day planning taking place, not in party headquarters, but in the office of the leader; the growing dominance of television and other electronic media; and, largely as a result of the commercial demands of television, the gradual replacement of ideology and policy with a focus on personality and the qualities of a leader. Over the course of time, the traditional emphasis on manifestos and formal party meetings has been largely replaced by more presidential activities, including: walkabouts; studio interviews and sound bites; carefully orchestrated campaign opening and closing ceremonies, to which only the party faithful are invited; and the ubiquitous leaders' debates.

However, it would be unwise to overstate the impact of a more presidential style of leadership on the nation's electoral and institutional politics. As we have seen in other chapters, although voters cast the first of their two votes for their preferred party and the second for the electorate candidate of their choice, they do not elect the Prime Minister, nor do they elect the leaders of the various political parties, unless, of course, they happen to be paid-up members of the party concerned. While the personal skills and qualities of each leader receive much closer media attention than they did in the pre-television age, it is important to remember that the

Prime Minister has limited formal powers and can be removed from office by a simple majority of the party caucus. And while the Prime Minister chairs Cabinet and is free to speak on all matters of government policy, final authority rests, not with the Prime Minister, but with the collective will of Cabinet.

A second factor that helps account for the growing emphasis on a more personal style of politics is the gradual transformation of the two large class-based parties into what have been described as 'catch-all' political movements (Katz and Mair, 1994). There was a time when a majority of voters identified so strongly with National or Labour that they would never even contemplate voting for another party. However, rather than continuing to represent the class identities that defined their early existence, the two main parties have broadened their appeal to include the more individualistic, self-interested and transient motivations of new generations of voters. Through the medium of television, party leaders are able to reach over the heads of their members with messages and imagery that are more closely aligned to the interests of the median voter. This growing tendency to converge on matters of doctrine and policy has given rise to attempts to find alternative points of differentiation, hence the emphasis on contrasting styles of leadership (Karvonen, 2010; Vowles, 2002).

A third and final influence on the growth of personality politics has been the changing environment of MMP. With the presence in Parliament of up to ten party leaders at any given time (the Green and Māori parties have co-leaders), and with several leaders of the small parties having built their movements around their own personal agendas, the temptation to focus on contrasting leadership styles becomes overwhelming. As we have seen, one productive area of enquiry has been to consider whether the leadership qualities deemed desirable prior to the introduction of MMP are still appropriate under present governing arrangements. The overwhelming body of opinion among those who study political leadership appears to be that the demand for a more consensual and transactional style of leadership has largely replaced the mobilising and transformational leadership of the pre-MMP two-party era.

Chapter Eight

Political Parties

While National and Labour have lost the monopoly they once enjoyed as mass parties, and have had their powers further reduced as a consequence of the mixed-member proportional (MMP) system, both have been able to withstand the inevitable ebbs and flows in electoral support. As a result, they continue to dominate electoral and governmental politics. At the 2002 election, National's share of the vote dropped to a mere 20 per cent, its worst result ever. Six years later it was in government, and by 2011 and 2014 it had exceeded 47 per cent, setting a new record of support for any party under MMP. With Labour's electoral fortunes tracking in the opposite direction, the combined two-party vote during the past decade has tended to lie between 75 and 80 per cent, not far short of where it was prior to the introduction of MMP. From this dominant position, the two parties are able to alternate in government, giving them the power to dictate the terms of the political agenda.

A puzzle at the centre of this chapter is why two-party support remains so high, especially given New Zealand's increasingly diverse society and the multiplicity of options available to voters, with twenty or more parties contesting each general election.* As we will see, continuing success owes

---

* In his study of two-party politics, Alan Ware described New Zealand's two-party system as having 'collapsed' (Ware, 2009: 15). This chapter argues that Ware overstates the decline of the former two-party system.

much to the two parties' legacy in government, their ability to draw on the loyalty of voters and their greater access to resources. The future of the small parties,* on the other hand, is more complex and difficult to predict. As we know from the collapse of the Alliance, Act and United Future, most have failed either to advance a sufficiently compelling message or to nurture their own particular sources of potential support, weaknesses that have become more pronounced the closer their ties to government (Miller and Curtin, 2011).

As well as considering the nature of New Zealand's multi-party system, this chapter will look within the parties themselves to examine their beliefs, how they are organised and the sorts of people they claim to represent. Given the highly competitive nature of the party system, especially the pressure on parties to maximise their vote, how important is it that they continue to be defined by their core values and beliefs? A further important consideration of this chapter is the impact of declining membership on the ability of parties to represent the interests of the voting public, especially when it comes to fulfilling the core functions of recruiting candidates, mobilising voters and raising the funds with which to launch a modern election campaign.

The Party System

A political party has been described as 'any group, however loosely organised, seeking to elect governmental officeholders under a given label' (Epstein, 1967: 9). In some respects parties are rather like interest groups – as well as representing commonly held values, both aim to achieve certain political outcomes. What makes parties different from interest groups, however, is their core function of electing candidates for public office, a responsibility that involves both competition and cooperation, as parties

---

* These parties are sometimes referred to as 'third' parties, on other occasions as either 'minor' or 'small' parties. To avoid relegating them to an insignificant role in Parliament and government, they will be referred to in this chapter as 'small' parties.

engage one with the other (Ware, 2009: 2; Webb, 2000: 1). This process of engagement requires that parties serve as a two-way link between the voting public and their elected leaders (Lawson and Merkl, 1988; Maor, 1997).

Together, parties make up what is referred to as the *party system*. One-party states, such as China, can hardly claim to have a party system, on the grounds that there are no other parties with which to cooperate or compete. Despite its large and diverse population, the United States, with its long-established Democratic and Republican parties, remains the most prominent exponent of two-party politics. At election after election, almost every vote cast in the Electoral College – an arcane body that officially elects the president – has been for the two large parties. Several former two-party systems, such as the United Kingdom, Canada and even Australia, have developed a multiplicity of parties, whose particular causes, such as regionalism and nationalism, are no longer capable of being accommodated within the two-party system. Multi-party systems may be moderate in size, with fewer than six elected parties, or follow the Israeli model of being highly fragmented. New Zealand can be described as having a moderate party system – although it has had as many as eight elected parties, at least three are so small as to create something of a 'multi-party mirage' (Curtin and Miller, 2012: 132).

While party systems are products of a number of influences, a nation's social structure and electoral system are the most important. Social and cultural divisions or cleavages take a number of different forms and may be based on class, ethnicity, culture, language or religion. In deeply pluralistic societies, the presence of several different divisions is likely to be reflected in the diversity of the party system, as illustrated by the range of religious, linguistic and regional cleavages to be found in the multi-party systems of Belgium, Italy and Israel. In contrast, New Zealand was long considered a one-dimensional society, with socio-economic class providing the only significant cleavage in an otherwise homogeneous social structure. With the formation of a separate Māori party, Mana Motuhake, in 1980, the possibility of a second, ethnic, dimension began to be discussed. As it turned out, most Māori voters continued to support Labour until 1996, when New Zealand First, then the Māori and Mana parties, began their assault on the Māori seats.* While an urban/rural dimension was first detected in the early 1900s, it had always been closely associated with occupation and income, both of which were represented within the two-party system. The emergence of a number of new parties in the 1990s diverted attention from social structural divisions to more issues-based dimensions, such as post-materialism and economic interventionism, both of which might help explain the presence of three Green parties at the 1996 election, as well as the line-up of parties on either side of the free market divide (Nagel, 1994).

The second major influence on the nature of the party system are the electoral rules, with scholars claiming that a causal link exists between first-past-the-post (FPP)† voting and two-party systems on the one hand, and proportional voting and multi-party systems on the other (Duverger, 1964: 217). As we saw in chapter five, under FPP a vote for one of the less-fancied parties was deemed to be a wasted vote, advice that has been used to nobble the growth of small parties dating back to the earliest years of the Labour Party. Despite retaining a toehold in the party system, for the best part of fifty years Social Credit suffered the effects of being treated as an electoral irrelevance, a condition made worse by the widely dispersed nature of its support. When combined with New Zealand's particular version of the Westminster political structure (see chapter two), it became even more difficult for small parties to survive, let alone prosper. In the absence of either a federal structure of government or an elected upper house, and with a long tradition of non-partisanship (at least formally) in local government, the only opportunity to gain representation was through election to the House of Representatives. In the sixteen general elections that took place between 1945 and 1992, the year of the first

---

* Tau Henare (New Zealand First) won the seat of Northern Maori in 1993, and three years later the party defeated Labour in the remaining Māori seats.

† Another term for first-past-the-post is plurality voting. According to the rules of FPP, to win an electorate contest the candidate must receive at least one more vote than the second-running candidate, even if the vote falls short of a majority (Farrell, 1997: 12).

electoral referendum, a total of only five MPs were elected from the small parties. Most faced defeat after a mere one or two terms.*

In his seminal study of political parties, Maurice Duverger made the claim that proportional representation 'always coincides with a multi-party system: in no country in the world has proportional representation given rise to a two-party system or kept one in existence' (Duverger, 1964: 245). One of the obvious reasons why small parties prosper in proportional electoral systems is the significantly lower threshold for representation, and hence the much smaller incidence of wasted votes. Instead of having to win a plurality of the votes in any given electorate, under proportional voting systems all a party has to do is reach the designated threshold, be it 5 per cent or some other figure, and it will receive representation in proportion to its share of the vote. The result, as Duverger points out, is that proportionality has a 'multiplicative tendency', causing new parties to be formed and established parties to divide and fragment. In the case of New Zealand, the decision to adopt two electoral thresholds had a greater effect on the multiplication of elected parties than any changes to the social structure (see chapter five).†

Development of the Party System

As we are about to see, throughout its history the party system has faced competing pressures to consolidate and fragment. Before the formation of New Zealand's first political party in the early 1890s, Parliament was made up of a number of factions, some of which were based on shared beliefs, while others were a product of personal or regional ties. Because these factions were mostly fluid arrangements, they lacked the accountability we normally associate with political parties. After coming to power in 1890,

---

* Four represented Social Credit: V. F. Cracknell (Hobson) 1966–69; B. C. Beetham (Rangitikei) 1978–84; G. T. Knapp (East Coast Bays) 1980–87; and N. J. Morrison (Pakuranga) 1984–87. J. P. Anderton (Sydenham), who was first elected as a Labour MP in 1984, contested the 1990 election under the NewLabour Party label.

† As we saw in chapter five, as well as a 5 per cent threshold, New Zealand's particular variant of MMP has a one-seat threshold for any party winning an electorate contest.

the Liberal government became aware of the benefits of having a more formal, disciplined and durable approach to political decision-making. As a result, it began to develop the rudimentary structure and policies of New Zealand's first political party. In the absence of an organised opposition, the fledgling party reached out to a broad electoral constituency: Māori and Pākehā; employers and trade unionists; city and provincial town dwellers; and self-employed farmers and farm workers. In short, the Liberals aimed to be the party of all New Zealanders. However, by the early 1900s, this broad electoral coalition was beginning to unravel, with prosperous farmers who opposed the government's leasehold land policy joining forces with more affluent members of the urban middle class to form the conservative Reform Party, and unionised workers on the left of the Liberal Party switching loyalties to the small radical and moderate electoral groups representing organised labour.

Following the formation of the Labour Party in 1916, a fully fledged party system began to take shape. The Reform and Liberal parties competed on the right of the political spectrum, appearing to give Labour ample opportunity to build its constituency on the left, with core support coming from unionised workers in the large urban electorates. However, creating an electorally popular workers' party proved to be a more difficult task than anticipated. Labour's political opponents were ruthlessly successful at characterising it as a party of extremists, a tactic made plausible by its radical stance on progressive taxation; state ownership of the means of production, distribution and exchange; and military conscription (Bassett, 1982). In pamphlets and other campaign material being disseminated by its opponents, Labour was depicted as a dangerously extreme and unpatriotic movement, even one that took its orders from Moscow.

With the advent of the Great Depression and the growing unpopularity of the Reform–Liberal coalition government, Labour began to moderate its message with a view to reaching beyond its core constituency to some unlikely sources of support. These included the politico-religious Rātana movement, which was led by the Māori prophet Tahupōtiki Rātana, together with the Social Credit Association. The latter was embraced by large numbers of struggling farmers and small business operators, who saw cheap credit as the answer to their financial woes. By the time of its

1935 landslide victory, Labour had built a mass-membership organisation, the first of its kind in New Zealand.

The beginning of the two-party era was marked by the fusion of the Reform and Liberal parties to create the National Party in 1936. Although the two conservative parties had maintained a close working relationship, which included a period of coalition government between 1931 and 1935, the electoral threat posed by Labour quickly rendered a formal merger an electoral necessity. By adopting Labour's organisational structure, National was able to build a formidable political force – on a *per capita* basis, the most successful mass party to be found in any Western democracy, with an estimated membership of 100,000 spread across 1000 branches within two years of its formation (Gustafson, 1986: 26). The building process continued for the next two decades. By 1960, when the party returned to government after three years in opposition, its membership had reached 230,000, or approximately 40 per cent of National's total vote (ibid.: 82–83). Just as Labour's identity was built on its predominantly urban and working-class base, so National's had its roots in the support of farmers, business proprietors and managers, together with the burgeoning middle class who had taken up residence in the metropolitan suburbs and provincial cities and towns. By presenting itself as the party of free enterprise, pragmatism and modernity, National hoped to broaden its appeal to all sections of the community.

In contrast, by the late 1940s it had become apparent that fourteen years in government, half of which had been occupied fighting a distant war, had taken their toll on an increasingly weary Labour administration. National held power for all but six of the next 34 years. For most of that time, while it campaigned on a promise of individual autonomy and limited government, its primary role was to manage the Keynesian welfare state introduced by Labour. To this end, its economic priorities included a commitment to high levels of state regulation, ownership and control. This broadly contradictory stance reaped significant electoral rewards, leaving Labour little opportunity to carve out a distinctive policy agenda from that of National.

A rare victory in 1972 allowed Labour to forge an independent foreign policy based on New Zealand's growing sense of nationhood and gradual shift of identity away from Britain and towards the South Pacific. But the new government also encountered growing economic problems, mostly resulting from successive rises in international oil prices and the loss of Britain as a major trading partner following its entry into the European Economic Community. By the late 1970s, voters viewed with increasing cynicism the perceived failure of the two major parties to deal with the effects of economic stagnation and high inflation. Although they had long prided themselves in their broad-church appeal to voters, the rise of the new social movements, notably the anti-Vietnam, anti-nuclear, feminist, environmental and anti-apartheid movements, and the resurgence of interest in New Zealand's perennial third party, Social Credit, had a corrosive effect on levels of support for National and Labour.

Although Social Credit managed to win only one parliamentary seat at the 1978 election, its 16 per cent share of the vote marked the beginning of a new era of electoral multipartism. At the following election, the party's vote increased to over 21 per cent, and in 1984 the libertarian New Zealand Party won 12 per cent of the vote but no seats. While the two-party vote returned to a familiar 92 per cent in 1987, several new anti-free-market parties were on the cusp of being formed, including NewLabour (1989) and the Green Party of Aotearoa New Zealand (1990). Having persuaded many Labour Party members and activists to defect, the leaders of the NewLabour Party were confident of a good result at the 1990 election. The party's 5 per cent share of the vote was disappointing, especially given that the more recently formed and loosely organised Green Party averaged 9 per cent in the seats it contested. The following year, NewLabour and the Greens reached an electoral accommodation with Social Credit (now called the Democrats) and Mana Motuhake, and later the Liberal Party, a small splinter movement from National. By nominating just one candidate per seat, this five-party Alliance hoped to reduce the incidence of vote splitting among the small parties. It had an immediate effect – in a by-election in the National stronghold of Tamaki, the Alliance came close to victory (Miller and Catt, 1993).

In February 1993, a former National Cabinet minister, Winston Peters, resigned his seat of Tauranga, thereby forcing a by-election, which he won as an Independent candidate. He then formed New Zealand First, a party that became known for its populist views on immigration, foreign investment and corruption. Although the combined vote for the small parties at the 1993 general election was 30 per cent (not far short of the 35 per cent received by National), with the Alliance receiving over 18 per cent of the vote, the small parties' reward was a mere four seats, compared with the 45 seats received by National.

In 1993 a small group of former MPs, including Roger Douglas, Richard Prebble and Derek Quigley, formed a libertarian pressure group, the Association of Consumers and Taxpayers, with a view to exerting pressure on the National government to complete the free market reform agenda begun by Labour. Although some senior figures in the association had campaigned against electoral reform, the referendum decision to adopt MMP forced a change of plan. In 1994, the association was converted into a fully fledged political party.

Table 8.1: Party Support in General Elections under MMP, 1996–2014

Party	Founded	1996	1999	2002	2005	2008	2011	2014
National	1936	33.8	30.5	20.9	39.1	44.9	47.3	47.0
Labour	1916	28.2	38.7	41.3	41.1	34.0	27.5	25.1
Green	1990		5.2	7.0	5.3	6.7	11.1	10.7
NZ First	1993	13.4	4.3	10.4	5.7	4.1	6.6	8.7
Māori	2004				2.1	2.4	1.4	1.3
Act	1994	6.1	7.0	7.1	1.5	3.7	1.1	0.7
United Future	2000			6.7	2.7	0.9	0.6	0.2
Mana	2011						1.1	1.4
Conservative	2011						2.7	4.0
Alliance	1991	10.1	7.7	1.3	0.1	0.1	0.1	

Source: New Zealand Electoral Commission, http://www.electionresults.govt.nz/.

The formation of the Act Party marked a watershed in the country's transition to a multi-party system. Whereas the first wave of multipartism had its roots in ideological conflict, the second pre-MMP wave was a product of political opportunism. Attracted by the anticipated congeniality of the MMP environment for small parties, a number of mainly backbench MPs reasoned that, by strategically positioning new parties on the left–right spectrum, they would be well placed to contribute to a future multi-party government. Among the new parties to be established in the run-up to the first MMP election were the Right of Centre Party (renamed the Conservative Party), Christian Democrats and United (later renamed United Future). At the 1996 election there were 22 registered parties and twelve unregistered parties. With the exception of Act, the only parties to win seats in the new MMP Parliament were those that had been established by sitting MPs (see Table 8.1, previous page, that shows party voting, 1996–2014).

Values and Policies

In this new crowded marketplace of parties, how was one party likely to be distinguished from another? There are two starkly different perspectives on the importance of ideology to the way parties compete. The first stresses the enduring quality of the party's founding principles, which are used to mobilise members and win the support of voters. According to this view, while parties adapt their message in response to changing conditions, as well as the changing views of followers, they remain true to their founding principles. As one scholar has put it, parties are 'prisoners of their own history as an institution' (Ware, 1996: 18). An alternative perspective comes from the work of Anthony Downs (1957), who regarded parties as being primarily motivated by a desire to win votes. Unlike the enduring ideological qualities associated with the first approach to party competition, the vote-maximising model views the electorate as a political marketplace where entrepreneurial parties compete by offering products they believe the voting public need and want.

Ideological Model
In his analysis of the continuing importance of a party's founding aspirations and beliefs, Ware identifies a number of party 'families', including

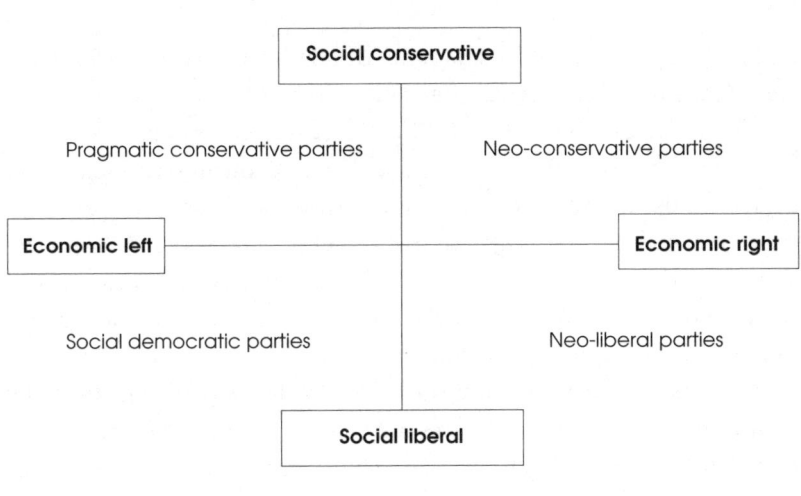

Figure 8.1: Ideological Dimensions Matrix
Source: Adapted from Mulgan (2004: 249).

a social democratic family and a conservative family, as well as families based on ethnicity, religion and the environment (Ware, 1996: 22).* What the members of each family have in common is a commitment to a shared set of values. This clustering of party families can be expressed by way of a matrix, with the horizontal line showing the left–right extremes of economic intervention and the free market, and the vertical line representing the extremes of social conservatism and liberalism (see Figure 8.1). While social democratic parties endorse the basic principles of capitalism, they believe that the excesses of the capitalist economy should be subject to some state intervention and control, hence their use of taxation as a way of reducing disparities of wealth and income. Neo-liberal parties, on the other hand, believe in a minimalist state. Their libertarian values preclude any significant role for the government in regulating the economy, delivering welfare, or dictating one's moral or social beliefs. Rather, the only meaningful role for the state is in the protection of the life, liberty

---

* The notion of party families has been adopted in a number of studies, including Esaiasson and Heidar, 2000: 456.

and property of its citizens. Examples of neo-liberal parties include the New Zealand and Act parties, together with the Libertarianz.

The distinction between neo-liberal and neo-conservative parties is best seen in the beliefs of Margaret Thatcher and Ronald Reagan, political leaders whose brand of conservatism included a commitment to traditional social values, a strong military capability, and the upholding of law and order. Their particular combination of economic liberalism and social conservatism appealed to a broad range of political and religious groups including, in Reagan's case, members of the influential 'Moral Majority'.

Pragmatic conservative parties, on the other hand, are distinguished by their commitment to expediency rather than principle, a stance best exemplified by Robert Muldoon's 1975 campaign slogan 'New Zealand the way you want it' (Gustafson, 1986: 121) and promise to voters that he would leave the country no worse off than the way he found it. His commitment to the status quo included strong intervention in the economy, especially with a view to continuing to fund a universal welfare state, together with a pledge to uphold traditional social values on such matters as race relations, homosexual law reform and abortion. As Richard Mulgan has observed, the broad-church nature of both National and Labour helps explain why they appear in more than one category (Mulgan, 2004: 248; and see Figure 8.2). Whereas Muldoon was an unquestioned pragmatic conservative, other members of his party included economic or social liberals, notably Derek Quigley (who went on to help found the Act Party), Jim McLay (Muldoon's successor as leader) and Marilyn Waring.

Among the goals Labour can be described as sharing with social democratic parties in other countries are a more cooperative society, political and economic equality, a just distribution of wealth from an active and interventionist state, Keynesian economics, comprehensive and universal welfare, and the protection of human rights. When in 2014 the party leader, David Cunliffe, described what the party stood for, he reached back to a legacy built on a fair distribution of wealth, carefully moderated by a benevolent state: 'The rich are getting richer, the middle are struggling, the poor are going backwards. That is the human face of trickle-down economics – the daft idea that if you give more to the people at the top, eventually things will get better for the rest' (Cunliffe, 2014).

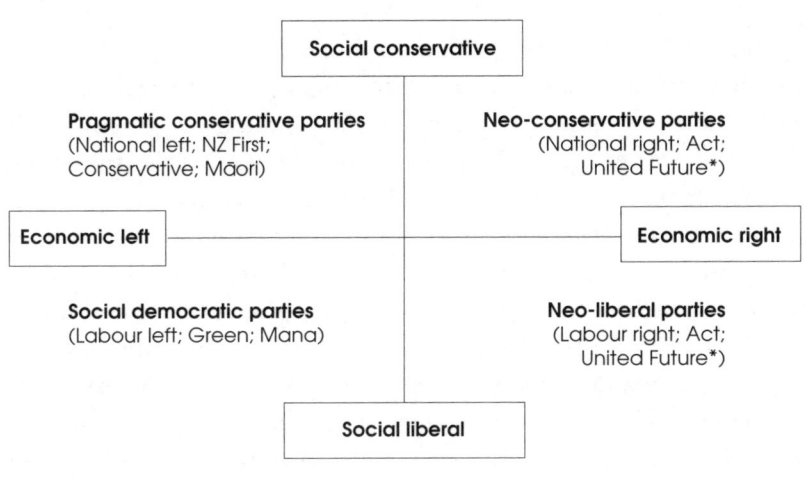

Figure 8.2: Ideological Dimensions and Political Parties

Source: Adapted from Mulgan (2004: 249).

* Parties often fall into more than one ideological category, for example the Act Party or the 'centrist' party United Future, which at various times has attempted to attract support from liberals, ethnic minorities, Christians and conservatives.

Instead of representing the modernisation of social democracy, the Lange government's experiment with right-wing economic reform was regarded by critics as a violation of the movement's founding principles of fairness, equality and social justice. Subsequent attempts to reconcile ideological tensions within party ranks included the decision of some senior politicians, including a government minister, Steve Maharey, to adopt the rhetoric, if not the substance, of what became known as the politics of the Third Way (Giddens, 1998; Giddens, 2000; Chatterjee et al., 1999). The notion of a Third Way had its roots in growing concern that social democratic parties were caught in a bind between the 'uncaring individualism' of the right and the 'ineffective collectivism' of the left. Its leading advocates, including President Bill Clinton and former British Prime Minister, Tony Blair, expressed support for the core values of social democracy, whilst at the same time recognising the importance of the global trend towards a more open and competitive marketplace. Evidence of the eclectic character of the movement could be seen in its commitment to the decentralisation and devolution of power, constitutional reform designed to make decision-making more democratic, and the encouragement of individual self-help through such means as 'welfare-to-work'. While advocates hold that the Third Way represents the revitalisation of social democracy, critics described it as an unsuccessful attempt to provide neo-liberalism with a human face.

In what some interpreted as a swing to the left, in 2014 Cunliffe announced a 'bread-and-butter' set of policy proposals, some of which involved a significant increase in the role of the state, including legislating to raise wage rates, controlling power prices, amending Reserve Bank legislation with a view to reducing mortgage interest and exchange rates, extending paid parental leave from fourteen weeks to six months, and introducing measures to address the problem of child poverty. While these policies were consistent with the party's founding principles, others, such as deep-sea oil drilling and mining on Crown land, both of which promised to deliver much needed jobs, were more problematic, raising tensions between the party's left and right wings, especially over Labour's likely strategy with respect to any future policy concessions to the Greens.

Not surprisingly, National draws its ideological inspiration from principles that are antithetical to those traditionally associated with Labour. These include individual freedom and self-reliance, the free market, limited government, enforcement of law and order, support for the monarchy and defence of the realm. While there is a consistency in the way these principles have been expressed, as we have seen, one of the hallmarks of National's style of government has been its ability to moderate its principles with a view to broadening its electoral appeal. In 2011, for example, any ideologically driven impulse towards the full privatisation of state-owned power companies was tempered by the need to claim a public mandate. The result was a pragmatic solution that preserved the government's controlling 51 per cent interest in each company. As one of the architects of the plan, the Minister of Economic Development, Steven Joyce, observed in relation to his own personal beliefs: 'I don't see myself as right wing. I've believed strongly in the ability of individuals to make decisions and make their own courses in terms of how they want to live their lives. I don't see that as particularly ideological' (Stuart, 2014). This is a view widely shared among the party's ministers and backbench MPs and helps explain National's commitment to a public–private partnership in areas such as education (for example, charter schools), health-care provision, and the ownership and management of prisons. It also explains National's continued support for a number of Labour initiatives, including its Working for Families scheme and interest-free loans for tertiary students.

Vote-maximisation Model

In his controversial study, *An Economic Theory of Democracy*, Anthony Downs (1957) advances the argument that the primary concern of political parties is the need to win votes. Whereas our first approach makes a case for the defining importance of a party's founding ethos and principles, the vote-maximising model views elections as something akin to a public market, where parties compete by offering products they believe the voting public need and want. In other words, instead of parties winning elections to make policy, according to Downs they make policy in order to win elections. In two-party-dominant systems, such as New Zealand, while the two main parties may range widely across the left–right spectrum with a view to eliminating competition, especially competition from the small parties on either flank, their primary target is the overwhelming majority of voters who converge in the ideological centre ground. As the two-way competition becomes more intense, they begin to adopt each other's policies, as well as appeal to the irrationality of voters by making their policies 'vague and ambiguous' (Downs, 1957: 115). This absence of policy divergence exposes the parties to the criticism of being little more than 'tweedledum and tweedledee'. According to this vote-centred approach, ideology is highly flexible and adaptable, and tends to be given much less emphasis than more immediate considerations, such as personality, leadership, branding, media presentation and the tools of mass marketing. In the event that policies meet with public resistance or rejection, they can be repackaged or replaced by others that are more appealing.

While this entrepreneurial approach to party competition may give an appearance of self-serving pragmatism devoid of principle, this is not entirely the case. According to Downs, parties would be unwise to abandon their founding values and beliefs, and for two main reasons. Because voters tend to lack the time to become well informed on specific party policies, they use a party's ideology as something of a signpost that guides them towards a voting decision. Furthermore, ideology has the benefit of constraining parties that attempt to leapfrog over each other with a view to simply maximising their vote. Downs argues that parties lose all credibility with voters if they are perceived to be making unprincipled manoeuvres along the ideological spectrum for the purpose of outflanking a potential rival.

As this discussion has suggested, the *ideological* and *vote-maximising* approaches are not entirely incompatible; indeed, while there are times when parties need to defend their principles in order to remain true to the beliefs of their members, they must also be responsive to shifting tides of opinion. As a result, both major parties not only monitor media coverage of issues and events, but also conduct their own internal polls, often before drafting and releasing new policy, and on other occasions for the purpose of executing policy U-turns. During National's 2011–14 term of government, these included reversing unpopular education reforms, such as the announced increase in class sizes, as well as the prohibition on the sale of 'legal highs' and the subsequent ban on the animal testing of synthetic drugs. Over the same period of time Labour also made a number of U-turns, including the removal of GST from fresh fruit and vegetables, as well as the decision not to tax the first $5,000 of income. All back-downs were a direct result of concern that the policies in question were proving unpopular with the voting public.

Whereas the major parties are sufficiently well resourced to conduct their own public opinion research, small parties tend to rely on political instinct, together with media reportage and commentary, as well as the word-of-mouth impressions of their members and elected officials. Their constituencies are small and highly susceptible to the personal agendas of their leaders, as illustrated by the case of Winston Peters, whose election speeches are calibrated to reignite the populist sentiment first expressed in 1996, when the party received 13 per cent of the vote and 17 seats. Peters' recurring targets include the free market, members of the political establishment, big business, immigrants, and foreign owners and investors. Although New Zealand First describes itself as a centre party capable of coalescing with either National or Labour, its electoral success is largely a product of its right-wing agenda. This has included opposition to biculturalism; the stereotyping of immigrants and refugees, especially from Asia; support for a smaller Parliament; and increased use of the instruments of direct democracy, particularly citizens'-initiated referenda (CIR). Because its message resonates with the nostalgia of times past, New Zealand First receives the bulk of its support from socially conservative New Zealanders, especially those over the age of 65. Having failed to meet the 5 per cent electoral threshold in 2008, the party returned to Parliament in 2011 with eight list seats and 7 per cent of the vote.

Another small party capable of carving out a distinct identity is Act. Although it began as a low-tax, small-state party committed to completing the free market revolution begun by Labour, for much of its existence it has been bogged down in a debate between its purists and pragmatists, with Douglas on one side and Prebble and perk-busting MP Rodney Hide taking a more electorally expedient, even populist, stand on such issues as race relations and law and order. Had the party maintained its ideological purity, it may well have retained the 6 to 7 per cent support it enjoyed at its first three elections. However, by diluting its radical economic agenda and adopting a number of populist policies that closely resembled those of New Zealand First, especially on political corruption, law and order, and race relations, the party lost much of its distinctiveness as an electoral organisation. With the removal of Hide as leader in 2011, followed by the departure of Don Brash the same year and John Banks in 2013, the party began the task of reinventing itself as a libertarian alternative to National. By then the level of public support had dropped to less than 1 per cent. Only National's decision, first made in 2005, to gift Act the electorate seat of Epsom kept it from losing its remaining seat in Parliament. Navigating the party back to its libertarian roots whilst at the same time trying to rediscover its electoral appeal proved to be a stern challenge for its then leader, Jamie Whyte, a political philosopher who was recruited from the United Kingdom in 2013. Shortly after assuming the leadership, Whyte expressed support for the legalisation of incestuous relationships between consenting adults, a stance that hardly augured well for the future of his leadership, or, indeed, that of his party.

Unlike Act and New Zealand First, the Greens have managed to maintain an uncompromising position with respect to their founding principles while continuing to enjoy consistently high levels of electoral support. The party has its roots in at least two ideological traditions, environmentalism and the collectivist values of social democracy, hence the occasional reference to the Greens as a red–green party. These two traditions are not always in harmony, especially on the frequent occasions when environmental priorities clash with the livelihood of workers, as exemplified by the public criticisms of the Greens by Labour's Shane Jones prior to his resignation from Parliament in 2014. Unlike materialists, who stress the importance of jobs, economic stability and growth, together with the home comforts we tend to associate with a prosperous economy (Inglehart, 1977), the Greens have been described as post-materialists, a term that is often used pejoratively to describe the liberal social values, middle-class lifestyles and environmental radicalism of a new generation of political activists. Having expressed a commitment to the principles of ecological sustainability and social responsibility, the Greens pursue a policy agenda that includes opposition to continuing investment in motorways and roads, the pollution of lakes and rivers, deep-sea oil drilling, the felling of indigenous forests and mining in national parks. Of course, they are also known for their initiatives on a range of social issues, including anti-smacking legislation, same-sex marriage, the rights of women and Māori sovereignty.

Party Participation

The growing influence of the electronic media, together with the trend towards more professionally planned and centralised election campaigns, has had a profound impact on the organisational capabilities of the two major parties. Whereas mass parties once operated as conveyor belts, with grassroots members providing the essential link between the voting public and their elected representatives, the advent of television made it possible for party leaders to reach over the heads of their members and speak directly to a mass audience. While members continued to have a role in raising funds and increasing voter turnout, other functions became less useful to the party leadership, especially in the areas of policy formation, public opinion monitoring and organising campaigns. Rather than relying on the skills of enthusiastic amateurs, the two major parties began to employ professionals, including advertising agencies, communications companies, public relations advisers, and professional marketers and fundraisers. To finance these services, parties became increasingly dependent on the resources of the state. As party leaders began to dilute their message with a view to appealing to a broader and less ideologically motivated and class-based electoral market, the mass party gradually disappeared, to be replaced by what is sometimes referred to as the 'catch-all' (Katz and Mair, 1994) or 'electoral-professional' party (Panebianco, 1988). As a result, there has been less incentive to maintain a strong grassroots organisation based on a large and active membership.

It would be wrong to lay all of the blame for these developments on the political parties themselves. When compared with previous generations, one of the most distinctive features of contemporary society has been the extent to which collective values have been replaced by more individualistic ones, a trend that has had a profound impact on levels of membership and activism, whether in voluntary service associations, sports clubs, youth groups, trade unions or political parties. While it might have been thought that the decline in civic engagement was a direct product of the move from villages to towns, and from provincial towns to the more impersonal city suburbs, disengagement has impacted on each and every part of the national community. Whereas one in four voters once belonged to a political party, today it is closer to two in a hundred.* It is a trend that affects the small parties as much as the large ones. Shortly before the 2014 election, for example, both United Future and Act found that their membership numbers had fallen temporarily below the 500-minimum required for continued registration with the New Zealand Electoral Commission.

---

* Because the two major parties refuse to disclose their party membership numbers, these proportions are only approximate and do not include trade union members who belong to the Labour Party by virtue of the fact that their union is an affiliated member.

Organisational Structure

Despite their falling memberships, the two main parties continue to maintain the organisations of mass parties. Complementing the parliamentary structure, which focuses on the party caucus and leader's office (see chapter four), is an extra-parliamentary organisation that is shaped like a pyramid and operates at the national, regional, electorate and branch levels. At the national level is the party president,* who presides over a board (National) or council (Labour). Each serves as the governing body of the party between annual conferences. National's board has nine members, including the president and party leader. Labour's council of some nineteen members includes seven regional representatives and two non-voting representatives of the parliamentary caucus. The membership of the council and board is determined by a vote of all delegates in attendance at each party's annual conference.

While each major party has a youth section, Labour maintains a number of 'special' branches, including women's, university, industrial, and Māori and Pasifika branches. Each party has a policy consultation committee or policy council, made up of a mixture of elected politicians and representatives of the extra-parliamentary party. One of the primary tasks of these policy committees is to produce a manifesto prior to each general election. Despite the tradition in both parties of policy remits being proposed by grassroots members for debate at the regional and national conferences, in recent years the time allocated for policy discussion has been greatly reduced, partly in recognition of the increasingly dominant policy-making role of the elected politicians, but also because of the extent to which party conferences are now stage-managed with a view to projecting a harmonious public image. Disagreement over aspects of party policy is seen to be inconsistent with that image.

By comparison with the complex structures of the two major parties, the organisations of the small parties are skeletal and tend to be located, if informally, in the parliamentary offices of the party leaders. Commonly

---

* Labour's president is Nigel Haworth and National's Peter Goodfellow.

experienced problems that limit the effectiveness of small parties are small budgets, low membership numbers and a thinly spread base of electoral support. Whereas the large parties, together with the business-friendly Act Party, are able attract substantial donations from corporations and wealthy individuals through a range of party fundraising activities, small parties tend to be regarded by potential donors as relatively unimportant, having comparatively little to offer by way of potential influence and power. As a result, a number have found it expedient either to reach an electoral accommodation with other small parties or to pool their resources, examples of which include the cooperation arrangement reached in the 1990s between the five parties of the Alliance, as well as the two parties making up the Christian Coalition, and, more recently, the financial assistance provided by Kim Dotcom's Internet Party to the cash-strapped Mana Party. Of course, new movements can also be largely bankrolled by their founding leaders, as illustrated by Colin Craig's Conservative Party in 2011 and 2014. Since leaving the Alliance in 1999, the Greens have been something of an exception. In addition to any indirect assistance provided by parliamentary and electorate staff, they have been able to maintain a sizeable paid-up membership and volunteer workforce. Their financial situation has been further assisted by the requirement that all Green MPs and other candidates for public office contribute one-tenth of their gross salary (excluding allowances) to the party. With foresight and prudent management, the party has been able to extend its organisational reach into areas of low growth, especially Auckland.

The Party-funding Debate

In recent years, two aspects of party finance have been the subject of close scrutiny and debate: first, the laws around the funding of election campaigns; and second, whether or not political parties should be funded solely by the state.

Financing Election Campaigns

Following its re-election in 2005, Helen Clark's Labour government introduced an Electoral (Finance Reform) Bill designed to prevent wealthy organisations from making sizeable donations in the months immediately preceding an election campaign. Labour's primary target was a small and shadowy religious sect, the Exclusive Brethren, whose members had donated an estimated one million dollars to National's 2005 election campaign with a view to bringing about a change of government (Hager, 2006). The secrecy with which this small religious organisation launched its publicity campaign, especially given the closely fought nature of the election, caused Labour to introduce legislation setting strict limits on the size of donations and the timespan involved. Spending limits for donor agencies or 'promoters' were set at $120,000 and the period when restrictions were to apply was extended from three months before an election to 1 January in the year of an election. Donations of over $12,000 had to be registered with the New Zealand Electoral Commission and were subject to financial disclosure. National and Act, along with a number of media, lobby group and professional bodies, such as the New Zealand Law Society, described the Finance Bill as an attack on democracy and free speech, with National promising to repeal it on becoming the government. The Electoral Amendment Act, which was passed in 2010, returned the pre-election period to three months and increased the limit donor organisations were permitted to spend on campaign advertising to $300,000. Donations to parties had to be disclosed only if they exceeded $15,000. Spending limits for parliamentary candidates were set at $25,000 and for parties $2.8 million.

State Versus Private Funding

In some countries, political parties are required to raise all their funds from private sources, while in others they are fully funded by the state. New Zealand has a long tradition of part-public part-private funding, with the state paying for any expenses involved in the registration and preparation of voters, as well as broadcasting time during the election campaign period. Indirectly, the state also meets the payment of expenses incurred by MPs during the course of the campaign, including salaries, travel, research and staffing resources. Because all other costs must be funded from private sources, parties engage in a number of activities, including everything from membership drives and fundraising events to direct appeals to wealthy individuals. Because recruiting new members is time-consuming and produces a relatively low financial return, there is an increasing tendency to rely on the donations of large corporations and interest groups, such as the trade unions, the business world and farmers' associations. Whenever it is alleged that donations are being received in exchange for political access and influence, there is a rekindling of the debate on the relative merits of public versus private funding.

Advocates of full state funding tend to focus on three main concerns: first, the increasing cost of campaigns; second, the need for a fair distribution of funding across all political parties, including those representing low-income groups; and third, the promise of greater transparency and accountability, especially with respect to anonymous donations. While *per capita* campaign costs are significantly lower in New Zealand than the United States, the rise of the professional campaign has had a costly impact on traditional party-funding sources. As we have seen, this has resulted in some inventive fundraising schemes, including 'meet and greet' occasions with government ministers (referred to by National as 'Cabinet Club' events), as well as direct approaches to wealthy corporations and individuals. Related to this issue of rising costs is the question of fairness in the distribution of funds across political parties. As the co-leader of the Green Party, Metiria Turei, reportedly stated, 'An election should be a battle of ideas, not a battle of who has the most money' (Trevett, 2010). To ensure that all parties get their message across, including non-parliamentary parties, which lack access to the state-funded largesse enjoyed by their parliamentary counterparts, it is argued that state funding should be made on a *pro rata* basis similar to the present allocation of broadcasting time.

The third and perhaps most important concern is that full state funding promises to remove any doubts the public might have about a lack of transparency and accountability. Despite a recent tightening of the rules around anonymous donations, David Cunliffe controversially set up a secret trust for the purpose of channelling anonymous donations into his campaign for the Labour Party leadership. Although arguments around 'money for access' tend to falter through the absence of any proof of a causal link, members of the public have a right to be concerned. In 2010, for example, Minister of Internal Affairs Nathan Guy, having been lobbied by a fellow minister, Maurice Williamson, as well as the mayor of Auckland, John Banks, granted New Zealand citizenship to a wealthy Chinese immigrant against the advice of his officials. It was followed by a visit by the Prime Minister and Williamson to open the first stage of Donghua Liu's hotel development. Liu subsequently made a $22,000 donation to the National Party as well as substantial donations to the election campaigns of National's Jami-Lee Ross (Botany) and Scott Simpson (Coromandel).

Opponents of financial reform, on the other hand, argue that state funding will do nothing to curb over-spending during election campaigns; indeed, they believe the history of state funding would suggest that, when organisations become beneficiaries of the taxpaying public, their spending habits become careless and excessive. In response to the allegation that private funding disadvantages small parties representing the interests of those on low incomes, opponents argue that fairness should be measured, not by size or access to resources, but rather by a party's commitment to hard work and initiative. One of the criticisms of state funding is that it encourages parties to rest on their laurels, glorying in past achievements rather than expending the sort of effort that is required to recruit new members, raise funds and vigorously contest elections. According to this argument, rather than providing greater accountability, full state funding will cause parties to stagnate. Finally, opponents of state funding argue that there is no evidence of a smoking gun or proven causal link between private donations and corrupt practices, certainly of the sort that might result in 'money for access' deals being done between donors and government ministers.

Candidate Selection

As we saw in chapter five, the Electoral Act's requirement that the parties adopt democratic rules for candidate selection is followed to varying degrees (Electoral Act, 1993: 46). In the case of the Act Party, for example, while an indicative ballot is conducted among party members, it is the board that decides the composition and ranks the party list. In contrast, the Greens conduct a ballot among party members, although with the proviso that the political leadership first presents them with an indicative list. There are a number of reasons why parties place restrictions on the level of involvement by grassroots party members. Quite apart from concerns about possible flaws in the democratic process, or the possibility that it might produce an inappropriate candidate, left-of-centre parties tend to be of the view that fair representation is best achieved through firm central guidance, if not control. It is for this reason that the Greens stipulate that the party has male and female co-leaders, and that women occupy at least every second place on the party list. Rather than adopting a quota system for meeting equity obligations, Labour's moderating committee stops periodically during the list-ranking process to conduct an equity review. Once the selection process has been completed, the decisions of the committee are final and not open to appeal.

Because National makes no formal provision for equity considerations, believing that decisions should be based on meritocratic criteria alone, the selection of electorate candidates is more devolved than for Labour. Following the example of political parties in the United Kingdom and elsewhere, National conducts an electoral college for prospective candidates, the purpose of which is to identify and provide advice and support for potential candidates, as well as to assist electorates in pre-selecting suitable candidates. During the pre-selection phase, the candidates are interviewed and reference-checked, after which the number of remaining candidates is reduced to a maximum of five. At the selection meeting, which is attended by 60 or more delegates, the candidates deliver short speeches and answer two questions, after which the delegates cast their votes. It is unusual for the party headquarters or political leadership to interfere with this process. Election within Labour, by comparison, is the responsibility of a small committee made up of local and central representatives – usually a combination of senior party officials and elected politicians. Where electorate membership numbers are small, or local committee members divided, it is not uncommon for head office to make the final decision. National's procedures for ranking the party list are similar to those of Labour, with final responsibility resting with a nationally appointed list-ranking committee.

In some of the small personality-driven parties, the rules around candidate selection are more flexible and subject to periodic intervention by the party leadership. Prior to the 2011 general election, for example, New Zealand First was charged with breaching its own rules on list selection by exempting its leader, Winston Peters, from the requirement that all list candidates also contest an electorate seat (Farrar, 2011). This was not the first time the leader was charged with personal intervention in the candidate selection process. In 1996, Peters was said to have personally ranked the New Zealand First party list (Laws, 1998: 342), and three years later he was accused of controversially dropping two women MPs, Robyn McDonald and Jenny Bloxham, to unelectable positions on the list.

Conclusion

This chapter began by asking why the two major parties continue to prosper in the more competitive multi-party environment of MMP. It proposed three possible explanations: the ability of National and Labour to draw on the loyalty of voters, their legacy in government and the benefits derived from their superior resources.

Having almost completed the transition from the class-based politics of the mass party era to the catch-all politics of today, National and Labour seek to maximise their appeal to voters by competing in the ideological centre ground. In contrast, their rivals are forced to garner support from much smaller electoral communities, including ethnic and religious minorities, environmentalists and those on either side of the neo-liberal divide. Frustrated by their failure to create a sufficiently large niche of potential support, these parties are either pushed towards the extremities of left and right or relegated to a lopsided battle with the large parties for the support of the median voter.

A second reason for the continuing strength of the two main parties is their legacy in government. For close to half a century under FPP they were able to maintain an aura of privilege and power. Their credibility was enhanced by the existence of an array of networks that included the public service, the media and a vast range of special interest groups. In contrast, small parties tended to be relegated to the role of political outsiders, leaving them with little or no prospect of gaining seats in Parliament, let alone Cabinet. As a result, they were widely perceived to be of no particular value to the political process, apart from acting as agents of protest. Against all expectations, this two-party mindset persists to the present day, with the result that small parties receive few accolades for their contribution to stable and effective government. Recognising the electoral risks of being seen to be partners in government, their leaders are less likely to accept ministerial positions within Cabinet and hence, from their perspective, inside government. From this vantage point they are able to preserve some limited autonomy, while continuing to struggle to build any real sense of political legitimacy.

A final reason for the dominance of the two major parties is their superior resources. As our discussion on candidate selection demonstrates, the major parties are able to draw on a much larger and more thoroughly vetted pool of potential candidates than the small parties, some of which struggle to find candidates. A problem that impacts on all parties is the conflation of diminishing resources and rising costs, a situation largely accounted for by the trend towards more centrally controlled, professional and expensive campaigns. As we know, although all parties suffer from a loss of paid-up members, the major parties enjoy better access to large corporate donations, as well as the benefits that flow from the state's largesse. In addition to receiving the lion's share of the state-funded broadcasting allocation, they are able to draw on a range of state-funded benefits, including MPs' salaries, travel expenses, telephone and postage allowances, and staff resources. Together, these resources place the major parties in a position of privilege, reinforcing their dominance within the political system.

Chapter Nine

Māori Electoral Politics

Democratic representation and decision-making are fundamental to the way we practise politics. To make democracy work for the benefit of all, there must be agreed mechanisms by which power is shared equally. While the New Zealand Parliament serves as a model of the long-established principle of majority rule, an important challenge facing any democracy is the need to give due recognition to the rights of minorities. Nowhere is this more apparent than in the protection of the rights of Māori who, as well as constituting some 15 per cent of the total population, have legitimate claims based on their status as the tangata whenua or indigenous people of New Zealand. Without due recognition being given to their collective status, as well as to that of other ethnic and minority groups, democracy could well degenerate into what Alexis de Tocqueville once described as the 'tyranny of the majority' (de Tocqueville, 1837).

New Zealand has a mixed record of providing equal electoral rights for Māori. As we saw in chapter one, along with other adult males, Māori males were granted the right to cast a vote in 1852. Fifteen years later, the decision was made to create four dedicated Māori seats. Until quite recently, these initiatives were widely viewed as evidence of the government's commitment to a racially inclusive society, in contrast to the long history of discrimination suffered by the Aboriginal population of Australia. What was less well known, however, was the extent to which Māori were under-represented by virtue of being restricted to only four seats. As the historian Keith Sorrenson has calculated (Sorrenson, 2014:

172), had the number of Māori seats been based on the same population per seat as their European equivalents, the entitlement would have been at least fourteen seats rather than the allotted four.* Nor were the motives behind the idea of separate representation entirely pure. For European advocates of separate representation, creating stand-alone Māori seats served the useful purpose of ensuring that some of the 70 European electorates were not 'swamped' by Māori voters (Martin, 2004: 60). As the electoral system evolved, other inequalities became apparent. Although granted the right to cast a vote, most Māori males were excluded from voting, having failed to meet a property qualification based on individual rather than communal ownership of land. Whereas the secret ballot was first introduced in the European seats in 1871, it was not made compulsory in Māori seats for a further 66 years. Māori deemed half-caste or more were not permitted to vote in European seats; Māori and non-Māori voters did not vote on the same day until 1951; registration of Māori voters was not made compulsory until 1956 (29 years later than for Europeans); and Māori were not permitted to register in either the Māori or renamed 'General roll' until 1975 (New Zealand Electoral Commission, 2002: 189–91).

This chapter will consider the past, present and future of Māori electoral politics. More than ever before, almost every parliamentary party now includes Māori in its line-up of parliamentary candidates, with generally positive effects on the overall proportions of Māori MPs and ministers. In particular, the presence of two registered Māori political parties, namely the Māori and Mana parties, offers a distinctly Māori perspective to the executive and legislative agendas. However, without the protection of a codified constitution, advances in the levels of Māori representation and influence can quickly disappear, as illustrated by the decline of an earlier Māori party, the Mana Motuhake movement, in the early 2000s, and the Mana Party's loss of its one parliamentary seat in 2014. In its investigation into the current state of Māori politics, the Constitutional Advisory Panel (2013), which was established as a

---

* Citing somewhat different population figures, Ranginui Walker argued that Māori were entitled to some twenty seats (Walker, 1984: 4; 1990: 144).

result of the Māori Party's post-election negotiations with National in 2008, considered arguments for the retention and abolition of the seven Māori electorates, as well as suggestions for the further enhancement of Māori representation, including entrenchment of the Māori seats, creation of a second legislative chamber, and the devolution of designated powers to specially created tribal authorities or parliaments. Two contrasting views have been brought to the resulting discussions: on the one hand, the view made famous in the Orewa speech of National's Don Brash and first captured in the words of Captain Hobson in 1840 when he announced that 'we are now one people' (Mulgan, 1989b: 6); and the other, the bicultural argument that New Zealand is made up of two distinct peoples, with Māori claiming 'the right to a parity of status with the ruling majority' (Vasil, 2000: 216), or, as Donna Awatere put it, a society in which 'taha Maori receives an equal consideration with, and equally determines the course of this country as taha Pakeha' (quoted in Walker, 1983: 6). Finally, given the historically low levels of participation in the electoral process, no study of electoral politics is complete without some consideration of the vexed question of voter turnout.

Early Māori Representation

Much of the early Māori opposition to government policy had its roots in colonisation, notably the imposition of a dominant European political and cultural identity, the extensive transfer of aboriginal land into the hands of the settlers and the 'token' provision of seats under the terms of the 1867 Maori Representation Act (Walker, 1990: 144). Early attempts to fill the four designated Māori seats were poorly executed by the returning officers concerned, with the result that some elections were uncontested, while others attracted few votes. A gradual expansion in the number of polling places had a positive effect on rates of participation, as well as on the competitiveness of the contests (Sorrenson, 2014: 176–77). But despite offering a distinctly Māori perspective, the influence of the four Māori MPs on parliamentary decision-making remained small. Meanwhile, a number of attempts were made to establish small tribal independence movements, as well as a trans-tribal Māori parliament committed to the devolution of political and economic power.

As MPs began to replace their independent and factional instincts with an attachment to a new phenomenon – a party system – Māori voters and MPs went in one of two directions, with some aligning themselves with the Liberal Party, while others supported its more conservative offshoot, Reform. Most prominent among the Māori politicians of that era were the Liberal Party's James Carroll, Hone Heke, Pita Te Rangi Hīroa (Peter Buck), Tame Parata and Āpirana Ngata, together with Reform's Māui Pōmare.* They were an impressive group – most were highly educated, professionally trained, and thoroughly prepared for a career in politics – with Carroll, Ngata and Pōmare receiving appointments as Cabinet ministers. Whereas Pōmare was known for his assimilationist views on race relations (Sorrenson, 2014: 183), the others, especially Ngata, devoted their political careers to improving living standards and opportunities for Māori. However, their views were always going to be those of a tiny minority within the party and its parliamentary caucus. As Sorrenson has observed, 'Ngata's parliamentary career demonstrated more clearly than those of any of his colleagues both the opportunities but also the ultimate limitations of the existing system of Maori representation in Parliament' (Sorrenson, 2014: 187). These limitations were most graphically seen in the failure of Ngata and his colleagues to slow down, let alone prevent, the wholesale alienation of Māori land.

Electoral Alliance with Labour

The next stage in the history of Māori electoral politics was marked by the forging of an alliance between Labour and the 25,000-member Rātana Church (Walker, 1984: 8), an arrangement that gave the two movements

---

* James Carroll (MP for Waiapu, then Gisborne, 1893–1919), Hone Heke (Northern Maori, 1893–1909), Tame Parata (Southern Maori, 1893–1911), Te Rangi Hīroa (Peter Buck) (Northern Maori, 1909–1914) and Āpirana Ngata (Eastern Maori, 1905–1936), together with Reform's Māui Pōmare (Western Maori, 1911–1930). Parata and Carroll were first elected as Independents, the former in 1885 and Carroll in 1887.

a plurality of votes in all four Māori seats for the next fifty years.* In the early 1920s, a Māori electoral movement was formed under the name of its founder, the faith healer and religious prophet Tahupōtiki Wiremu Rātana. On winning its first seat of Southern Maori in 1932, Rātana's new MP, Eruera Tirikātene, made an unsuccessful attempt to convince the Labour leader, Harry Holland, that the two movements would benefit from a formal alliance (Gustafson, 1986: 188). Labour's concern appeared to centre on any possible damage an alliance might cause to existing relationships with other Māori organisations, particularly the King Movement, which treated Rātana with disdain (ibid.: 190). Three years later, Rātana won a second victory, after which its two MPs formally ratified the new government's legislative agenda and began to attend its weekly caucus meetings. At the 1943 general election, the Rātana–Labour alliance won all four Māori seats. This electoral monopoly survived until New Zealand First's victory in the seat of Northern Maori in 1993.

Quite apart from its religious mission, the Rātana movement was founded on a commitment to improving the health, welfare and employment opportunities of a population suffering from both the confiscation of tribal land and race-based inequality in the provision of government welfare (Chapman, 1963: 249). In the words of one commentator, this new movement of the poor and dispossessed represented a transition 'from the old tribally based alliances, astutely managed by a prestigious parliamentary leader like Carroll and later Ngata, to a class-based grassroots movement, organised by a network of Ratana branches and in due course firmly aligned to the Labour Party' (Sorrenson, 2014: 192). Rātana himself claimed to represent 'the shoemaker, the blacksmith, the watchmaker, carpenters, orphans and widows' (quoted in Sinclair, 1980: 274). Among the political objectives of the new movement was a commitment to recognise the terms of the Treaty, the settlement of issues around the confiscation of tribal land, and an increase in the number of Māori seats from four to six (Chapman, 1986: B-43).

---

* The one exception to this Labour–Rātana alliance was the election of a Mormon, Puti Tipene (Steve) Watene, to the seat of Eastern Maori, a position he held between 1963 and 1967.

Although the Rātana MPs provided Labour with its governing majority on two separate occasions (1946–49 and 1957–60), their impact on government policy, as well as on the portfolio of Maori Affairs, fell some way short of what their potential influence might suggest. Advances were made in the provision of Māori education, housing and employment, but little or no headway was made towards achieving Rātana's political goals, especially the ratification of the Treaty, increase in the number of seats and repossession of alienated land (Ward, 1999: 21–22). Reflecting something of the paternalism with which Labour tended to treat its Māori allies, the position of Maori Affairs Minister was held by a succession of Pākehā politicians, including Prime Ministers Peter Fraser and Walter Nash; indeed, Matiu Rata, who became Maori Affairs Minister in 1972, had the distinction of being the first Māori to occupy that position in over one hundred years. Meanwhile Māori voters in the four Māori seats continued to deliver Labour substantial majorities. At the 1946 election, for example, whereas Labour's overall share of the valid vote was 51 per cent, in the Māori seats it was 64 per cent (Chapman, 1986: B-45). When calculated over a total of ten elections, the consistency with which the Māori seats were delivered to Labour becomes even more clear-cut. For example, whereas the average overall vote for Labour between 1946 and 1972 was 45.8 per cent (see General Election, 1890–1993, New Zealand Electoral Commission website), in the Māori seats it was 68 per cent (ibid.: Graph 1).

The first significant threat to the longstanding electoral alignment between Māori and Labour occurred in 1980 and took the form of a breakaway Māori party, which was led by Rata and took the name Mana Motuhake. Rata, who was first elected to Parliament in 1963, represented the disillusionment of a growing number of young Māori activists, many of whom had migrated to the urban centres in search of education and work, and who believed that Labour had paid insufficient attention to their cultural, political and economic aspirations, particularly with respect to Māori self-determination. Rata, who had been relegated to the backbenches, resigned from the Labour caucus and forced a by-election in the Northern Maori electorate, which he lost, although his 37.9 per cent share of the vote sent a strong warning to Labour, whose share of the vote reduced from 71.5 per cent to 52.4 per cent. As Walker has pointed out,

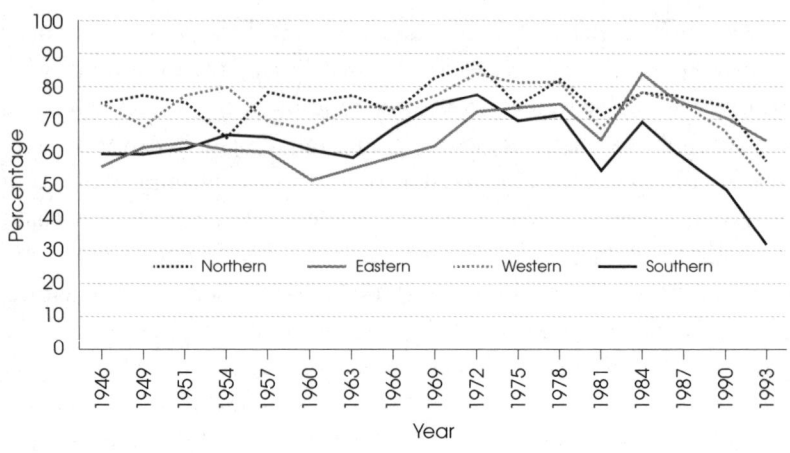

Figure 9.1: Electoral Support for Labour–Rātana, 1946–1993

Source: New Zealand Electoral Commission, http://www.electionresults.govt.nz/.

Rata's decision marked 'the divorce of the Ratana Church from the Labour party and the determination of the activists to capture and control the four Maori seats' (1983: 6). At the 1981 general election, Mana Motuhake came second in all four Māori seats. Although Rata's share of the vote in Northern Maori continued to grow, his party was unable to win a seat until 1993, when its new leader, Sandra Lee, took the General seat of Auckland Central as a member of the five-party Alliance. At the same election, New Zealand First's Tau Henare captured the seat of Northern Maori. This was the first occasion in which Labour had lost a Māori seat in five decades of electoral competition.*

In 1993, a change in the electoral law paved the way for a recalculation of the number of Māori electorates based on the size of the Māori population registering on the Māori roll. As a result, the number of seats increased to five in 1996, six in 1999 and seven in 2002. At the 1996 election, New Zealand First won all five seats on the back of the sudden rise in its popular support. Led by a Māori leader and deputy leader, the new

---

* Labour–Rātana picked up the last of the four Māori seats, that of Eastern Maori, in 1943.

Table 9.1: Results in Māori Seats, 1996–2014

	1996	1999	2002	2005	2008	2011	2014
Te Tai Tokerau	NZ First	Labour	Labour	Māori	Māori	Mana	Labour
Tāmaki Makaurau*			Labour	Māori	Māori	Māori	Labour
Tainui†	NZ First	Labour	Labour	Labour	Labour	Labour	Labour
Waiariki		Labour	Labour	Māori	Māori	Māori	Māori
Ikaroa-Rāwhiti	NZ First	Labour	Labour	Labour	Labour	Labour	Labour
Te Tai Hauāuru	NZ First	Labour	Labour	Māori	Māori	Māori	Labour
Te Tai Tonga	NZ First	Labour	Labour	Labour	Māori	Labour	Labour

* Tāmaki Makaurau was referred to as Hauraki before 2002.
† Tainui became Hauraki-Waikato in 2008.

party campaigned on an anti-immigration and anti-foreign-investment agenda that appealed to many Māori voters (see Figure 9.1 and Table 9.1). Despite its success, New Zealand First later expressed a commitment to the abolition of the Māori seats.

The collapse of the National–New Zealand First coalition in 1998 left the latter party divided, with eight MPs, including the five occupants of the Māori seats, choosing to prop up Prime Minister Jenny Shipley's minority National government. A similar fate befell the Labour–Alliance coalition in 2002, leaving the Mana Motuhake movement to contest the Māori seats as a separate party. Its candidates came second in three of the seven Māori electorates, with an average of 10.6 per cent of the vote in the seats being contested. This was to be the last occasion on which the Mana Motuhake movement contested a general election.

Māori Party

Having recaptured all seven Māori seats from New Zealand First in 1999, the incoming Helen Clark-led Labour government appointed three Māori to its new ministry: Parekura Horomia (Māori Affairs), Tariana Turia (State), and Mana Motuhake's Sandra Lee (Conservation and Local Government). Clark, who had strengthened Labour's links with the Rātana movement, gave every appearance of understanding the grounds upon which Māori had deserted Labour at the previous election. However, as subsequent events were to show, neither Clark nor her senior ministers fully comprehended the highly conditional nature of the Māori voting public's return to Labour in 1999, and again in 2002.

Conflict between Clark and a number of her Māori MPs had its origins in the government's response to a decision by the Court of Appeal upholding the right of eight South Island iwi to proceed with a claim to the Māori Land Court establishing customary rights to the foreshore and seabed of the Marlborough Sounds. In its landmark findings, the court ruled that customary title had not been extinguished by statute or common law and that the case should proceed to the Māori Land Court. After first adopting the position that customary title properly belonged with the Crown, Clark began to substitute any reference to the Crown with the words 'public domain'. Clearly, she was concerned about the adverse impact the court's decision would have on public opinion, especially given the New Zealand public's historic assumption of free and open access to the coastline for recreational purposes, including swimming, boating and fishing. Attempts by the government to win the support of Māori proved unsuccessful and resulted in disagreement and threats of rebellion. Such was the bitterness that Clark refused to meet a hīkoi of some 15,000 to 20,000 people who marched to Parliament to protest the government's decision, describing them in the media as a group of 'haters and wreckers' (Sharples, 2007: 285).

The New Zealand First Party agreed to support the minority government's Foreshore and Seabed Act 2004 on condition that ownership was vested solely in the Crown, thereby putting an end to the softer option of placing ownership in the 'public domain'. The government's reaction, including the subsequent legislation, was described by one legal scholar as 'ham-fisted' and 'ill-judged' (M. Palmer, 2006: 204). Tariana Turia refused to support the Bill and was dismissed from her ministerial responsibilities, and another Labour MP, Nanaia Mahuta, broke ranks with her colleagues, also voting against it following the first and second reading of the Bill, before switching back to support the government in the third reading. In May 2004, Turia forced a by-election in the seat of Te Tai Hauāuru. Neither of the two major parties was prepared to put up a candidate, leaving Turia to win with a majority of 92.3 per cent. Immediately following the by-election the formation of a new electoral vehicle, the Māori Party, was announced. Turia was joined as co-leader by Pita Sharples, and in 2005 the new party won four of the seven Māori seats. In January 2006 they were welcomed onto the grounds of the Rātana Church, a move that signalled a symbolic end to Rātana's special relationship with Labour.

New parties often struggle to develop a coherent set of principles and policies to justify credibly the claim to having a reason for being. For the Māori Party, the immediate goal was repeal of the Foreshore and Seabed Act and its replacement with legislation reversing the 'confiscation' of iwi ownership and customary rights. However, a major first statement that was released following the Te Tai Hauāuru by-election outlined three broad principles: first, social solidarity and mutual respect (manaakitanga); second, self-determination (rangatiratanga); and third, the nurturing of a spiritual identity that was closely connected with the land (wairuatanga). Policy proposals were summarised under two broad themes: constitutional reform, and Māori economic and social advancement. A statement published in 2004 specified a number of constitutional changes the party would pursue in Parliament and government, including entrenching the Treaty of Waitangi, speeding up and strengthening the Treaty settlement process, and entrenching the Māori seats. The party pledged to introduce measures designed to promote employment training, support the teaching of te reo Māori in schools, and provide free education from pre-school up to and including tertiary education. The party also undertook to 'provide support, advocacy, and practical assistance in working with families, community and schools to address the impact of poverty upon families and children' (Māori Party, 2004). A follow-up statement in October 2008 further pledged to pursue the initiatives of a constitutional convention and the introduction of a public health agenda focusing on preventative care, especially in areas such as alcohol and drug abuse. Quoting Ranginui Walker, it described the failure to entrench the Māori seats in the Electoral Act as 'perhaps the most discriminatory measure of all in the application of the law to Māori representation' (Māori Party, 2008).

The party's success in winning five of the seven Māori seats at the 2008 election provided an opportunity to secure an agreement with the incoming National government. In exchange for a pledge to support the government on matters of confidence and supply, the party received two ministerial positions outside of Cabinet, as well as support for a number of its policy initiatives. Although National and the Māori Party were far from being 'ideologically connected' (Arseneau, 2010: 289), by forging a similar arrangement with the five-member Act Party, National was able to keep the Māori Party 'at arm's length from the government's most important [economic] decisions' (Miller and Curtin, 2011: 118). This was a far cry from Clark's assertion prior to the 2005 election that the Māori Party would be the 'last cab off the rank' in any post-election negotiations with a Labour-led government (Boston, 2007: 393).

Despite the absence of any tradition of support for National by Māori voters, there were clear benefits to be gained from the governing arrangements entered into by both parties following the 2008, 2011 and 2014 elections. While National was not prepared to abandon its pledge to abolish the Māori seats, it agreed not to proceed in the meantime. The Foreshore and Seabed Act was repealed and replaced by the Marine and Coastal Area Act 2011. The new law restored the right of iwi to lay claims for customary title through the courts. At the same time it guaranteed access to all New Zealanders for existing uses, such as fishing and boating. Although welcomed by the Māori Party, the legislation was strongly opposed by those on both extremes of the debate, with the Act MPs attempting to filibuster the vote and the Green co-leader, Metiria Turei, accusing the Māori Party of having sold out any right to customary title. On the other hand, the government agreed to fund a number of Māori Party initiatives in education, health and welfare, including the much anticipated Whānau Ora programme. Together, these achievements made the Māori Party arguably the most successful support party in the short history of MMP.

But success can also bring failure, as illustrated by the defection in 2011 of the Te Tai Tokerau member, Hone Harawira, to form the rival Mana movement. As the most ideologically radical member of the caucus, Harawira had become increasingly uncomfortable with the Māori Party's partnership with National, particularly in light of the alleged impact the government's austerity measures were having on the poorest members of his North Auckland electorate. Disillusionment with the Māori Party's decision to support the Marine and Coastal Area Act further alienated Harawira from his erstwhile colleagues, leading not only to his resignation from the party, but also the decision to resign his seat and force a by-election, which he won with a 49.2 per cent share of the vote (compared with 40.1 per cent for the Labour candidate, Kelvin Davis, and a mere 8.8 per cent of the vote for the Māori Party candidate, Tipene Solomon). Harawira repeated this victory at the general election later the same year (see Table 9.2). An even bigger threat to the continuing popularity of the Māori Party occurred in 2014 when, following the retirement from politics of the party's co-leaders, Tariana Turia and Pita Sharples, the Mana movement joined forces with the generously funded Internet Party with the intention of exploiting the controversial one-seat electoral threshold. Were it to have been successful, the two parties' plan would have resulted in one or more list candidate from each party being elected on Harawira's coat-tails, including the leader of the Internet Party, Laila Harré (see chapter ten). On polling day the controversial arrangement backfired badly, with Harawira losing his Te Tai Tokerau seat to Labour's Davis and the combined Internet/Mana party vote falling well below (at 1.4 per cent) the other, 5 per cent, electoral threshold.

Table 9.2: Māori Party and Labour Party Competition in the Seven Māori Seats, 2005–2014

	2005		2008		2011*		2014	
	MP	LP	MP	LP	MP	LP	MP	LP
Te Tai Tokerau	50.9	32.5	60.3	28.7	15.8	35.4	11.7	43.8
Tāmaki Makaurau	51.4	40.5	64.4	26.7	38.8	33.7	30.2	37.5
Tainui/Hauraki-Waikato	40.9	50.9	45.7	50.5	16.3	54.8	21.9	59.3
Ikaroa-Rāwhiti	41.7	52.3	42.0	50.3	21.9	57.6	17.8	45.2
Waiariki	52.8	38.2	65.8	30.7	40.8	23.2	44.6	26.8
Te Tai Hauāuru	60.9	32.4	68.2	28.4	46.3	28.6	32.5	40.2
Te Tai Tonga	45.7	33.0	45.7	40.4	30.3	38.7	24.2	41.8
Total	47.3	41.7	56.1	36.4	30.0	38.7	26.1	42.1

Source: New Zealand Electoral Commission, http://www.electionresults.govt.nz/.
* Mana vote in 2011 was 20.1 per cent.

The dramatic decline of the Māori Party vote in 2011 (see Table 9.2) points to a major challenge facing all support parties, even those that remain at arm's length from a formal coalition (see chapter six). The nature of a support party's relationship with the government has been described as a product of three competing goals: office, policy and votes (Muller and Strom, 1999). A party that is primarily concerned with holding ministerial office may have to sacrifice some of its policy goals, and perhaps face declining support at the next election. Policy-seeking parties, on the other hand, are less concerned with ministerial office and votes than maximising their policy gains, especially those deemed non-negotiable; these are sometimes referred to by politicians as being their bottom-line policies, with the implication that they will not be negotiated away in any government formation talks. Then there are the vote-seeking parties, such as the Greens, who, despite being shut out of office and deprived of substantial policy gains, have demonstrated an ability to grow their vote in opposition by adopting the role of 'conscience and critic'. This brings us back to the Māori Party, which has had an uneasy relationship in the company of National and Act (Miller and Curtin, 2011). The party's substantial policy gains and ministerial positions notwithstanding, before the 2014 election it was on the wrong side of Māori public opinion, with a substantial majority of Māori voters preferring a partnership with Labour rather than National.* To draw attention to the Māori Party's discomfort, Mana positioned itself as the party of the disadvantaged, with an end to child poverty and a more just distribution of the nation's wealth heading its list of policy priorities.

Future of the Māori Seats

As part of the 2008 confidence and supply agreement between the Māori Party and National, the two parties convened an advisory panel to consider a number of constitutional issues, including ways in which Māori

---

* Surveys of Māori public opinion before the 2014 election reveal a consistent pattern of two-thirds support for a coalition with Labour, rather than National. See Māori Reid Research Polls, 18 August–5 September 2014: Trevett, 2014.

representation might be made more effective. During 2013, the advisory panel conducted a 'conversation' with a wide variety of New Zealanders, including Māori. Not surprisingly, it found that opinion was divided on whether the designated Māori seats should be abolished or retained. In its report, the panel concluded that 'there is no immediate need to change the current arrangements for Māori representation in Parliament. The Māori seats are effectively self-regulating, as Māori can determine, through the Māori Electoral Option, whether or not they continue' (Constitutional Advisory Panel, 2013: 24). The panel observed that a number of those submitters favouring abolition made reference to the findings of the 1986 Report of the Royal Commission on the Electoral System, which of course had recommended the introduction of MMP. Whilst acknowledging that the seats had special significance for Māori (Wallace, 1986: 85), the report had taken the view that Māori voters would benefit from MMP to the extent that 'it is likely there would always be substantially more Māori MPs than at present and that they would be spread across several parties' (ibid.: 102). In line with this view, the report concluded that there would be no further need for separate representation under an MMP electoral system (ibid.: 113).

Support for the abolition of separate seats is based on four main arguments: first, the democratic argument that making 'special' provision for one segment of society, albeit a significant one, undermines the principle of equality; second, the somewhat contradictory argument that, beginning in 1867 and continuing through to the present, separate representation has created something akin to a form of apartheid, with those representing the Māori seats being relegated to separate and diminished roles within Parliament and government; third, that maintaining separate provision for Māori undermines the multicultural nature of New Zealand society and is unfair to other ethnic groups, notably Pacific peoples and, more recently, Asians; and fourth, as predicted by the Royal Commission, that under MMP Māori have received representation broadly equivalent to their share of the population, and thus no longer require the protection of dedicated seats.

The anti-democratic argument is based on the assumption that providing dedicated seats is inherently unequal, since it privileges Māori over all other categories of voters. However, as Mulgan (1989b: 82–86) points out, providing the principle of 'one person, one vote' is observed, it matters not whether constituencies are based on geography, occupation, language, race or some other shared characteristic. While the 70 electoral districts under MMP are determined by geographical proximity and 'community of interest', they could just as easily be based on other criteria, as is implicit in decisions around the selection and ranking of party lists, with some parties giving priority to gender and ethnicity, while others make selections based on service to the party and community. Furthermore, as with all other voters, Māori are entitled to only two votes, one for the party of their choice, the other for their preferred electorate MP. Regardless of whether these two votes are cast on the General roll or the Māori roll, all eligible voters are bound by the same electoral rules.

There is ample evidence in support of the second general argument for abolition, the view that Māori have been relegated to a separate and diminished role electorally, as well as in Parliament and government. As we have seen, it took until the latter part of the twentieth century for Māori voters and parliamentary candidates to be accorded the same democratic rights as non-Māori, with the most glaring inequity being the fixed number of Māori seats (Walker, 1990: 144–45). As a result, Māori were relegated, according to law professor Andrew Geddis, to 'something of a representational ghetto: there are too few Māori MPs to impose their constituents' views on an otherwise unresponsive non-Māori majority, and so they can only achieve progress on these issues if that non-Māori majority deigns to notice the issue and lend them a hand' (Geddis, 2006: 360). As the Royal Commission warned some two decades earlier, the will of the non-Māori majority has too often been wielded against that of the Māori minority, a result that 'has had particularly adverse effects on the ability of the Māori MPs to protect the interests of their people' (Wallace, 1986: 90).

A third argument in support of abolition is based on the view that, since New Zealand is now a multicultural society, fairness dictates that the privileged status of Māori be removed. While a number of parties subscribe to a one-New Zealand policy, including National, New Zealand First, Act and the Conservatives, it was most powerfully expressed by the former National Party leader Don Brash when, in a speech in Orewa in

January 2004, he condemned 'racial separatism' and called for the abolition of all race-based legislation, including the designated Māori seats. Although his right-wing economic agenda enjoyed only limited support, by adopting a right-wing populist message on race he was able to appeal to a much broader constituency. Within a matter of weeks, National's support leaped from 17 per cent to 45 per cent, the largest single increase in the history of polling in New Zealand. As Table 9.3 suggests, these views on race-based politics tapped into a rich vein of support among centre-right voters.

Table 9.3: Voter Attitudes Towards Future of Māori Seats by Party (per cent)

	National	Labour	Green	NZ First	Māori Party
Abolish	54	26	16	36	1
Retain	33	44	57	36	27
Increase	3	20	14	20	71
Don't know	10	10	14	9	0

Source: New Zealand Election Study, 2011.

A final major argument for abolition reflects the Royal Commission's prediction that competition for votes under MMP would motivate parties to select Māori candidates high on the party list, as well as in marginal and safe electorates (Wallace, 1986: 102). This prediction is confirmed by the data in Table 9.4 (overleaf): with the exception of New Zealand First the proportions of those who have acknowledged their Māori ancestry are highest among parties of the centre-left. In 2014, some 19 per cent of all MPs claimed Māori ethnicity, with ten MPs coming from party lists and a further six from the General seats. Thus, a case can be made for the view that, under MMP, Māori are being represented in reasonable proportion to their share of the population (although the total figure of 23 Māori MPs includes those from the seven dedicated seats).

Support for the retention of separate Māori seats is strongest among Māori (98 per cent), Green (71 per cent) and Labour (64 per cent) party voters (see Table 9.3). Of particular interest is the finding that a majority of New Zealand First voters (56 per cent) are at odds with their leader,

Table 9.4: Māori Representation, 1990–2014

	1990	1996	2002	2005	2011	2014
National	1	1	1	3	6	7
Labour	4	4	9	9	8	8
NZ First		8	5	4	2	3
Māori				4	3	2
Alliance		2				
Green			1	1	2	2
Mana					1	0
Act		1	1			0
Total	5 (5.2%)*	16 (13%)	17 (14%)	21 (17%)	22 (18%)	22 (18%)

Source: New Zealand Electoral Commission, http://www.electionresults.govt.nz/.

* Percentages in parentheses represent share of total seats in Parliament.

Winston Peters, and his parliamentary colleagues on the issue. Those supporting retention do so on the basis of three main arguments: first, the constitutional argument, which draws on the Treaty principles of partnership and self-determination, or tino rangitiratanga; second, the historic argument, which is built on the distinctive nature of the arrangement and the opportunity it affords to bring a uniquely Māori perspective to representation; and third, the view that, although Māori are reasonably well represented under present conditions, there is no guarantee that these levels will continue. Whereas the numbers of Māori achieving winnable places in the General seats and on the party lists are dependent on the goodwill of party elites, separate representation is something over which Māori voters alone can exercise control.

For many Māori, retaining dedicated seats has great symbolic as well as practical importance, since it represents, if inadequately, the Treaty partnership that exists between Māori and the Crown. The principles of the Treaty make it imperative that both partners participate in the decision-making process, and the sovereign Parliament is an obvious place for this to happen. It is for this reason that the Māori Party supports the entrenchment of the relevant section of the Electoral Act, action that would prevent any future government from abolishing the seats unless it could achieve a 75 per cent parliamentary majority. This said, while retention of the Māori seats may be viewed as a necessary step, it is hardly sufficient to guarantee full Treaty partnership as understood by many Māori. In the event that self-determination under present constitutional arrangements fails to eventuate, other more radical possibilities include the creation of an indigenous parliament, and the right of veto over legislation directly relevant to Māori, or, as Mason Durie describes it (Durie, 2000; 2003), devolution of power leading to the creation of a separate Māori nation-state. One structure that gives due recognition to the notion of partnership is Whata Winiata's three-house parliament, with legislative proposals emanating from the two lower houses, Tikanga Māori and Tikanga Pākehā, and proceeding to an upper Treaty of Waitangi house, whose membership would include both Māori and Pākehā (Winiata, 2000).

As we have seen, while the influence of the early Māori MPs was limited, their very presence in the colonial Parliament served as an important reminder of the distinct culture and identity of Māori, as well as the obligations of the Crown under the Treaty (Wallace, 1986: 86). The historic link going back to Carroll, Ngata, Pōmare and Rātana provides a powerful argument for the preservation of an institutional arrangement uniquely dedicated to representing Māori interests. In contrast, all the MPs chosen to represent General seats, as well as those elected on the party lists, are required to serve the interests of diverse constituencies. The potential for conflict posed by these differing sets of obligations is perhaps best illustrated in relation to Labour's Foreshore and Seabed legislation. Although two MPs representing Māori seats – Tariana Turia (Te Tai Hauāuru) and Nanaia Mahuta (Tainui) – indicated they would defy the instructions of the Prime Minister and vote against the legislation, a Māori MP representing the General seat of Wairarapa was put under immense pressure to support the government. Georgina Beyer argued that her Māori ancestry dictated that she should abstain. However, her local Labour Party executive insisted that she was not delegated to represent Māori, but rather the voters of Wairarapa. In the end Beyer decided to support the Bill.

While the recent increases in levels of Māori representation appear to confirm the prediction made by the Royal Commission on the Electoral System when it first proposed the adoption of MMP (see Table 9.4), the vagaries of electoral politics make predictions difficult, especially given the fluctuating fortunes of parties such as National and New Zealand First, both of which have promoted Māori candidates in their General seats and on their lists. Were the dedicated seats to be abolished, what guarantees would there be that alternative opportunities for representation would be opened up to compensate? But there is the further problem of what the future might hold for race-based parties, notably the Māori and Mana parties, both of which gained seats in Parliament by virtue of having won dedicated Māori seats. Should these seats be abolished, there is every chance that neither party could survive, especially under the 5 per cent electoral threshold currently in place.

Perhaps as great a threat to the survival of dedicated seats is the contagion effect of declining voter participation on the Māori Electoral Option, and hence the number of Māori seats. As it has been argued (for example, by Sullivan et al., 2014), low turnout is a product of several factors, including age, low socio-economic income and high mobility, together with the absence of inter-party competition (on the assumption that competition motivates people to vote). As we have seen, prior to the advent of MMP, Labour had substantial majorities in all four Māori seats. This lack of competitive pressure contributed to a steady decline in participation rates, a situation that was halted, if temporarily, by the success of New Zealand First in capturing all five Māori seats in 1996. In recent years participation rates have been spiralling downwards, more as a result of the cumulative effect of social trends than an absence of electoral competition. In 2011, turnout had dropped to a mere 58 per cent, compared to an historically low but nevertheless superior 75.5 per cent in the general electorates (ibid.: 143). Unless this trend is reversed, retaining (let alone increasing) the present number of dedicated seats will become increasingly problematic. In recognition of the importance of this issue, the Constitutional Advisory Panel recommended that steps be taken to both promote the electoral option and educate voters on existing electoral arrangements (Constitutional Advisory Panel, 2013: 25).

Conclusion

The advent of MMP has had a number of positive effects on Māori electoral politics, including: a significant rise in the number of Māori MPs, a corresponding increase in the proportion of Māori ministers in Cabinet and the wider executive,* and some substantial policy gains negotiated as part of the government formation process. Furthermore, in contrast to the two-party era of the early postwar years, Māori voters have been represented across a range of party organisations, including the two elected Māori parties. While accepting ministerial office is likely to incur electoral costs, an experience hardly unique to the Māori Party, remaining in opposition creates its own frustrations. On a less positive note, despite some modest achievements in the direction of devolved power, partly as a result of the Waitangi Tribunal process, but also policy innovations such as Whānau Ora, Māori are not substantially closer to the Treaty goals of partnership and tino rangatiratanga than they were under previous constitutional and governing arrangements.

Although the National, New Zealand First, Conservative and Act parties remain committed to the abolition of the Māori seats, National has agreed to postpone any decision while it remains in a governing arrangement with the Māori Party. Of course, this begs the question of who will make the final decision, with the obvious alternatives being either a unilateral decision by the government of the day on the grounds of a claimed mandate; a referendum of all voters; or, as recommended by both the Royal Commission on the Electoral System (1986) and the Constitutional Advisory Panel (2013), a referendum restricted to Māori voters. Only the latter alternative offers protection to the rights of New Zealand's indigenous minority.

---

* The five Māori ministers in National's 2011–14 government were: in Cabinet, Hekia Parata (Education), Paula Bennett (Social Development) and Simon Bridges (Energy and Resources from 2013); and in the wider executive, Tariana Turia (Disability Issues) and Pita Sharples (Māori Affairs).

Chapter Ten

Elections and Voters

New Zealand elections have long been known for their inclusiveness. By extending participation to all non-citizen adults of twelve months' residency or more, they have helped to foster a sense of collective participation, as well as shared national identity, with all segments of the population taking part on the same day and under the same democratic principle of 'one person, one vote, one value'. But open and free elections are also judged by the extent to which they provide genuine choice. In contrast to the experience of one-party states, democratic elections provide an opportunity for political parties to compete for support by offering alternative visions of the good society. Whereas the former first-past-the-post (FPP) electoral system largely limited the contest to the two main parties, under the rules of the mixed-member proportional (MMP) system many parties compete and relatively few votes are wasted, with the result that Parliament is closer to becoming a microcosm of New Zealand society than at any time in its history.

Elections serve two essential functions: first, to elect MPs who will represent their constituents in the legislative chamber and intercede on their behalf with government ministers and the public service; and second, to choose a government. The process of electing MPs is reasonably straightforward, with individual members being elected by a system of plurality voting in geographical constituencies – of which there are 71 – or, alternatively, selected from the party lists in proportion to each party's share of the party vote. On the other hand, the role of elections in choosing a government is potentially problematic, especially under the multi-party arrangements of MMP. While some voters may take their cue from what they regard to be ideologically compatible governing blocs, others are guided by campaign events, including the steady release of opinion polls that track levels of party support. These influences notwithstanding, there have been occasions when the precise shape of the governing options has remained unclear until after the election results have been declared. This was most graphically illustrated by the two months of parallel negotiations between New Zealand First and the two major parties following the 1996 election. It is experiences like these that give rise to the complaint that, in contrast to the two-party either/or option provided under FPP, it is now the politicians rather than the voters who actually choose the government.

This chapter will discuss the way modern election campaigns are conducted, with the 2014 campaign serving as our central case study.

Setting the Rules

To help ensure that all votes are of approximately equal value, every five years, and following completion of the Census of the Population, New Zealand's Representation Commission conducts a review of the boundaries for each electorate (see chapter five). Among the considerations of the commission's 2014 review were the effects of the Canterbury earthquakes on population movements within and around Christchurch. As with previous reviews, it also considered the number and distribution of electorate seats in light of the continuing population growth in metropolitan Auckland. This resulted in some significant boundary changes, including the creation of a new seat in Auckland's western suburbs. Before releasing its final review, the commission is required to engage in a consultation process with voters. One source of public concern in 2014, for example, was the proposal to combine part of south Epsom with the seat of Mt Roskill. Objectors expressed concern about the likely impact of the proposed merger on school boundaries, and hence property prices in the suburb of Epsom. On further reflection, the commission decided not to proceed with the merger.

As well as reviewing the General seats, the Representation Commission determines the boundaries for the Māori electoral districts. It is preceded by an advertising campaign to make all voters of Māori descent aware that they can register on either the Māori roll or the General roll. All eligible voters are sent a form, asking them to choose between the two options.* At the 2014 election, first-time Māori voters opted to go on the Māori roll in a ratio of more than two to one. However, with 55 per cent (228,718 voters) choosing the Māori roll and 45 per cent (184,630) the General roll, the number of Māori seats remained at seven (New Zealand Electoral Commission, 2013).

At each general election, the Electoral Enrolment Centre conducts an enrolment of all electors, either online or by post. An extensive publicity campaign is mounted during the months preceding the election with a view to increasing the proportion of voters, especially first-time voters, registering on the electoral roll. In 2014, the names of those who had not registered by Writ Day (20 August) were not included on the register of electors. Of course, those individuals were still able to vote provided they registered by the Friday before polling day. By that time, 91.7 per cent of eligible voters had registered, down slightly on the 93.4 per cent in 2011. Although registration is compulsory under New Zealand law, with a $100 charge for first-time offenders, imposing such a penalty is rare. A relaxation of the voting regulations around advance voting resulted in a sharp increase in the incidence of early voting, from 270,427 in 2008 to 717,579 in 2014 (New Zealand Electoral Commission, 2014a).

Modern Media Campaign

There has been much debate over who actually controls the campaign agenda. Until recently, each political party claimed ownership of its policy proposals and took primary responsibility for the management of its campaign. For their part, the various media sources served as a conduit

---

* Because of the Canterbury earthquakes, the 2011 census was delayed by two years, thereby delaying the Māori Electoral Option by the same length of time.

or channel through which the parties competed for the hearts and minds of voters. As the influence of the media, especially television, grew, news producers began to take a stronger role in defining and interrogating the issues of the campaign, an approach that called for decisions as to the newsworthiness of one issue or event relative to another. Not to be outdone, the politicians resorted to political 'spin' as a means of reasserting their control, with highly paid public relations and communications advisers playing an increasingly prominent role in monitoring public opinion and taking control of the day-to-day management of the party's campaign.

This struggle for control of the campaign agenda can be illustrated with reference to four developments, all of which had a major influence on the 2014 election campaign: first, the growth of what has become known as the 'permanent' campaign; second, its increasing personalisation relative to other factors, notably policy issues; third, the vulnerability of the campaign timetable to unforeseen media-driven interventions and events; and finally, the hollowing out of party membership on party activism and campaign funding, giving impetus to the trend towards a more professional and media-focused campaign.

Advent of the 'Permanent' Campaign

According to convention, the campaign proper commences on 'Writ Day', when the Governor-General instructs the Electoral Commission to hold an election and the televised advertising campaign begins. These formalities notwithstanding, it is clear that the activities we normally associate with an election campaign begin to take place many months before the designated campaign launch. In announcing the date of the 2014 election in March – some six months before the September election – the Prime Minister was merely confirming that the contest was underway, with policy announcements on a projected surplus and hints of future tax reductions having occurred as early as the previous year. Some international studies have even argued that any attempt to nominate a starting date in the era of the professional campaign can be misleading (for example, Farrell and Webb, 2000). The notion of a 'permanent' campaign has its roots in the American presidential system, where candidates are required to establish name recognition and build their campaign organisations from scratch, a process that may take as long as from one election to the next. Even personalities as prominent and well-resourced as Hillary Clinton and Jeb Bush were under pressure to declare their candidacy and begin campaigning a full two years before the formal 2016 presidential contest.

This notion of a permanent campaign can be contrasted with the era of largely amateur campaigns, when New Zealand's political parties lacked the necessary organisation, personnel and resources to conduct a prolonged campaign. Quite apart from the personal demands associated with managing a government, successive prime ministers assigned themselves Cabinet responsibilities that placed additional burdens on their time, keeping them close to their Wellington office and staff until the commencement of the formal campaign. Examples include Prime Minister Robert Muldoon, who took on the demanding portfolio of Finance (1975–84), and David Lange who, as well as serving as Prime Minister, assumed responsibility for Foreign Affairs (1984–87), followed by Education (1987–89). This was a practice their successors were keen to avoid. Between elections, a less encumbered Jim Bolger took the media on his Heartland tour of New Zealand, and later, Jenny Shipley and Helen Clark adopted the same practice of crisscrossing the country several times each for the preceding months, all the while engaging in activities virtually identical to those we have come to associate with an election campaign.

Although their resources are much more constrained, the leaders of the opposition parties have been forced to conduct their own semi-permanent campaigns by largely shadowing the activities of the Prime Minister. When Don Brash, as the Leader of the Opposition, delivered his controversial Orewa speech on race relations in January 2004, it was immediately apparent that this was the beginning of National's campaign to both lift Brash's personal profile and generate a surge in the polls in advance of the 2005 election. Similarly, on replacing Brash as Leader of the Opposition in 2006, Key began an intense nationwide two-year campaign geared towards achieving victory for National in 2008. Whilst activity among the leaders of the small parties is less comprehensive and more spasmodic, all have embraced the challenges posed by an ongoing campaign. In the case of Winston Peters in particular, creating the perception of a 'three-horse race' in 2005 required that he maintain an active schedule of meetings and related events quite outside the four-week campaign, especially among the party's middle-aged and elderly supporters (Edwards, 2007).

Growth of Personality Politics

It is hard to exaggerate the centrality of the personalities of Helen Clark and, especially, John Key to their parties' election campaigns in the period since 1999. More than ever before, the two parties' campaigns were consciously built around the personal qualities and popularity of their leader. As the National Party's campaign manager, Steven Joyce, once observed, 'It has been well documented that the modern political campaign is all about the leader. More often than not, it is the party leader in which [sic] the voters place their trust . . . Of course that means the party leader has to personify the party brand; in John Key, National has a leader who does just that' (Joyce, 2010: 66).

This emphasis on a more personal style of campaigning is largely due to the influence of television, a medium that is strongly identified with the new personality-driven celebrity culture and thus is better suited to presentational than issue-based politics. That said, studies on the media coverage of elections in Western Europe have found that evidence on the prominence of personality tells more than one story, with some studies observing a move away from parties and towards personalities, while others have found the evidence to be mixed, with discernible movement in some countries but not in others (Karvonen, 2010; Kriesi, 2012). For example, while some parliamentary systems, including those of Britain and New Zealand, show evidence of an increasing personalisation of campaigns, others, such as Canada, do not. One New Zealand trend that resonates with international experience is the growing gap in the media attention given to the prime minister relative to the leaders of the opposition parties (Kriesi, 2012: 841).

Despite the attention being given to the personal attributes of the leader, is there evidence to suggest that leadership has a major influence on the way people vote? Clearly, the campaign officials and professional consultants believe there is, otherwise they would give less attention to making the leader the personification of the party's brand. Again, however, evidence is mixed, with some studies arguing in favour of a leadership effect, while others prefer to describe the evidence as inconclusive. In their analysis of leadership and voting in New Zealand, Jack Vowles and Peter Aimer agree that available evidence leads to 'only modest and guarded conclusions' (Vowles and Aimer, 2004: 175). Although the data cited are somewhat dated, they suggest a minimal 'net leadership effect' of between 1 and 3 per cent. As the two authors point out, however, even small percentages like these can potentially determine the outcome of very close elections.

Unforeseen Interventions in the Campaign

A feature of the modern campaign is the scarcity of substantive policy announcements and pre-planned events in what is becoming an increasingly lean schedule of photo opportunities, sound bites, one-on-one interviews and somewhat contrived televised leaders' debates.* This approach to campaigning contrasts with the more 'educative' approach of an earlier age (Gardner, 2009: 30), a style that doubtless provided greater opportunity for public engagement through such means as door-to-door canvassing and the scheduling of open forums for public discussion and debate – unlike the invitation-only campaign opening and closing addresses of today. Although it would be an exaggeration to suggest that New Zealand ever achieved the highest standards of civic engagement, clearly campaigns provided opportunities for citizen participation that were less cynical and remote than those of today.

One development that has impacted on the campaign agenda has been the injection of largely unforeseen events, thereby effectively disrupting the campaign schedule, including debate over party policy. The first such event occurred in 2002 and involved the investigative journalist Nicky Hager. His book, *Seeds of Distrust*, which was released part way through the campaign, alleged that there had been a conspiracy by the Labour-led government to withhold information concerning the accidental and illegal release of genetically engineered corn. If proven, the allegations were likely to have had serious implications for the outcome of the election. In its response, the government condemned the tactics adopted by the

---

* In 2014, Key refused to include the leaders of the small parties, including the Greens and New Zealand First, in the televised debates.

broadcaster who broke the story, TV3's John Campbell. It argued that, having not been given advance warning of the nature of the interview, the Prime Minister had effectively been 'ambushed' by Campbell and TV3 (Atkinson, 2004). The subsequent attacks on the integrity of the Prime Minister continued to haunt Clark and her government for the remainder of the campaign.

A second unforeseen intervention occurred in 2005 and involved an attempt to influence the outcome of the election by an obscure religious sect known as the Exclusive Brethren. Their decision to spend more than a million dollars on an advertising campaign attacking Labour and the Greens might have attracted less attention had it not been for the allegation that the church's financial and canvassing support came with the knowledge and blessing of National's most senior politicians and strategists. When the party leader was asked if he had any prior knowledge of the group's activities, Brash replied that he did not. He was later forced to admit under pressure that there had been a brief meeting, and that it had taken place a few weeks earlier. In *The Hollow Men*, which was published after the election, Hager claimed that the meeting referred to by Brash was one of a number conducted with members of the Exclusive Brethren Church over many months. Indeed, according to Hager, Brash had even received advance warning when the religious group's advertising material was about to be released (Hager, 2006: 246). Brash's attempt to conceal any knowledge of the Exclusive Brethren's activities is said to have contributed to National's narrow defeat at the hands of Labour (Levine and Roberts, 2005).

A further example of an unanticipated intervention that subsequently dominated an election campaign occurred in 2011 and followed an informal meeting between Prime Minister Key and Epsom's Act candidate, John Banks, with a view to signalling to Epsom's National voters that they should give their electorate vote to Act. In what became known as the 'Teapot Tape' affair, the two politicians sat at a table inside a Mt Eden café while an assemblage of cameras recorded the meeting from the outside. Unbeknown to Key and Banks – and, allegedly, the operator of a small recording device that had been left on the table – the politicians' conversation was recorded and subsequently retained by the media organisation concerned, a decision that resulted in a police investigation and legal action by both the cameraman involved and the Prime Minister. As well as dominating media coverage of the final two weeks of the campaign, the affair gave Winston Peters a platform from which to attack the government, on the grounds that he knew the content of the conversation, and that some of the comments made on the tape had been unkind to elderly voters, as well as to Act's then leader, Don Brash. The unforeseen publicity that flowed from these alleged revelations provided New Zealand First, a party that had been out of Parliament for three years, with unexpected publicity and a welcome lift in the polls. While Key and National appeared not to be hurt by the affair (indeed, Key's allegations of media bias may well have made him more popular), late support for New Zealand First took it above the 5 per cent threshold, rewarding it with eight seats on polling day.

Doubtless the most highly publicised of the unanticipated interventions occurred in 2014 and involved separate attacks on the credibility of the government and the Prime Minister by Hager and the wealthy internet entrepreneur, Kim Dotcom. The impact of these interventions will be considered in our discussion of the 2014 campaign.

The Professional Campaign

By the time the parties had co-opted the assistance of professionally trained campaign consultants and advisers, the era of the mass-membership party was well and truly over. In their heyday the two major parties were able to claim the membership, either directly or in Labour's case through its union affiliates, in excess of 25 per cent of all voters (see chapter eight). Today, the figure is likely to be less than 2 per cent, giving rise to speculation that, unless trends are reversed, party organisations are well on the way to becoming largely memberless oligarchies. Whereas its members once numbered in excess of 60,000, Labour's membership at the time of the 2014 election is estimated to have been less than 7000.* Hence, it has

---

* Unlike parties in many other Western democracies, New Zealand's two major parties maintain the confidentiality of membership numbers. As a general rule, membership numbers increase in election year and then drop off in the following two years.

been through a combination of declining membership, increasing engagement with the media, including social media, and the need for expert help and advice that the parties have moved in the direction of centralised campaign planning and control. There was a time when much of the responsibility for the day-to-day running of the campaign was devolved to local electorate committees, with oversight from the extra-parliamentary organisation. In recent years that responsibility has shifted to the party's political wing, in particular the office of the party leader. In the case of the governing party, this makes perfect sense, especially since the party leader has access to additional public funding by virtue of being the party leader, but also because of the number of personnel, such as IT specialists, political analysts, speechwriters and press secretaries, who are on hand long before the campaign begins. Additional professional agencies whose services are used by the better-funded parties during the campaign include focus group facilitators and pollsters, political advertising and marketing consultants, distribution networks (to mail out party literature), together with public relations and commercial fundraising companies. While most of the small parties lack sufficient resources to employ a wide range of professional and commercial expertise, some, like the Greens, utilise the skills of party members and supporters, especially those employed in the IT and communications industries, an arrangement that comes at little or no cost to the party budget.

Under MMP there is a strong incentive to maintain tight central control over campaign planning and execution. Unlike the former FPP system, success is measured by how well the parties go about mobilising their nationwide vote. Campaign officials were once able to focus their attention on the most marginal seats, on the grounds that they were the ones that largely determined the outcome of the election. Today, in contrast, parties must maximise their party vote regardless of where it is located. This means that a party vote in a totally unwinnable electorate has precisely the same value as a party vote in the most marginal of seats. To this can be added the sheer intensity of multi-party competition under MMP, something that is best managed within a centralised and coordinated organisational structure. Party branding is becoming an increasingly important feature of this competition, partly because it helps to distinguish one party from another, but also because, with the decline in levels of party identification and voter loyalty, a party's defining characteristics need to be clearly understood.

Voting

While the study of voting choice has a long tradition, it is not always clear why people vote the way they do. In postwar Britain, it was generally thought that the dominant influence on voting choice was social class, with working-class voters supporting Labour, and middle- and upper-middle-class voters the Conservatives. As a result, experts in the study of voting measured the importance of social and economic characteristics, such as social status, income and education, on the development of party preferences. Although class differences are less pronounced in New Zealand, the same socio-economic division has been used to help explain the continuing strength of the two main parties. Whereas National voters tend to be self-employed farmers, professionals and business proprietors on relatively high incomes, Labour's core constituency is unionised low-to-medium-income workers, most of whom are employed in manual and service occupations, together with Māori, beneficiaries and state house tenants.

In the early 1960s, Robert Chapman added the urban versus rural division to the socio-economic mix. In his view, the sectional interests separating New Zealand cities from the provincial towns and rural hinterland delineate 'different psychologies arising from two sorts of experience of life' (Chapman, 1962: 235). Thus the divisions of wealthier/poorer and rural/urban became the 'twin axes' that largely explained why people voted for one party rather than the other (Chapman, 1963: 227). By dividing the nation into distinct social sections – richer, poorer and mixed city electorates; provincial cities and towns; and rural electorates – Chapman was able to make generalisations about patterns of voting within each category.

By the 1960s, the importance of psychological and social attachments had become the subject of groundbreaking American research. A small group of social psychologists at the University of Michigan identified a number of causal factors they believed largely influenced voting choice. While these included socio-economic class, they also extended to other long-term characteristics, such as ethnicity, social and sectional interests, and family and friends (Campbell et al., 1964). By the 1970s, however, it was becoming clear that the old partisan alignments were beginning to weaken, a phenomenon that turned the attention of researchers towards alternative, more short-term explanations for voting choice.

While the *social psychological* model continued to enjoy support, there was renewed interest in the alternative *rational voter* model, the most well-known exponents of which were Anthony Downs (1957) and V. O. Key (1966). According to Downs, voters behave rationally by making largely short-term choices based on self-interest, a process that involves weighing up the relative merits of the alternative policy agendas on offer. Despite their rationality, however, voters are not always well informed, and indeed in many cases require signposts of the sort one might experience during an election campaign, a short-cut that might help them to reduce their 'information costs' (Downs, 1957: 113). In order to maximise their appeal to the median voter, the two main parties may jettison some policies and adopt others, an election-winning strategy that is high in pragmatism and low in deeply held beliefs. According to Downs, such is their desire to win that they may even 'deliberately change their platforms so that they resemble one another' (ibid.: 115).

Unlike the aggregative approach of Chapman and others of his generation, more recent work has been based on mass survey research, drawing on the declared choices and opinions of individual voters. Examples of this method include the pre-election surveys conducted by Stephen Levine and Nigel Roberts of Victoria University of Wellington, and the New Zealand Election Study (NZES), led by Jack Vowles. In a series of surveys stretching back over two decades, the NZES has discovered that the influence of short-term factors has continued to rise, at the expense of more long-term social psychological factors, confirming an early observation that, in addition to the well-known long-term influences, 'a whole host of other factors influence voting choice' (Vowles et al., 1995: 12). The potential importance of this multiplicity of short-term factors is confirmed by survey data showing that a significant proportion of New Zealand voters – upwards of 40 per cent – make their final decision during the course of the campaign (Vowles, 2014: 33).

To summarise, while the hypothetical 'average' voter may be susceptible to short-term events, many of which are likely to occur during the course of a campaign, there is always the possibility that they may be weakened or over-ridden by a predisposition to vote in a particular way. Factors contributing to this early decision may include upbringing, occupation, income and involvement in the local community (see Figure 10.1). Conversely, perhaps the most compelling evidence for the growing importance of short-term influences is the decline of party identification – from over 70 per cent of voters in the 1980s to 52 per cent in 2011 (Vowles, 2014: 46–47).

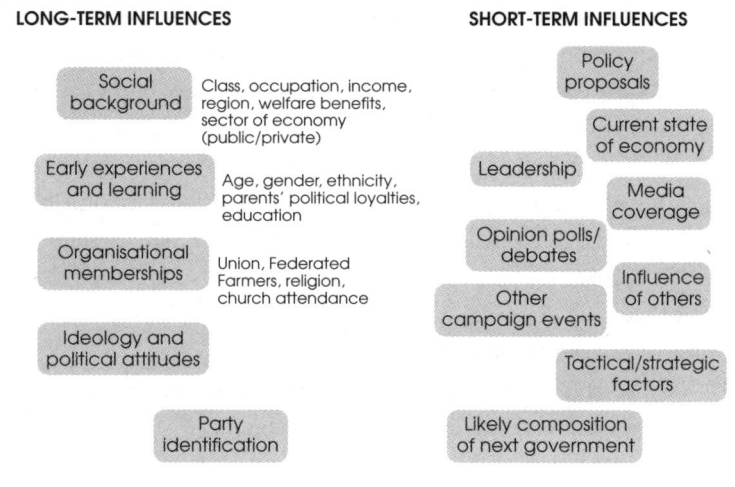

Figure 10.1: Influences on Voting Choice

Source: Adapted from Vowles et al., 1995: 11.

2014 Campaign

There was never any doubt that the 2014 election was National's to lose. In poll after poll, it had maintained a significant lead over Labour, so much so that most of the informed pre-election speculation had less to do with the contest between the two traditional rivals than the likely composition of the next National-led government. Would National be able to continue to govern with the support of its three small support parties, Māori, Act and United Future, or would it be forced to negotiate a confidence and supply agreement with the Conservatives or Winston Peters and New Zealand First? While National's level of support in pre-election polls had reached a flattering 50 to 52 per cent, giving rise to the prediction that it might be able to govern alone, no party had ever won a majority of seats under MMP, and to do so after six years in government was widely regarded to be a near-impossible task. On the other hand, while Labour had a mathematical chance of leading a multi-party government, such an outcome would be conditional on the support of four or five small parties, a potentially unstable arrangement that National's advertising campaign was quick to exploit.

National had good reason to be cautiously optimistic. With the two previous MMP governments having served for nine years, there was reason to believe that medium- to long-term voting patterns reflected a preference for stability and continuity over change. National's confidence had received an initial boost in 2011, when it gained a 47.3 per cent share of the vote, the largest of any party under MMP, and was further buoyed by its lead of 15 to 20-plus points in opinion polls, a margin that remained remarkably constant for the next three years. In contrast, following Clark's narrow election victory in 2005, electoral support for Labour began to stagnate at below 35 per cent, a situation that grew steadily worse under her three successors as party leader. The party's remaining hope of forming a centre-left government depended on a further consolidation of support for the Greens at approximately 15 per cent of the vote, together with a workable three-way agreement with New Zealand First, notwithstanding Peters' earlier refusal to support a government that included the Greens.

Brand Key

Over the preceding six years, National had elevated the personality of its leader to a level rarely seen in New Zealand politics. Leadership polls had confirmed him to be the party's most important asset, so much so that the Key 'brand' became the defining feature of the campaign, and arguably the primary agent of National's success. Key's image featured prominently in a billboard campaign that included the slogan 'Working for New Zealand:

Party Vote National'. His campaign appearances were the subject of meticulous planning with a view to reducing, if not eliminating, all risk, a strategy that kept him away from potentially hostile situations that might provide the opportunity for public disagreement or protest. In keeping with his reputation for approachability and authenticity, planned activities included targeted visits to successful businesses, especially those in the export sector; and to schools and kindergartens; as well as guest appearances at party and community events. Complementing these more formal occasions was the frequent use of walkabouts, where Key met members of the public and posed for the ubiquitous selfies. Consistent with his carefully nurtured image as a celebrity figure, Key also mixed with and received endorsements from a wide variety of prominent citizens and sportspeople, including past and present All Blacks. The natural way in which these interactions occurred contrasted sharply with the perceived awkwardness of the Labour leader, David Cunliffe, whose public appearances were often problematic, as illustrated by the public relations disaster surrounding his apology to a family violence conference for being a man, an admission that haunted him throughout the campaign and coincided with a sharp decline in the party's appeal to male voters.

By focusing its billboard campaign on the party's electorate contests, Labour caused the public gaze to be diverted from the all-important party vote, a strategy that had dire consequences for the election prospects of a number of high-ranking Labour list candidates. Television advertisements featured the faces of ordinary New Zealanders, as they responded to questions around such issues as affordable housing, jobs, wages and the pressures of time on family life. The emotional nature of the party's television campaign contrasted with National's humorous portrayal of the opposition parties as an assortment of inexperienced rowers trying to steer their dinghy in several different directions. Hardly surprisingly, National's television advertisements depicted the party as a team of competitive athletes all rowing in perfect harmony. Voters were urged to 'keep the team that's working'. Unlike Labour's strangely unfocused advertising strategy, the Green and New Zealand First parties concentrated their resources on maximising the party vote. The Green Party's provocative billboard campaign featured the words 'Love New Zealand', along with pictures of under-nourished children, oil spills and traffic jams. New Zealand First billboards adopted the slogan 'It's Common Sense', which appeared alongside a picture of Peters, far and away the party's greatest political asset.

Although Labour's rather clumsy admonition to 'Vote Positive' was designed to reinforce the party's commitment to a clean and constructive campaign, the absence of any direct reference to the leader had the unintended consequence of focusing attention on divisions within the party caucus and wider party organisation. As the campaign progressed, the Vote Positive message clearly inhibited Cunliffe's ability to deal with allegations of dirty tricks within National, opening the door for Key to complain that Cunliffe was focusing on dirty tricks at the expense of the 'real issues' of the campaign. This claim of hypocrisy on the part of Labour provided an opening for the media-savvy Green and New Zealand First parties to spearhead the attack on National.

Policy Issues

Consistent with its risk-averse approach to all aspects of the campaign, National announced the bulk of its policies well in advance of the formal campaign launch. An exception was the Prime Minister's promise of future tax cuts, the purpose of which was to differentiate National from the alleged 'tax and spend' policies of Labour. This was confirmed by the Finance Minister's clumsily expressed charge that the opposition parties' spending promises were symptomatic of a 'random dumb spending approach' (Bennett, 2014: A3). National's more measured promises in health and education included the extension of free doctors' visits to children under the age of thirteen and the introduction of 'merit' pay for the most highly rated principals and teachers. Under growing public pressure to introduce measures to reverse the steep rise in house prices, particularly in Auckland, the government promised a suite of policies, including reform of the Resource Management Act with a view to speeding up the consent process, as well as a vaguely worded commitment to the concept of social housing, the radical nature of which became apparent only after the election. To provide some limited assistance for potential first-home buyers, the government introduced a KiwiSaver Homestart scheme designed to make small grants available for those on modest incomes. As with most other policy proposals, the government's plan was to spread any limited increases in state spending to as wide a proportion of the population as possible.

Despite the absence of public support for Labour's tax and retirement policies at the 2011 election, they did not disappear, but rather were revived in good time for the 2014 campaign, a decision that reflected a desire to be principled and responsible, but also a belief that controversial policies could be repackaged in such a way as to make them more attractive the second time around. However, long before the mid-point in the formal campaign it had become clear that the proposal to raise the age of entitlement for superannuation from 65 to 67 was not going down well with older voters, despite Labour's other plans for the retired, including the proposal that doctors' visits be provided free of charge. Whereas 60 per cent of those over the age of 65 years planned to give their party vote to National, only 18 per cent intended voting for Labour. Similar results were found among 40–64-year-olds, with 50 per cent supporting National and 27 per cent Labour (Young, 2014: A3). Nor were there grounds for optimism that the proposed rise in the top tax rate (from 32 to 36 per cent) and the introduction of a capital gains tax were enjoying popular support, especially following Cunliffe's failure to clarify immediately the suggestion that the family home might not be excluded from the 15 per cent levy. On the other hand, as the Labour Party's Finance spokesperson, David Parker, was quick to explain, public policy promises incur significant costs, making increases in tax revenue imperative for any Labour-led government. Such policies included increasing the number of teachers by 2000, reducing the teacher-student ratio, extending parental leave, creating more apprenticeships, and addressing the problems of poor housing and poverty.

Whereas the policy demands of National's likely support parties were reasonably easy to accommodate, Act's being largely limited to the expansion of charter schools, the abolition of the Resource Management Act and tougher penalties for repeat offenders, the Greens provided National with an easy target, despite the claim that their spending plans had been costed with some care. On more than one occasion, for example, the Prime Minister made the unsubstantiated claim that the combined promises of the two centre-left parties would cost up to $28 billion dollars (Bonallack, 2014: A15). Most of the Greens' spending priorities were in the areas of support for low-income families, public transport, and substantial funding increases for education and the environment. On the other hand, National's allegations of excessive spending were carefully targeted to exclude New Zealand First, a party the Prime Minister might have needed in the event that the existing support parties failed to provide National with a legislative majority. New Zealand First's proposals had a familiar ring, especially its planned restrictions on the foreign ownership of houses and land, the tightening of immigration laws, low-interest loans for first-home buyers, and increased spending on health and education.

Dirty Politics

In keeping with the hallmark secrecy that accompanied his previous investigations, the release of Nicky Hager's *Dirty Politics* partway through the campaign caught National's strategists by surprise. The explosive nature of the book's content, especially the graphic language and threats to harm political opponents, raised concerns about declining ethical standards in politics. Potentially more damaging for National, however, were the alleged links between the central figure in the attacks, right-wing blogger Cameron Slater, and senior members of the government, especially the Justice Minister, Judith Collins, and Jason Ede, who was a senior communications adviser in the Office of the Prime Minister.

Although Key was not directly implicated in the alleged dirty tricks, the charge of guilt by association continued to haunt him throughout the campaign. In the words of Hager: 'Sitting in the midst of the negative politics was John Key. For years Jason Ede had been working in his office, two doors along the corridor, coordinating attack politics for the National government' (Hager, 2014: 132). Even in the absence of a smoking gun, Hager's allegations had the potential to tarnish the reputation of the Prime Minister, and perhaps even change the outcome of the election.

After defending his Justice Minister for two weeks, Key eventually accepted Collins' resignation from Cabinet, claiming that he was in receipt of new evidence implicating her in a campaign to discredit the previous head of the Serious Fraud Office, Adam Feeley (Savage and O'Sullivan, 2014: A2–A3). In an unrelated matter, Collins admitted to having leaked private information to Slater on yet another public servant, who later received death threats. Although the subsequent release of further emails from an anonymous source continued to keep the 'dirty politics' allegations in the public domain, by early September it was becoming clear that the government had weathered the worst of the storm.

In contrast to the secrecy surrounding the release of *Dirty Politics*, Kim Dotcom's personal attacks on the Prime Minister and his promise to provide damning evidence to back up his various claims a mere five days before polling day were signalled so far in advance as to remove much of the dramatic effect, as well as any significant public interest. That notwithstanding, much of National's time and energy during the final two weeks of the campaign was devoted to dispelling the Kim Dotcom threat, especially the possible impact of any allegations about international and domestic surveillance on last-minute voters. At the scheduled event in the Auckland Town Hall, Dotcom failed to deliver reliable evidence in support of his claim that Key had lied when he claimed no knowledge of Dotcom's existence prior to the armed raid on his Coatesville mansion in January 2012. On the other hand, he was able to mount a spirited attack on the government's role in intelligence gathering by recruiting the Pulitzer Prize-winning author Glenn Greenwald and American whistle-blower Edward Snowden, to provide testimony as to its involvement in collecting data, especially on New Zealand citizens. Despite extensive media coverage of the event, by the final week of the campaign it had become clear that the Dotcom persona and litany of allegations had largely exhausted all remaining public interest.

Despite both the serious nature of the allegations and the attention given to them by the media, neither *Dirty Politics* nor the Dotcom allegations appear to have had any measurable impact on public opinion (see Figure 10.2). Even allowing for the possibility of a slight lag effect on opinion, by 22 August (some nine days after the book's release) there was little to suggest that either source of attack was hurting National's re-election chances. As research by Colin James has revealed, by averaging out the last four polls across the six most prominent polling

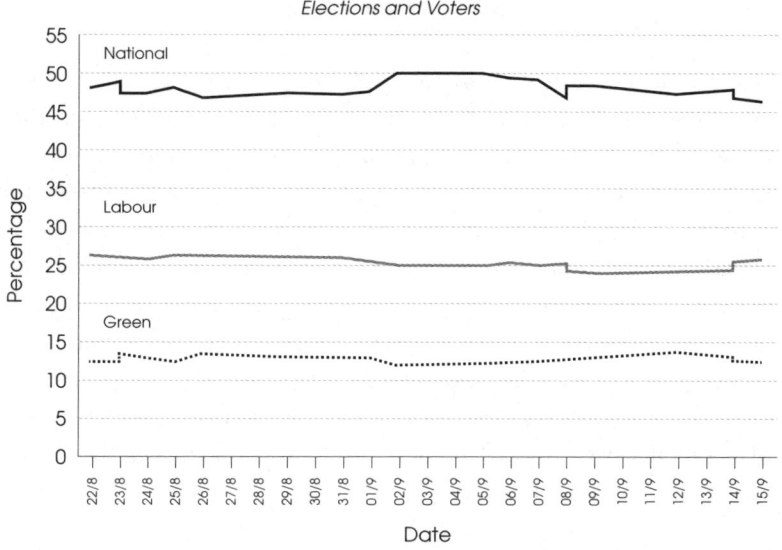

Figure 10.2: Average Last Four Polls, 20 August to 15 September 2014
Source: James, 2014.

agencies,* it is possible to detect only one significant dip in support, and that was in the final few days of the campaign – a common experience among governing parties, as illustrated by the decline in support for Labour late in the 2002 campaign, and National in 2011 (James, 2014). By the same token, both Labour and the Greens failed to benefit from any perception that they were innocent bystanders in the unseemly turn of campaign events. Indeed, even strong performances by Cunliffe in at least three of the four televised leaders' debates appeared to provide no lift in Labour's level of support.

There are several plausible explanations for the lack of any measurable effect of *Dirty Politics* on public opinion. Based on survey research, it is clear that many voters make up their minds how they are going to cast their two votes long before the formal campaign actually begins. In the previous two elections of 2008 and 2011, up to 60 per cent of voters were

---

* TV1 Colmar Brunton, TV3 Reid Research, Fairfax Media-Ipsos, New Zealand Herald DigiPoll, Roy Morgan New Zealand and UMR Research.

early deciders (Vowles, 2014: 33). There is no reason to believe it was any different in 2014; indeed, the long-term nature of Labour's electoral decline might suggest that the proportion of early deciders was even higher. Of course, it is also possible that, having given some thought to the nature of the allegations, many voters were not convinced, either on the grounds that they found the assurances of the Prime Minister to be more credible, or because they simply dismissed Hager as a radical opportunist with a political agenda. A further explanation, and one that is potentially the most disturbing, is the possibility that the public have become so disengaged from campaigns that they are no longer attentive to day-to-day developments, even those that might test their confidence in the current state of New Zealand democracy.

2014 Results

On election night, National received 48.1 per cent of the vote and an overall majority of 61 seats, a particularly noteworthy result, and one that set a record for a modern government contesting its third election in succession. Comparisons have often been drawn between the popularity of Keith Holyoake's four-term National government (1960–72) and that of National under Key. What made the 2014 provisional results even more impressive than those of the Holyoake government was not simply the fact that they were achieved in an MMP multi-party environment, but also because this was National's third successive election increase – from 44.9 per cent in 2008 and 47.3 per cent in 2011, to a provisional total of 48.1 per cent in 2014. In contrast, the Holyoake government's share of the vote actually declined at each election it contested – from 47.6 per cent in 1960, to 47.1 per cent in 1963 and 43.6 per cent in 1966. In what must be considered a night of records, Labour's share of the vote (24.7 per cent) was its lowest since 1922 (23.7 per cent), giving rise to calls for the resignation of the leader and a fundamental overhaul of the party's organisation and policies. Although the Greens might have expected to be the major beneficiary of Labour's misfortune, their 10 per cent share of the vote was lower than the polls had been indicating (see Figure 10.2), and also lower than the 11.1 per cent result achieved in 2011.

When the final results were announced some two weeks after polling day (see Table 10.1), National's share of the vote slipped back to 47 per cent and 60 seats, a result that did not alter its previously announced plan to sign support agreements with the three parties it had worked with over the preceding six years, namely Act, the Māori Party and United Future. As well as minimising the risk of defections or by-election defeats during the course of the next three years, bringing the MPs from the small parties on board came at little cost to the government, their bargaining strength having been weakened by the gradual attrition in their numbers over the preceding six years (from a total of eleven MPs in 2008 to five in 2011 and four in 2014). Although unable to add to its 32 seats, Labour did experience a small increase in its overall share of the vote. The Greens recovered slightly, gaining a list seat to add to their initial complement of thirteen seats (one fewer than in 2011).

Table 10.1: Results of the 2008, 2011 and 2014 Elections

	2008				2011				2014			
	Vote	Elect.	List	Total	Vote	Elect.	List	Total	Vote	Elect.	List	Total
National	44.93	41	17	58	47.31	42	17	59	47.04	41	19	60
Labour	33.99	21	22	43	27.46	22	12	34	25.13	27	5	32
Greens	6.72	0	9	9	11.06	0	14	14	10.70	0	14	14
NZ First	4.07	0	0	0	6.59	0	8	8	8.66	0	11	11
Act	3.65	1	4	5	1.07	1	0	1	0.69	1	0	1
Māori	2.39	5	0	5	1.43	3	0	3	1.32	1	1	2
Progressive	0.91	1	0	1								
United Future	0.87	1	0	1	0.60	1	0	1	0.22	1	0	1
Internet/Mana					1.08	1	0	1	1.42	0	0	0
Conservative					2.65	0	0	0	3.97	0	0	0
Other	6.54	0	0	0	0.75	0	0	0	0.85	0	0	0
Total	100.0	70	52	122	100.0	70	51	121	100.0	71	50	121

Source: New Zealand Electoral Commission, 2008, 2011 and 2014.

Table 10.2: Two-Party Results in Auckland, 2014

	National		Labour	
	Party Vote	Electorate Vote	Party Vote	Electorate Vote
North Shore	58.2	60.0	16.6	19.3
Auckland City	46.3	36.5	26.9	41.0
Eastern Suburbs	62.3	65.4	16.4	19.1
West Auckland	43.0	43.9	30.8	39.6
South Auckland	29.9	28.0	50.3	54.3

Source: New Zealand Electoral Commission, 2014b.

One major consequence of the election results was National's success in driving back Labour to its fortress seats in West and South Auckland, Wellington and Dunedin. As Table 10.2 shows, National made a clean sweep of Auckland's North Shore and Eastern Suburbs electorates, defeating Labour in all its marginally held seats. Even in safe Labour electorates, National achieved success after success in the all-important party vote: of the total number of 64 General seats nationwide, Labour managed to win the party vote in only four (Kelston, Māngere, Manukau East and Manurewa), all of them situated in West and South Auckland. In the traditionally safe Auckland seat of Mt Albert, for example (a seat held by the former Labour leader David Shearer), National received 39 per cent of the party vote and Labour 29 per cent. In Mt Roskill, where the incumbent was another former Labour leader, Phil Goff, the margin was 42 per cent to 35 per cent (see Appendix). The same pattern prevailed in the Auckland seat of New Lynn, where the Labour candidate was party leader David Cunliffe. In Wellington, where Labour has a strong record of success, the average party vote for National was 41 per cent, compared with 29 per cent for Labour. In Trevor Mallard's seat of Hutt South, for example, National received 45 per cent of the party vote and Labour 28 per cent.

But perhaps the greatest challenge facing Labour in the period 2014–17 is that of regaining lost ground in the provincial towns and cities of both islands. In 2002, when Labour was close to its prime, it managed to win eighteen provincial seats, including Invercargill, Aoraki, Wairarapa, Whanganui, New Plymouth, Taupo, Rotorua, and Hamilton East and West. In 2014 the party won only three: Napier, Palmerston North and

West Coast-Tasman. Even more concerning for Labour is the steep decline in its share of the party vote, with only one in five voters in the provinces giving their party vote to Labour (see Table 10.3).

Table 10.3: Two-party Results by Region, 2014

	National		Labour	
	Party Vote	Electorate Vote	Party Vote	Electorate Vote
Auckland	49.1	47.7	26.8	33.3
Wellington	41.1	29.9	28.7	47.6
Christchurch	46.5	43.3	25.4	40.6
Dunedin	36.1	34.3	32.5	47.9
Provincial North Island	52.2	54.4	20.3	27.7
Provincial South Island	54.5	56.2	19.6	27.7
Māori Seats	7.9	0.0*	40.8	42.1

Source: New Zealand Electoral Commission, 2014b.

* National did not contest Māori electorates.

Given these wide margins between Labour's party and electorate votes, it is hardly surprising that the proportion of voters who split their votes nationwide was slightly greater in 2014 than in 2011, at some 31.6 per cent. Even less surprising is that the greatest split occurred in the Auckland seat of Epsom, with 60.1 per cent of National voters giving their electorate vote to the Act candidate, David Seymour (New Zealand Electoral Commission, 2014b).

Conclusion

More than at any previous election, the 2014 campaign exemplified the importance of four major developments: the growth of the 'permanent' campaign; increasing personalisation relative to more substantive issues, especially party values and policies; the vulnerability of the campaign timetable to unplanned interventions and events; and the trend towards a more professional, media-focused campaign. Although New Zealand's small and intimate society might have been expected to insulate it from the most disengaging effects of international trends, this has not been the case; indeed, campaigns are in danger of becoming as cynical, vacuous and remote as they are in much larger democracies. In light of National's thin policy agenda and even thinner campaign schedule, the Prime Minister's complaint that journalists and political opponents who interrogated Hager's allegations were being distracted by mere sideshows can best be described as disingenuous.

How might we account for the absence of any discernible public response to the charges made by Hager and others about the future of New Zealand democracy? As we have seen, one obvious explanation is that the level of public goodwill felt towards Key was more than sufficient to withstand what were widely regarded to be attacks on his character, especially from such polarising figures as Hager and Dotcom. Instead of challenging the central claims of Hager's argument, the Prime Minister attacked the author as a conspiracy theorist, left-wing agitator and attention-seeker who, by basing his claims on 'stolen' emails, was as guilty of misconduct as the alleged perpetrators of the dirty tricks campaign. Dotcom proved to be an even easier target, especially given the obvious self-interest that lay behind his attacks. Despite some initial fascination with the David-versus-Goliath battle the internet entrepreneur was conducting with the Hollywood film industry and United States government, by 2014 many of his supporters had begun to tire of the largely unsubstantiated nature of his personal attacks and the determination with which he exploited the unpopular coat-tails provision of MMP on behalf of the new Internet/Mana Party.*

The lack of any voter backlash against National may also reflect a widely held belief that attack politics, while far from desirable, are common to all political parties, a claim the Prime Minister exploited to good effect. His success may help explain why Labour and the Greens failed to derive any lift in popular support, despite promising a cleaner style of politics under a centre-left government. Of course, there is the further possibility that a significant proportion of the electorate were so thoroughly

---

* Under the one-seat threshold provisions of MMP, had Hone Harawira been re-elected in the northern Māori seat of Te Tai Tokerau he may conceivably have brought one or two Internet Party list candidates into Parliament with him, even in the event that the Internet/Mana vote failed to reach the other threshold of 5 per cent.

disengaged from the campaign that any allegations made by Hager or Dotcom simply had no bearing on the way they intended casting their vote – or not casting it at all.

In the end, the country got the government most pundits had been predicting. Throughout the preceding three years, opinion polls had been reporting a preference for continuity over change. New Zealand had successfully weathered the storm of financial crisis, much of the credit for which had been claimed by the National-led government. It is also the case that electoral history was very much on the government's side. With only one exception (the Fourth Labour Government of 1984–90), every government formed during the past four decades has been re-elected for a total of three terms or nine years. The only significant cloud on the horizon was the unpopularity of National's three support parties, Act, United Future and the Māori Party. With all three winning seats, National's re-election for a third term was assured.

Labour's performance, on the other hand, suffered as a result of internal division, weak and unstable leadership (with four different leaders in the space of six years), some poorly conceived and presented policies, and a flawed campaign. Having failed to use its time in opposition to renew its caucus, redefine its message, and build a credible working relationship with the Greens, at no stage in the campaign did Labour look like upsetting National's claim to a third term.

For National, the only cloud on the horizon was a by-election in the hitherto safe seat of Northland in March 2015. Because conditions under which by-elections occur are vastly different from those of a general election, their outcomes are hard to predict. As studies have shown (see Miller and Catt, 1993), by-elections afford voters the opportunity to send the government an anti-government message without placing the immediate future of the government at risk. In Winston Peters, Northland voters had a populist campaigner with an unparalleled ability to exploit feelings of resentment and neglect. On the other hand, National chose a candidate who was almost entirely unknown outside the local party organisation. Despite the close attention given by senior party officials and government ministers, including the Prime Minister, National's 9000-vote majority at the 2014 election turned into a 4000-vote by-election loss.

Chapter Eleven

Future of Democracy

It is possible to provide at least two contrasting, even contradictory, discourses on democracy in New Zealand. The first is overwhelmingly positive and begins with international rankings revealing New Zealand to be one of the most democratic and least corrupt nations in the world.* Confirmation of this high standing is provided by way of public opinion, with between 65 and 70 per cent of voters expressing satisfaction with the practice of democracy in New Zealand. Attitudes towards the act of voting are also highly positive, with 85 per cent of survey respondents believing it to be a citizen's duty to vote, a view confirmed by historic data, with over 90 per cent of eligible voters regularly turning out to vote (see chapter one, Table 1.5). At the height of the mass party era, an estimated one in four voters belonged to a political party, a proportion without equal in the Western world. By measuring satisfaction from the somewhat different angle of 'subjective well-being', social psychologists rank New Zealand high on any scale of public happiness or satisfaction (for example, Inglehart et al., 2008).

There are a number of possible explanations for these results. New Zealand's small and physically remote population has created expectations of intimacy and a sense of belonging that would be unrealistic in much larger democracies. Elected politicians who fail to provide open,

---

* Transparency International's Accountability index ranks New Zealand among the world's two or three most accountable countries: see Transparency International website.

accessible and transparent leadership risk facing a public backlash, including defeat at the next election. Public expectations are reinforced by a range of constitutional and institutional safeguards, including: triennial elections; small electoral districts; proportional elections; a socially and politically diverse Parliament; the constraining influence of minority government; together with avenues of direct action, including parliamentary submissions, petitions and citizens'-initiated referenda (CIR).

Despite this legacy of intimacy and accountability, at the heart of our second, contrasting view of democracy are growing levels of disengagement from the political process. Paralleling patterns found in other Western democracies, participation rates are in decline, elected officials struggle to retain the public's trust, and the gap between rich and poor is widening (see Organisation for Economic Co-operation and Development [OECD], 2014). Despite the proliferation of parliamentary parties, with up to seven or eight parties holding seats at any one time, there has been a hollowing out of party membership and activism. As a result, traditional links between party organisations and the communities they represent have been attenuating. The decline in voter turnout among the young has been an issue of particular concern, especially given the growing evidence that it is part of a new pattern of generational disengagement. Equally dangerous are the inherent risks to be found in the more gladiatorial leader-driven nature of modern election campaigns. With party branding and personal style so often trumping substance, the voting public is being deprived of informed policy choice. The extent to which voters have become disengaged is illustrated by the absence of any discernible public reaction to the media's interrogation of the dirty politics and mass surveillance allegations that dominated the 2014 campaign.

In light of these developments, one of the central tasks of this chapter is to ask who runs New Zealand, and in whose interests. Does political power reside with the people or is it more narrowly based? There are those who argue that power is in the hands of a congenial elite consisting of government ministers and their key advisers and bureaucrats, together with the captains of business and finance. Despite New Zealand's highly educated population and record of democratic engagement, much of the demand for constitutional and institutional reform has originated with those in positions of political influence and power, to the virtual exclusion of public discussion and debate. Examples of top-down reform include the abolition of the upper house, privatisation of state-owned assets, adoption of a Bill of Rights and the replacement of Britain's Privy Council as the highest court of appeal with a local Supreme Court.

Conversely, it is important to remind ourselves of the role once played by public opinion in reshaping the political structure in a direction more compatible with New Zealand's increasingly pluralistic society. The decision by popular referendum to replace the first-past-the-post (FPP) or plurality voting system had a number of important consequences, notably the consolidation of new multi-party arrangements and the advent of coalition government. As we have seen, the preferred mixed-member proportional (MMP) voting system also attracted its fair share of critics, mainly on the grounds that it was likely to shift the balance of power in the direction of small parties, giving rise to predictions of unstable and ineffective government.

This chapter will consider a number of quite distinct, even contradictory, conceptions of what democracy actually means. As well as telling us something about the many different approaches to the way scholars view and understand politics, they also provide insight into the methods and strategies being adopted by practitioners – in other words, those who operate in the real world of politics.

Pluralist Democracy

When New Zealand's politicians are asked to describe how their system of democracy works, they invariably resort to the imagery, if not the language, of pluralism. Democratic pluralism is based on two main assumptions: that society is split up into a number of different segments or interests; and that political power is widely dispersed. It is the right of all individuals to join together and have their interests represented by independent organisations, such as trade unions, employers' associations, and ethnic and environmental groups. It is the role of government, on the other hand, to act as an impartial referee or umpire, giving fair treatment to the needs and interests of these groups. Because there is likely to be competition for influence between, let's say, employers and unionised workers, or mining lobby groups and environmentalists, it is the task of government to mediate the debate with a view to reaching a just decision. Controversially, early pluralists were of the view that interest groups of equivalent size had a roughly equal ability to be heard and to influence government decisions (Dahl, 1956). They also believed that the overall outcome of the bargaining process was a state of stability or 'equilibrium' between the various groups (Dahl, 1982: 152).

To press their claims with the government, interest groups carry out a variety of tasks, including: lobbying politicians and other decision-makers; conducting and disseminating their own research; launching media campaigns with a view to influencing public opinion; and even taking to the streets in protest, as illustrated by the marches in 2010 by opponents of the government's plan to allow mining exploration in national parks and on high-level conservation land. The reform of New Zealand's liquor laws was another issue that sparked activity among competing interest groups. In April 2010, the government-funded New Zealand Law Commission released a report entitled 'Alcohol in our Lives: Curbing the Harm'. The report, which made 153 recommendations, including lifting the excise tax on alcohol and increasing the minimum age for the purchase of alcohol from eighteen to twenty years, attracted intense public interest (with 3000 submissions) and lobbying from both sides in the debate. Among the most vocal lobby or interest groups were the well-resourced Hospitality Industry Association and the advertising industry on the one hand, and public health and safety groups, the police and the Alcohol Advisory Council (ALAC) on the other.

Writing in the late 1980s, Richard Mulgan argued that political power was distributed among three interconnected institutions: Parliament, including the political parties; interest groups; and local government (Mulgan, 1989a: 37–55). Society, he argued, was characterised by both diversity, as reflected in the range of social groups and interests, and a sense of unity and shared values. At the core of support for the two major parties, for example, were distinct ethnic, socio-economic and occupational groups, with National representing those on higher incomes in the farming, business and professional sectors, and Labour the lower paid, largely unionised urban workers and beneficiaries, as well as members of the Māori and Pasifika communities. Despite these differences, for much of their early history both parties adopted a moderate and pragmatic approach to reform, as well as having a shared commitment to those policies we have come to associate with the mixed economy and Keynesian welfare state. This consensus of opinion applied as much to foreign and defence policy as to domestic politics. Successive postwar governments expressed their loyalty to the British monarchy and Commonwealth, as well as support for defence ties with the United States. The golden weather lasted until the early 1970s and was characterised by political stability, economic prosperity and employment for all.

By the late 1970s it was becoming clear that New Zealand's postwar consensus was beginning to unravel. Global economic recession, much of it brought on by successive increases in the price of oil, placed severe pressure on New Zealand's domestic economy. A combination of high inflation, negative growth and rising unemployment might reasonably have resulted in a rigorous review of the government's spending commitments. Instead, Prime Minister Robert Muldoon embarked on a series of major energy-based industrial developments, euphemistically entitled 'Think Big'. To fund these projects, Muldoon borrowed heavily from overseas at high rates of interest. Voter disillusionment with the personal costs of economic recession and the polarising leadership of Muldoon resulted in the gradual decline in levels of support for the two main parties. Many voters began to turn their attention instead to the small parties, as well as the growing array of social movements. The civil rights and anti-Vietnam protests of the 1960s had helped spawn a number of new social movements, including the anti-nuclear, environmental, women's, anti-apartheid and Māori civil rights movements. Although they remained on the periphery of the political system, their various causes being largely rejected by the two main parties, these new movements attracted support in the tens, if not the hundreds, of thousands. Examples of protest action by these movements included the 1975 Maori Land March from Northland to Wellington and the disruption to rugby games caused by the 1981 anti-Springbok protests.

The emergence of these and other social movements represented a significant new challenge to classical pluralism.

Pluralism's failure to provide a truly persuasive account for the unequal distribution of power caused critics to turn to more radical explanations, including elite theory and Marxism. Robert Michels, a German sociologist, famously referred to the 'iron law of oligarchy' in describing his belief in the inevitability of elite rule (Michels, 1962). Another sociologist, C. Wright Mills, argued that, instead of being widely dispersed, political decision-making in the United States was controlled by a socially homogeneous 'power elite' consisting of the most senior leaders in the spheres of politics, the military establishment and business. While Mills did not entirely dismiss the influence of political parties and interest groups on the policy process, he relegated their importance to that of middle managers within a large organisation (Mills, 1956). Ordinary citizens, on the other hand, were largely excluded from any participation in the decision-making process. Writing in a similar vein, the New Zealand social critic Bruce Jesson asserted that the New Zealand business elite, which he variously described as 'a particular social class' and the 'bourgeoisie', had seized the levers of power (Jesson, 1987: 12; Jesson, 1989).

Marxism goes much further than elite theory in offering a view of history in which there is a causal link between capitalism and the exercise of political power. Marx argued that advanced capitalism contains within it the seeds of its own destruction, evidence for which can be seen in the exploitative behaviour of the capitalist class, resulting in ever-increasing levels of class-consciousness and alienation. He predicted that a revolutionary struggle would take place between the capitalist class, or bourgeoisie, and the financially powerless industrial proletariat, the outcome of which would be a radical redistribution of political and economic power and the death of capitalism (Dryzek and Dunleavy, 2009: 79–99). In his Marxist critique of capitalism, Brian Roper draws parallels between Marx's evidence for class struggle and capitalist decline and economic trends in New Zealand. These are said to include economic stagnation and inflation (often referred to as 'stagflation'); rising unemployment; an increase in the incidence of strike action and other forms of class struggle; declining incomes, especially among the low-waged; and growing personal and public debt. While there have been efforts to address some of these problems, ultimately the capitalist system is deemed by Marxist scholars to be 'inherently and unalterably exploitative', thereby restricting 'the participation of the working class majority in the governance of the economy, society, and polity' (Roper, 2001: 553).

Where pluralism faced its most difficult challenge, however, was in responding to the right-wing ethos behind the free market reforms of the 1980s and 1990s. Implicit in the arguments for reform were a number of assumptions. The postwar Keynesian consensus, with its emphasis on social and economic equality and an active state, was allegedly fundamentally flawed. Citizens were not equal, nor did they enjoy equal access to power. While the state had a duty to defend the life, liberty and property of the citizens, it was not its place to intervene in the economy with a view to achieving a more equal society. Consistent with public choice theory, which was at the heart of the free market reforms, group interests were 'vested' interests and as such must give way to the rights of the individual (Mulgan, 1994: 8–9). As New Zealand's leading architect of free market reform, Roger Douglas, stated, 'Governments would do best by keeping foremost in mind the interests of taxpayers and consumers – the small people – not those of producers and special-interest groups' (Douglas, 1993: 3). According to this view, 'the collective is about imposing your values on others, and as such is undesirable since all values are subjective, a matter of individual choice' (Stoker, 2006: 204). This focus on the individual rather than the collective applies as much to political parties as it does to interest groups, which helps explain Douglas's frequent disagreements with the members of his own extra-parliamentary party who dared to oppose his reforms.

There is no doubt that these critiques exposed some fundamental weaknesses in the pluralist model of democracy. Those of a *neo-pluralist* persuasion now concede that groups are manifestly unequal, both in terms of resources and access to those in positions of power. Those representing corporate capitalism, for example, are in a naturally favourable position by virtue of their influence over prices, profits and jobs. The choice of either keeping their businesses in New Zealand or relocating overseas provides a further source of influence. As Charles Lindlom has warned, the power of the big corporations is such that 'They can . . . insist that government meet their demands, even if these demands run counter to those of citizens' (Lindlom, 1977: 356).

As well as acknowledging that groups are unequal, neo-pluralists repudiate any claims to the neutrality of the state. In the process of setting and prioritising their agendas, governments are subject to a variety of influences, especially from groups representing their electoral constituencies, such as Federated Farmers in the case of National, and the Council of Trade Unions in that of Labour. But politicians also have their own interests to protect. This is particularly so in an MMP Parliament and government. As well as satisfying the demands of various community and special interest groups, they must protect and advance the political interests of their own party, as illustrated by the government formation negotiations that follow each election. In the post-election negotiations of 2011 and 2014, for example, National was its own interest group, as were the Act, Māori and United Future parties. None could be regarded as either impartial or neutral as they advanced their own policy and office-seeking agendas.

Although the overall influence of interest groups remains strong, there has been a decline in levels of membership and support, as exemplified by the drop in the number of trade union members, from 683,000 in 1985 (Street, 2003: 381) to 371,000 or 16.6 per cent of the labour force in 2013 (New Zealand Companies Office, 2013). This same trend can be found in voluntary organisations, as well as independent community-based associations, many of which had long played an invaluable role in both shaping public policy and curbing the powers of government. In his book *Bowling Alone*, Robert Putnam describes 'social capital' as the vast array of voluntary associations to which members of the public belong (Putnam, 2000). In recent years, it has become clear that citizens' links with sports, recreational, religious, professional and other independent groups have been weakening. The reasons are complex and include the growth of a more secular and atomised society, the privatisation of leisure activities, and increased social mobility and access to travel.

Of at least equal concern for the future of pluralist democracy has been the decline of political parties as mass-membership organisations.

As we saw in chapter eight, parties once fulfilled the role of conveyor belts, transmitting the views of voters and grassroots members to the elected politicians, who in turn deployed party activists and members to proselytise the voting public. Following a similar pattern to that experienced in other Western democracies, beginning in the 1970s and 1980s party membership numbers began to decline. Part of the explanation for this trend has to do with the rise of television, which was better able to filter and interpret political information and opinion between the governing elite and the voting public. In contrast to the class-based politics of the mass party era, the new 'electoral-professional' parties of the television age deployed professional expertise with a view to broadening their appeal across a wide range of social groups. Having been largely deprived of a more significant role, the old mass-membership parties were transformed into small oligarchies, largely run by and in the interests of party officials and elected politicians.

Direct Democracy

Despite the obvious strengths of the neo-pluralist model of democracy, there is evidence of a substantial constituency for a more direct, voter-initiated and voter-controlled system of democracy. Some form of direct democracy is recognised in several of the standard definitions of democracy. According to one, democracy is 'the direct rule of the people themselves as a body without superior authority set over them' (Hirst, 1990: 23). In tracing the roots of modern democracy, theorists take us back to the city-states of ancient Greece, medieval Italy, the colonial American settlements of New England and, more recently, the Swiss plebiscitary system of democracy.

Although precise information on how Athenian democracy worked is sketchy, we do know that it consisted of regular (perhaps weekly or fortnightly) assemblies of citizens for the purpose of making decisions on such matters as law and order, public finance, and war and peace. It is easy to imagine protracted and oft-times passionate discussions, frequently involving fundamental disagreement, and culminating in a vote of all those present. A requirement of all citizens was that they placed the public good ahead of personal self-interest. Among the civic aspirations they were expected to uphold was a willingness to stand for political office and subscribe to the shared values of liberty, equality and the rule of law. With the names of potential office-holders being drawn at random, there was little prospect of individual candidates being re-elected, let alone becoming entrenched in positions of power.

Could this model of direct democracy be made to work in a nation-state the size of New Zealand? Despite the claim that political power in ancient Athens resided in the 'whole people', it bore no resemblance to modern conceptions of majority rule (Held, 2006: 16–17; Held, 1993: 16). All women, slaves and immigrants were excluded from participation, leaving political power in the hands of a small minority of free men. Furthermore, with attendance at assemblies numbering in the thousands (Held, 2006: 17), audiences were highly susceptible to manipulation by those with the strongest voices, as well as the greatest social status and wealth. In the end, any comparison between then and now must take into account differences of scale. The American political scientist Robert Dahl has put some perspective on the relative sizes of the Greek city-states and the modern nation-state by observing that 'New Zealand, one of the least populous democratic countries, has a hundred times more citizens than did fifth century Athens or medieval Padua. In territory, the difference in magnitude is even greater' (Dahl, 1982: 8).

But what about the New England states, which continue to practise direct democracy in many of their municipalities or towns? While attendances at town meetings are often small and decisions limited to matters affecting the immediate community, their symbolism continues to attract attention, as illustrated by the appearance of a former United States President, Jimmy Carter, at a number of such meetings during the late 1970s. However, it is hard to imagine how such an intimate model of decision-making could be expanded beyond small municipalities to include cosmopolitan centres the size of Boston, let alone something of the scale of a provincial or federal government.

A more common form of direct democracy, indeed one practised in approximately half of all American states, involves the use of referenda or ballot initiatives. Prominent examples include Proposition 13 (1978), which capped the property taxes of Californian residents, and Colorado's Initiative 25 (2010), which sought to make abortions in the state illegal. By vesting greater authority in ordinary citizens, initiatives can provide an effective brake on the powers of the governing elite. Referenda are of two types: those initiated by the government and those by ordinary citizens. In New Zealand, government initiatives have been used for constitutional and policy issues deemed to be of national importance. These include triennial polls on liquor licensing laws (last held in 1987), increasing the parliamentary term from three to four years (1967 and 1990), making retirement savings compulsory (1997), and changes to the electoral system (1992, 1993 and 2011). In a speech at the opening of the 2012 Political Science conference in Wellington, Prime Minister John Key expressed the view that, instead of holding a referendum on MMP at the previous election, the government should have sought voter opinion on increasing the parliamentary term to four years (Key, 2012). He later announced that there would indeed be another government-initiated referendum, not on the parliamentary term, but rather the replacement of the national flag with one deemed more appropriate for an independent New Zealand.

In contrast to the largely constitutional matters raised in government-initiated referenda, most of the petitions calling for CIRs have been on matters of public policy.*

In arguing for CIRs, a former New Zealand Member of Parliament made the claim that 'ordinary voters are sovereign and the government is essentially there to do their bidding' (Newman, 2010). Swiss democracy, with its long history of decision-making by referenda, is commended for its effectiveness in both 'limiting the influence of politically powerful minority pressure groups, by weighing up their demands against the costs to society as a whole', and 'stopping in its tracks the hijacking of the political process by party politics' (ibid.). According to this argument, while voters may lack confidence in political parties, interest groups and elected politicians,

---

* Exceptions include a small number of constitutional petitions, including one to reduce the size of the Parliament from 120 to 99 members (1997) and another calling for a written constitution (1997).

they do trust themselves. But referenda are also praised for their ability to hold governments to account. As one analysis on referenda has observed, 'what better way to maximize responsiveness of rulers to the ruled than by fostering a system in which the ruled themselves make the decisions?' (M. Saward, quoted in Parkinson, 2010: 579).

Critics of referenda express concern that ordinary citizens lack sufficient competence to make informed decisions, especially on complex matters of public policy. As a result, they are deemed to be vulnerable to manipulation by self-interested and wealthy individuals and groups. However, this view is now being challenged by empirical research[*] which shows that: first, voters are better informed than previously thought; secondly, they are able to compensate for limited information by taking 'information shortcuts', such as seeking sound advice; and thirdly, where they feel insufficiently informed, the tendency is to vote for the status quo rather than change (Lupia and Matsusaka, 2004). On the question of the influence of money, recent studies tend to show that, while it can have important consequences for referendum outcomes, results are more mixed than previously imagined, with heavy spending proving more effective in the defeat of referendum initiatives than in their success (ibid.).

Unless they are binding, referenda tend to be ignored by politicians, a result that fuels rather than extinguishes public feelings of disillusionment and exclusion. In 2009, voters were presented with a CIR seeking to repeal legislation prohibiting the use of physical force for the purpose of child correction or discipline. While the 'anti-smacking' Bill[†] received overwhelming parliamentary support, the vote among MPs being 113 for and seven against, its opponents managed to obtain the signatures of the required 10 per cent of registered voters in order to petition Parliament to hold a referendum. Critics of the referendum have drawn attention to the relatively low turnout of 56 per cent and emotive wording of the question, which asked 'Should a smack as part of good parental correction be a criminal offence in New Zealand?' Their objections notwithstanding,

---

[*] For a full discussion on research into voting in referenda and initiatives, see Lupia and Matsusaka, 2004.
[†] Officially known as the Crimes (Substituted Section 59) Amendment Bill 2007.

the 87 per cent 'no' vote provided dramatic evidence of a yawning gap between elite and public opinion on an important question of individual versus state rights. Following Prime Minister Key's assurance that he believed the anti-smacking law was working well, the organisers of the referendum proposed a further non-binding referendum to make all citizen-initiated referenda binding. It provoked the *New Zealand Herald* to warn, 'Binding referendums would simply magnify the potential for damage to good governance. Administrations trying to develop coherent public policy could easily have their hands tied by pre-emptive plebiscites' (Editorial, *New Zealand Herald*, 2010: A10.)

In addition to the anti-smacking result, majorities in excess of 80 per cent have been achieved for referenda aimed at reducing the size of Parliament from 120 to 99 members and imposing harsher penalties for violent crime. Despite these substantial majorities, no CIR has succeeded in changing the will of Parliament since the CIR Act was passed into law in 1993. In rejecting these emphatic majorities, opponents of decision-making by referendum have been quick to point out several potential shortcomings. These include: how to reduce complex issues into straightforward questions requiring an either/or answer; the largely unregulated and unmediated nature of referendum campaigns; the inability of referenda to measure intensity of opinion; the problem of low voter turnout, especially for referenda scheduled outside a general election; and the implications for minorities of being ruled by the majority, however that majority may be defined.

Yet another approach to achieving a workable system of direct democracy is through the devolution of political power from central government to democratically elected self-governing units or voluntary associations (Hirst, 1990). Advocates of 'associative democracy' attribute voter apathy and dissatisfaction to central government's stranglehold on political power (Hirst, 2001: 16). Quite apart from the need to re-engage the public, devolving decisions down to self-governing organisations is premised on the belief that governing has become too complex and society too diverse to justify the concentration of power (ibid.: 15–30). Policy areas over which these associations can be said to play a constructive role in cooperation with central government include health, education, pensions and welfare

(Hirst, 1997). Significantly, in most welfare systems the state bureaucracy has been criticised for its unfair and ineffective management of social policy decisions. To guarantee their legitimacy and independence, it is argued that voluntary associations need to be given their own budgets and full self-management of their affairs.

For a contemporary example of how associative democracy might work, we need go no further than the assumptions that lie behind the Whānau Ora scheme.* The main aim of Whānau Ora is to address the needs of dysfunctional (primarily Māori) families in such areas as school truancy, housing conditions, primary health care, employment and justice. The taskforce commissioned to investigate the scheme took the view that the financial, social and cultural needs of targeted families be devolved from central government to local private service providers. Its report reasoned that decisions 'should occur as close as possible to local communities and should be able to recognise particular requirements that may not be relevant to all regions' (Durie, 2010: 15). Designated providers would include local iwi, non-governmental organisations (NGOs) and private community organisations, such as West Auckland's Te Whānau o Waipareira Trust and Hamilton's Te Rūranga o Kirikiriroa. Although overall management and financial control was placed in the hands of the Ministry of Māori Development rather than an independent body, as recommended by the taskforce, Whānau Ora is a potentially potent example of how democratic decision-making around welfare provision can be devolved to local voluntary associations.

Deliberative Democracy

For an alternative approach to direct democracy, we turn to a relatively recent branch of democratic theory and practice. Deliberative democracy's starting point is the assumption that opinion is less important than the

---

* Whānau has been defined by the Whānau Ora taskforce to mean 'a multi-generational collective made up of many households that are supported and strengthened by a wider network of relatives' (Durie, 2010: 15).

process by which it is formed. Instead of the snap opinions of 'millions of atomistic citizens who bounce back unreflective preferences from the mass media' (Fishkin, 1991: 19), deliberative democracy promotes reflective, impartial and informed political dialogue. Drawing on the Athenian model of direct democracy, deliberative democrats reason that citizens need to be more actively engaged in the give-and-take of political debate. While those who participate will vary from issue to issue, they are likely to include individuals, as well as representatives of various cultural and interest-based groups, together with social movements. With the aim of conducting conversations in which all are treated equally, free from prejudice based on education, wealth or political influence, John Dryzek emphasises the need to include disadvantaged groups, particularly ethnic minorities (Dryzek, 2000: 81–114). Prominent among the goals of any deliberation is a spirit of tolerance towards the views of others, as well as a sense of 'reciprocity' with respect to any decisions reached (Dryzek and Dunleavy, 2009: 224). Examples of recent issues that might well be the subject of such debate include climate change, electoral finance laws and review of the MMP electoral system. It is hoped that any outcomes from this discursive process receive public endorsement.

There is an understandable tendency to associate deliberative democracy with the parliamentary debating chamber and its select committees, including the public submissions process. Those countries with an upper house are likely to look upon it as a house of review, although, as Dryzek and Dunleavy point out, party discipline may limit the opportunities for impartial debate in both chambers (Dryzek and Dunleavy, 2009: 220). But deliberative democracy also occurs in forums quite outside the realm of the state. These include citizens' juries and assemblies, as well as deliberative polls. The idea of citizens' juries comes from ancient Athens, where around 500 citizens per jury were chosen by a system of lots. This random method of selection ensured that jurors were unlikely to be re-appointed in subsequent elections (Fishkin, 1991: 87). The jury complemented the work of the much larger Athenian Assembly, although its deliberative function and the frequency with which it met ensured that its influence held sway over that of the assembly (ibid.: 88). In modern times, citizens' juries typically have a dozen or so members and meet frequently over a short period of time. Because of their size, they are well suited to deliberate on quite specific policy matters, examples of which might include the minimum drinking age and regulations around the use of tobacco. Their functions are to receive information and evidence, often from expert witnesses; to cross-examine witnesses; to debate the relevant issues; and report to the government or other body on their findings and recommendations. While the modern version of citizens' juries was pioneered in the United States, it is best associated with the democratic reforms of the Blair and Brown governments in Britain (Goodin, 2008: 16).

Unlike juries, citizens' assemblies are suited to more wide-ranging constitutional concerns, such as whether or not to entrench the Bill of Rights, the place of the Treaty of Waitangi in New Zealand's constitutional arrangements, arguments around the creation of an upper house and changes to the electoral system. Although selected in a similar way to that of juries, assemblies tend to be much larger, generally having upwards of a hundred members, and meet less often and over a longer time period. The Canadian provincial governments of British Columbia and Ontario created citizens' assemblies in 2003 and 2006 respectively to debate the issue of electoral reform. In 2008, the outgoing Clark government appointed a panel of experts to advise a citizens' assembly on possible changes to New Zealand's electoral finance laws in the wake of widespread public opposition to the Electoral Finance Act 2007. Following the election of the Key government, the expert panel was disbanded and the Act repealed. As a result, the citizens' assembly, which had been a Green Party initiative, was never convened.

The idea of deliberative polls is associated with James Fishkin of the University of Texas. Unlike conventional opinion polls, deliberative polls are designed to engage participants in face-to-face discussion on a given issue, usually over several days, after which a poll is taken. The deliberation process involves listening to a range of expert opinion, receiving other relevant information and engaging in debate with other participants. Because each participant will have completed a pre-deliberation poll, it is possible to assess the extent to which the deliberation process has changed opinions. As with citizens' assemblies, deliberative polls are based on the random selection of participants, chosen by lot, with the proviso that the

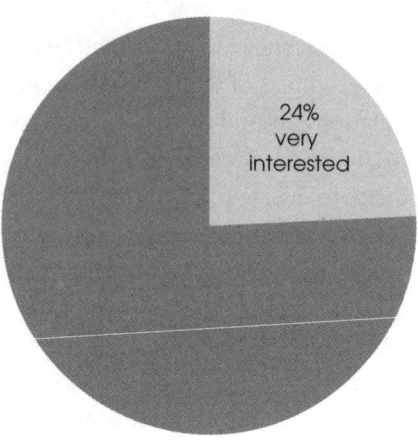

Figure 11.1: Very Interested in Politics, 2014
Source: New Zealand Election Study, 2014.

sample must be representative of the population as a whole (including ethnic breakdown, gender, age, residency and so on). Such polls have been used in the United States and Europe. Because of the emphasis on open and reflective discussion, opinions have been known to change over the course of the deliberative process. Examples of issues that might lend themselves to a deliberative poll include levels of direct and indirect taxation, the Emissions Trading Scheme, the so-called anti-smacking legislation that was the subject of a CIR, and local body decisions on water and electricity supply, as well as public transport.

While sceptics believe that the claims of deliberative democracy are pie in the sky, partly on the grounds that few citizens would ever want to be involved in time-consuming decision-making processes, the results of the New Zealand Election Study tend to suggest otherwise. When asked if they were interested in politics, one in four voters expressed a keen interest (see Figure 11.1). Remarkably large numbers of respondents to this national survey also claimed to be close followers of the media coverage of the 2014 election campaign, with one in three voters agreeing that they frequently sought out news about politics from the two major media sources, namely the TV One news programme and the newspapers (either hard copy or online). When these results are combined with those for occasional consumers of the campaign news, it is clear that at least two-thirds of survey respondents paid some attention to the media's coverage of the 2014 campaign.

Conclusion

A central theme of this book has been that political decision-making in New Zealand involves a complex interaction of citizen participation and the governing elite, with the latter ultimately holding the upper hand. There are numerous means by which the public can have their say, from traditional methods such as election campaigns, pressure groups and citizens'-initiated referenda, through to more immediate measures of opinion, including opinion polls and new media. These avenues for public influence notwithstanding, most constitutional and political reforms have been advocated by the political elite in advance of any public pressure or endorsement. The advent of MMP was widely interpreted as a victory for the citizens over their political masters. It must be remembered, however, that the impetus for change came, not from the voting public, but rather the Minister of Justice and Deputy Prime Minister, Geoffrey Palmer. While the eventual outcome of this decision was a more representative Parliament, and one better able to hold the government to account, Labour's principal motivation was the perceived unfairness of an electoral system that rewarded National with a majority of seats, despite its gaining fewer votes than Labour.* The complex interaction between government initiative and public response can be further illustrated with respect to the 2011 referendum on whether to retain or replace MMP. The initial decision to hold a referendum was made by the government, presumably in conversation with groups opposed to MMP. It promised that, in the event of a majority vote for the retention of MMP, a public review would be

---

* Although proportional representation had been advocated by the Social Credit Party for a number of years prior to 1984, it took Palmer's appointment of a Royal Commission to put it onto the political agenda.

conducted by the Electoral Commission with a view to presenting options for its improvement. On receiving these recommendations, the Minister of Justice announced that the government would not be proceeding with their implementation.

For some constitutional scholars, including Palmer, the greatest weakness in the New Zealand system of democracy is a lack of formal constitutional checks and balances, a result of which is the concentration of political power in the hands of the executive. Recent examples of excessive central control are said to include the Canterbury Earthquake Recovery Act 2011, which stripped local government of a number of its democratic functions, as well as the Environment Canterbury Act 2010, which replaced democratically elected members of Environment Canterbury with government appointees (G. Palmer, 2012). The justification for this latter decision was incompetence in the management of the supply of water. Other criticisms levelled at autocratic government decision-making in the wake of the Canterbury earthquakes include the lack of public consultation around the Minister of Education's decision to close and merge a number of Christchurch schools.

Other alleged abuses of the democratic process include the partial privatisation of a number of state-owned energy companies, such as Mighty River Power, Meridian and Genesis Energy. Opponents of the decision accused the National government of ignoring the will of the majority, opinion polls having recorded strong public opposition to the privatisation decision. For its part, the government argued that a strong performance at the 2011 election (47 per cent, compared with 27 per cent for Labour) provided the necessary mandate to proceed, the planned sell-off having been extensively debated in the lead-up to the election. Opposition parties called for a citizens'-initiated referendum, the results of which provided evidence for both sides of the argument: opponents highlighted the 67 per cent opposition vote, while supporters drew attention to the low 47 per cent turnout,* as well as the fact that asset sales were a *fait accompli*, the sales process having begun several months earlier.

---

* It was, in fact, a postal ballot. The referendum was conducted between 22 November and 13 December 2013.

Despite these and other criticisms of the practice of New Zealand democracy, empirical measures of public satisfaction point to some obvious strengths. In contrast to the sense of powerlessness and alienation found in some much larger Western democracies, smallness engenders a sense of intimacy and belonging, as well as confidence in the responsiveness of political parties and elected officials to the wishes of the voting public. While concerns have been expressed over the high number of elected politicians, the quality of representation they provide is one of Parliament's obvious strengths. Public satisfaction can be measured in a number of ways, including the act of voting and the strength of voters' belief that their vote really counts. Perhaps most reassuring of all, however, is the level of public interest, with one in four voters expressing a deep interest in politics, together with elections and their outcomes.

Appendix: Two-Party Results in the 2014 Election

	Result	National Party Vote		National Electorate Vote		Labour Party Vote		Labour Electorate Vote	
AUCKLAND SEATS (22)									
Auckland Central	N	12,652	44.78	12,494	45.51	6,101	21.59	11,894	43.32
Botany	N	20,016	59.42	21,044	63.84	7,473	22.19	7,549	22.9
East Coast Bays	N	20,895	63.24	19,957	61.3	4,005	12.12	3,915	12.03
Epsom	A	23,904	63.45	11,716	31.61	5,045	13.61	3,470	9.36
Helensville	N	20,689	58.39	22,720	65.17	4,430	12.5	4,425	12.69
Hunua	N	22,929	63.7	23,621	66.87	4,699	13.06	6,245	17.68
Kelston	L	9,924	32.14	9,724	32.35	12,934	41.88	15,091	50.2
Māngere	L	4,281	15.51	3,975	14.95	18,470	66.93	18,908	71.09
Manukau East	L	5,392	19.92	4,422	17.01	16,925	62.52	17,876	68.77
Manurewa	L	7,612	27.49	7,636	28.96	14,579	52.66	14,038	53.24
Maungakiekie	N	14,394	41.33	16,132	47.61	12,199	35.02	13,784	40.68
Mt Albert	L	14,359	38.89	10,314	28.61	10,823	29.31	20,970	58.17
Mt Roskill	L	14,275	41.87	10,546	31.58	12,086	35.45	18,637	55.81
New Lynn	L	13,136	39.02	11,977	36.28	12,085	35.9	16,534	50.08
North Shore	N	23,762	61.58	23,783	62.47	5,473	14.18	7,280	19.12
Northcote	N	17,900	50.54	19,696	56.52	7,803	22.03	10,032	28.79
Pakuranga	N	20,854	60.24	20,388	59.75	5,511	15.92	7,521	22.04
Papakura	N	17,733	51	15,588	46.07	8,967	25.79	10,469	30.94
Rodney	N	24,051	61.02	24,519	63	4,847	12.3	4,289	11.02
Tāmaki	N	24,091	65.56	25,539	70.57	5,431	14.78	5,118	14.14
Te Atatū	L	13,614	40.84	12,863	39.48	11,603	34.81	15,676	48.11
Upper Harbour	N	18,122	54.25	18,315	55.95	7,803	23.36	8,623	26.34
TOTAL			49.06		47.73		26.82		33.34
WELLINGTON SEATS (6)									
Hutt South	L	17,648	45.07	16,127	41.66	10,903	27.84	16,836	43.49
Mana	L	14,850	40.36	11,698	32.27	12,601	34.25	19,651	54.22
Rongotai	L	12,606	32.55	9,223	24.2	11,754	30.35	18,840	49.43
Rimutaka	L	15,352	41.28	12,622	34.37	12,176	32.74	19,286	52.51
Ōhāriu	UF	18,810	50.23	6,120	16.5	8,771	23.42	12,859	34.66
Wellington Central	L	14,689	37.54	11,540	30.09	9,306	23.78	19,807	51.64
TOTAL			41.13		29.89		28.68		47.63
CHRISTCHURCH SEATS (5)									
Christchurch Central	N	15,301	44.52	15,346	45.83	8,995	26.17	12,926	38.6
Christchurch East	L	12,928	39.62	11,148	34.77	10,450	32.03	15,221	47.48
Ilam	N	20,377	57.6	19,981	57.33	6,238	17.63	8,083	23.19
Port Hills	L	18,719	46.83	15,933	40.46	9,514	23.8	18,161	46.11
Wigram	N	13,117	42.72	11,189	37.22	8,764	28.54	14,519	48.3
TOTAL			46.48		43.33		25.4		40.57
DUNEDIN SEATS (2)									
Dunedin North	L	11,302	32.17	10,398	30.02	11,147	31.73	16,315	47.1
Dunedin South	L	15,003	39.7	14,324	38.26	12,518	33.13	18,182	48.56
TOTAL			36.07		34.3		32.45		47.86

Appendix

	Result	National Party Vote		National Electorate Vote		Labour Party Vote		Labour Electorate Vote	
PROVINCIAL NORTH ISLAND (20)									
Bay of Plenty	N	21,096	57.52	21,735	60.05	4,783	13.04	6,639	18.34
Coromandel	N	20,547	54	21,934	58.24	5,980	15.72	4,236	11.25
East Coast	N	17,152	48.42	18,074	51.92	8,022	22.64	10,140	29.13
Hamilton East	N	17,395	49.8	19,393	56.88	8,264	23.66	9,194	26.96
Hamilton West	N	16,072	47.51	17,382	52.5	8,649	25.57	11,598	35.03
Napier	L	18,005	49.19	11,493	31.77	9,466	25.86	15,343	42.41
New Plymouth	N	20,969	55.65	21,566	57.74	7,947	21.09	11,788	31.56
Northland	N	17,412	48.76	18,269	52.11	5,913	16.56	8,969	25.58
Ōtaki	N	18,854	48.71	20,980	54.8	9,543	24.65	13,198	34.47
Palmerston North	L	14,835	43.09	14,673	43.19	10,632	30.88	16,885	49.7
Rangitīkei	N	18,596	53.46	20,487	59.72	6,408	18.42	9,427	27.48
Rotorua	N	17,660	51.87	18,715	55.79	7,181	21.09	11,297	33.67
Taranaki-King Country	N	20,637	61.28	22,328	67.22	4,483	13.31	5,555	16.72
Taupō	N	20,703	56.94	22,448	62.59	6,752	18.57	7,402	20.64
Tauranga	N	20,728	55.58	20,711	56.4	5,361	14.37	5,869	15.98
Tukituki	N	18,680	51.81	18,537	52.01	8,205	22.76	12,047	33.8
Waikato	N	21,598	60	22,911	64.89	5,303	14.73	6,742	19.09
Wairarapa	N	19,634	52.32	16,223	43.61	7,712	20.55	9,452	25.41
Whanganui	N	16,687	47.13	18,649	53.15	9,012	25.45	14,144	40.31
Whangarei	N	18,503	50.08	20,111	55.07	6,575	17.79	6,942	19.01
TOTAL			52.18		54.44		20.3		27.72
PROVINCIAL SOUTH ISLAND (9)									
Clutha Southland	N	21,694	63.18	21,561	63.37	5,036	14.67	6,675	19.62
Invercargill	N	16,880	49.26	17,526	51.48	8,553	24.96	10,044	29.5
Kaikoura	N	20,770	56.45	20,857	57.18	6,269	17.04	8,287	22.72
Nelson	N	16,904	44.28	20,000	52.82	9,401	24.63	12,395	32.73
Rangitata	N	20,108	55.32	23,518	65.17	8,064	22.18	9,411	26.08
Selwyn	N	22,809	63.46	24,625	69.61	4,654	12.95	3,835	10.84
Waimakariri	N	20,734	57.33	17,263	48.34	6,835	18.9	14,757	41.32
Waitaki	N	22,656	56.97	24,547	62.23	7,162	18.01	7,879	19.97
West Coast Tasman	L	16,058	44.54	12,653	35.36	8,438	23.4	16,747	46.8
TOTAL			54.49		56.2		19.64		27.72
MĀORI SEATS (7)									
Hauraki-Waikato	L	1,583	7.46			9,724	45.83	12,191	59.34
Ikaroa-Rāwhiti	L	1,189	5.37			10,489	47.38	9,753	45.18
Tāmaki Makaurau	L	1,575	7.55			8,432	40.45	7,533	37.48
Te Tai Hauāuru	L	1,456	7.03			8,642	41.75	8,089	40.22
Te Tai Tokerau	L	1,938	8.46			8,034	35.07	9,712	43.88
Te Tai Tonga	L	2,977	14.36			7,607	36.7	8,445	41.77
Waiariki	M	1,120	5			8,595	38.38	5,837	26.78
TOTAL			7.89				40.79		42.09

Bibliography

Published Articles, Books and Papers

Allen, J. (2000), 'No to a Written Constitution', in C. James (ed.), *Building the Constitution*, Wellington, Institute of Policy Studies: 391–96.
Anckar, C. (2008), 'Size, Islandness and Democracy: A Global Comparison', *International Political Science Review*, 29/4: 433–59.
Anson, S. (1991), *Hawke: An Emotional Life*, Victoria, Penguin.
Arseneau, T. (1990), 'A Bill of Rights', in M. Holland and J. Boston (eds), *The Fourth Labour Government: Politics and Policy in New Zealand*, Auckland, Oxford University Press, 2nd edn: 22–40.
Arseneau, T. (2010), '2008: National's Winning Strategy', in S. Levine and N. S. Roberts (eds), *Key to Victory: The New Zealand General Election of 2008*, Wellington, Victoria University Press: 272–94.
Atkinson, J. (2004), 'The Campaign on Television', in J. Vowles, P. Aimer, S. Banducci, J. Karp and R. Miller (eds), *Voters' Veto: The 2002 Election in New Zealand and the Consolidation of Minority Government*, Auckland, Auckland University Press: 48–67.
Balfour Declaration (1926), Imperial Conference, London, http://www.foundingdocs.gov.au/resources/transcripts/cth11_doc_1926.pdf (accessed 20 December 2014).
Baptist, Simon (2014), 'The 'Flaws' of French Democracy', *BBC News Magazine*, 11 June, http://www.bbc.com/news/magazine-27310566 (accessed 24 December 2014).
Bassett, M. (1982), *Three Party Politics in New Zealand, 1911–1931*, Auckland, Historical Publications.
Bassett, M. (1995), *Coates of Kaipara*, Auckland, Auckland University Press.
Bassett, M. and M. King (2000), *Tomorrow Comes the Song: A Life of Peter Fraser*, Auckland, Penguin.
Bennett, A. (2014), 'English: Tax Cuts Ahead but No Pre-election Reveal', *New Zealand Herald*, 19 August, http://www.nzherald.co.nz/nz/news/article.cfm?c_id=1&objectid=11311137 (accessed 27 January 2015).
Bevir, M. (2009), *Key Concepts in Governance*, London, Sage Publications.
Bevir, M. (2010), *Democratic Governance*, Princeton, Princeton University Press.
Blondel, J. (1968), 'Party Systems and Patterns of Government in Western Democracies', *Canadian Journal of Political Science*, 1/2: 180–203.
Bolger, J. (1998), *Bolger: A View from the Top: My Seven Years as Prime Minister*, Auckland, Penguin.
Bonallack, A. (2014), 'Key Says Majority Government in Reach', *New Zealand Herald*, 21 August, http://www.nzherald.co.nz/wairarapa-times-age/news/article.cfm?c_id=1503414&objectid=11312041 (accessed 27 January 2015).
Boston, J. (2007), 'An Unusual Government: Coalition Politics and Inter-Party Arrangements Following the 2005 General Election', in S. Levine and N. S. Roberts (eds), *The Baubles of Office: The New Zealand General Election of 2005*, Wellington, Victoria University Press: 389–418.
Boston, J. and S. Chapple (2014), *Child Poverty in New Zealand*, Wellington, Bridget Williams Books.
Brash, D. (2004), 'Nationhood', Orewa Rotary Club, Auckland, 27 January, http://www.scoop.co.nz/stories/PA0401/S00220.htm (accessed 20 December 2014).

Brash, D. (2005), 'Orewa 2: Text of Speech by Don Brash', *National Business Review*, 26 January, http://www.nbr.co.nz/politics/orewa-2-text-speech-don-brash (accessed 2 October 2013).

Brookers (2012), *Brookers Public Law Handbook: Legislation and Constitutional Documents*, Wellington, Thomson Reuters.

Campbell, A., P. E. Converse, W. E. Miller and D. E. Stokes (1964), *The American Voter: An Abridgement*, New York, John Wiley & Sons.

Chapman, R. (1961), 'No Land is an Island: Twentieth Century Politics', in K. Sinclair (ed.), *Distance Looks Our Way: The Effects of Remoteness on New Zealand*, Auckland, University of Auckland: 42–62.

Chapman, R. (1962), 'The General Result', in R. Chapman, W. K. Jackson and A. V. Mitchell, *New Zealand Politics in Action: The 1960 General Election*, London, Oxford University Press: 235–96.

Chapman, R. (1963), 'The Response to Labour and the Question of Parallelism of Opinion, 1928–1960', in R. Chapman and K. Sinclair (eds), *Studies of a Small Democracy: Essays in Honour of Willis Airey*, Auckland, University of Auckland: 221–54.

Chapman, R. (1986), 'Voting in the Maori Political Sub-System, 1935–1984', in J. Wallace (Chair), *Report of the Royal Commission on the Electoral System: Towards a Better Democracy*, Wellington, Government Printer: B83–B108.

Chatterjee, S., P. Conway, P. Dalziel, C. Eichbaum, P. Harris, B. Philpott and R. Shaw (1999), *The New Politics: A Third Way for New Zealand*, Palmerston North, Dunmore Press.

Clark, H. (2000), 'Helen Clark Deplores Sunday Star-Times Attack', *Sunday Star-Times*, 4 September, http://www.scoop.co.nz/stories/PA0009/S00023.htm (accessed 10 December 2014).

Clark, H. (2009), Valedictory Speech, New Zealand Parliament, 8 April, http://www.stuff.co.nz/dominion-post/news/politics/2324599/Full-text-Helen-Clarks-valedictory-speech (accessed 9 June 2014).

Constitutional Advisory Panel (2012), 'New Zealand's Constitution: The Conversation So Far', New Zealand Government, September.

Constitutional Advisory Panel (2013), *New Zealand's Constitution: A Report on a Conversation. He Kotuinga Korero mo Te Kaupapa Ture o Aotearoa*, Wellington, New Zealand Government.

Cox, N. and R. Miller (2010), 'The Monarchy', in R. Miller (ed.), *New Zealand Politics and Government*, 5th edn, Melbourne, Oxford University Press: 130–44.

Cross, W. P. and A. Blais (2012), *Politics at the Centre: The Selection and Removal of Party Leaders in the Anglo Parliamentary Democracies*, Oxford, Oxford University Press.

Cunliffe, D. (2014), 'State of the Union', 26 January, https://www.labour.org.nz/stateofthenationvideo (accessed 24 November 2014).

Curtin, J. (2008), 'Comparing Pathways to Power: Women and Political Leadership in New Zealand', in P 't Hart and J. Uhr, *Public Leadership: Perspectives and Practices*, Canberra, ANU Press: 265–74.

Curtin, J. and R. Miller (2010), 'New Zealand's Party System: A Multi-Party Mirage?', in S. Levine and N. S. Roberts (eds), *Key to Victory: The New Zealand General Election of 2008*, Wellington, Victoria University Press: 120–36.

Dahl, R. A. (1956), *A Preface to Democratic Theory*, Chicago, University of Chicago Press.

Dahl, R. A. (1967), *Pluralist Democracy in the United States: Conflict and Consent*, Chicago, Rand McNally & Company.

Dahl, R. A. (1982), *Dilemmas of Pluralist Democracy: Autonomy vs Control*, New Haven, Yale University Press.

Dahl, R. A. and E. R. Tufte (1974), *Size and Democracy*, Stanford, California, Stanford University Press.
Dahlgren, P. (2009), *Media and Political Engagement: Citizens, Communication and Democracy*, New York, Cambridge University Press.
De Tocqueville, A. (1837), *Democracy in America*, London, Fontana Press.
Douglas, R. (1993), *Unfinished Business*, Auckland, Random House.
Downs, A. (1957), *An Economic Theory of Democracy*, New York, Harper & Row.
Dryzek, J. S. (2000), *Deliberative Democracy and Beyond: Liberals, Critics, Contestations*, Oxford, Oxford University Press.
Dryzek, J. S. and P. Dunleavy (2009), *Theories of the Democratic State*, Houndmills, Basingstoke, Palgrave Macmillan.
Dunleavy, P. (1986), 'Theories of the State in British Politics', in H. Drucker, P. Dunleavy, A. Gamble and G. Peels (eds), *Developments in British Politics*, Houndmills, Basingstoke, Macmillan Education, 2nd edn.
Dunleavy, P. (2006), 'The Westminster Model and the Distinctiveness of British Politics', in P. Dunleavy et al., *Developments in British Politics 8*, Houndmills, Basingstoke, Palgrave Macmillan.
Durie, M. H. (2000), 'A Framework for Considering Constitutional Change and the Position of Maori in Aotearoa', in C. James (ed.), *Building the Constitution*, Wellington, Institute of Policy Studies: 414–25.
Durie, M. H. (2003), 'Mana Māori Motuhake: The State of the Nation', in R. Miller (ed.), *New Zealand Government and Politics*, Melbourne, Oxford University Press, 3rd edn: 488–502.
Durie, M. H. (chair) (April 2010), 'Whānau Ora: Report of the Taskforce on Whānau-Centred Initiatives', Wellington, Taskforce on Whānau-Centred Initiatives.
Duverger, M. (1964), *Political Parties: Their Organisation and Activity in the Modern State*, London, Methuen.
Editorial, *Bay of Plenty Times* (2014), 'Keep the Flag to Honour Our Dead', *Bay of Plenty Times*, 1 November, http://www.nzherald.co.nz/bay-of-plenty-times/news/article.cfm?c_id=1503343&objectid=11351699 (accessed 29 December 2014).
Editorial, *New Zealand Herald* (2010), 'Hidden Danger of Rule by Poll', *New Zealand Herald*, 22 November, http://www.nzherald.co.nz/nz-government/news/article.cfm?c_id=144&objectid=10610805 (accessed 27 January 2015).
Edwards, B. (2010), 'Minor Parties', in R. Miller (ed.), *New Zealand Government and Politics*, Melbourne, Oxford University Press, 5th edn: 522–36.
Edwards, D. (2007), 'New Zealand First: Squeezed from Every Side', in S. Levine and N. S. Roberts (eds), *The Baubles of Office: The New Zealand General Election of 2005*, Wellington, Victoria University Press: 115–26.
Electoral Act (1993), Wellington, New Zealand Government. Marine and Coastal Area (Takutai Moana) Act 2011, http://www.legislation.govt.nz/act/public/2011/0003/latest/DLM3213131.html (accessed 21 January 2015).
Epstein, L. (1967), *Political Parties in Western Democracies*, New York, Frederick A. Praeger.
Esaiasson, P. and K. Heidar (eds) (2000), *Beyond Westminster and Congress: The Nordic Experience*, Columbus, Ohio State University Press.
Esler, G. (2012), *Lessons from the Top: How Successful Leaders Tell Stories to Get Ahead – and Stay There*, London, Profile Books.
Farrar, D. (2011), 'Peters an Illegal Candidate for New Zealand First', 25 November, http://www.kiwiblog.co.nz/2011/11/exclusive_peters_an_illegal_candidate_for_nz_first.html (accessed 19 May 2014).

Farrell, D. M. (1997), *Comparing Electoral Systems*, Hemel Hempstead, Hertfordshire, Prentice Hall/Harvester Wheatsheaf.
Farrell, D. M. and P. Webb (2000), 'Political Parties as Campaign Organisations', in R. J. Dalton and M. P. Wattenberg (eds), *Parties Without Partisans: Political Change in Advanced Industrial Democracies*, Oxford, Oxford University Press: 102–28.
Fishkin, J. S. (1991), *Democracy and Deliberation: New Directions for Democratic Reform*, New Haven, Yale University Press.
Foster, P. (2013), 'Obama on Course to Win Blame Game Against Tea Party Hardliners', *New Zealand Herald*, 2 October, A23.
Gardner, J. A. (2009), *What are Campaigns For? The Role of Persuasion in Electoral Law and Politics*, New York, Oxford University Press.
Garzia, D. (2011), 'The Personalization of Politics in Western Democracies: Causes and Consequences on Leader–Follower Relationships', *The Leadership Quarterly*, 22: 697–709.
Geddis, A. (2006), 'A Dual Track Democracy? The Symbolic Role of the Māori Seats in New Zealand's Electoral System', *Election Law Journal*, 5/4: 347–71.
Gibson, R. K. and I. McAllister (2011), 'Do Online Election Campaigns Win Votes? The 2007 Australian "You Tube" Election', *Political Communication*, 28/2: 227–44.
Giddens, A. (1998), *The Third Way: The Renewal of Social Democracy*, Cambridge, Polity Press.
Giddens, A. (2000), *The Third Way and its Critics*, Cambridge, Polity Press.
Goodin, R. E. (2008), *Innovating Democracy: Democratic Theory and Practice After the Deliberative Turn*, Oxford, Oxford University Press.
Gustafson, B. (1986a), *From the Cradle to the Grave: A Biography of Michael Joseph Savage*, Auckland, Reed Methuen.
Gustafson, B. (1986b), *The First Fifty Years: A History of the New Zealand National Party*, Auckland, Reed Methuen.
Gustafson, B. (2000), *His Way: A Biography of Robert Muldoon*, Auckland, Auckland University Press.
Gustafson, B. (2007), *Kiwi Keith: A Biography of Keith Holyoake*, Auckland, Auckland University Press.
Hager, N. (2002), *Seeds of Distrust*, Nelson, Craig Potton.
Hager, N. (2006), *The Hollow Men: A Study in the Politics of Deception*, Nelson, Craig Potton.
Hager, N. (2014), *Dirty Politics: How Attack Politics is Poisoning New Zealand's Political Environment*, Nelson, Craig Potton.
Hamilton, P. (2013), 'Speech by Peter Hamilton', *New Zealand Herald*, 2 November, http://www.nzherald.co.nz/nz/news/article.cfm?c_id=1&objectid=11150277 (accessed 27 January 2015).
Harris, B. V. (2004), 'The Constitutional Future of New Zealand', *New Zealand Law Review*: 269–312.
Hayward, J. and C. Rudd (eds) (2004), *Political Communications in New Zealand*, Auckland, Pearson/Prentice Hall.
Hayward, M. (2010), 'Leadership and the Prime Minister', in R. Miller (ed.), *New Zealand Government and Politics*, Melbourne, Oxford University Press, 5th edn: 226–42.
Held, D. (ed.) (1993), *Prospects for Democracy: North, South, East, West*, Cambridge, Polity Press.
Held, D. (2006), *Models of Democracy*, Cambridge, Polity Press, 3rd edn.

Henderson, J. (2003), 'The Prime Minister: Powers and Personality', in R. Miller (ed.), *New Zealand Government and Politics*, Melbourne, Oxford University Press, 3rd edn: 106–16.
Heppell, T. (ed.) (2012), *Leaders of the Opposition: From Churchill to Cameron*, Houndmills, Basingstoke, Palgrave Macmillan.
Hirst, P. (1990), *Representative Democracy and its Limits*, Cambridge, Polity Press.
Hirst, P. (1997), *From Statism to Pluralism: Democracy, Civil Society and Global Politics*, London, Routledge.
Hirst, P. (2001), 'Can Associationalism Come Back?', in P. Hirst and V. Bader (eds), *Associative Democracy: The Real Third Way*, London, Frank Cass.
Holland, M. and J. Boston (eds) (1990), *The Fourth Labour Government: Politics and Policy in New Zealand*, Auckland, Oxford University Press, 2nd edn.
Hutching, M. (1999), *Long Journey for Sevenpence: A Oral History of Assisted Immigration to New Zealand from the United Kingdom, 1947–93*, Wellington, Victoria University Press.
Inglehart, R. (1977), *The Silent Revolution: Changing Values and Political Styles Among Western Publics*, Princeton, Princeton University Press.
Inglehart, R., R. Foa, C. Paterson and C. Welzel (2008), 'Development, Freedom and Rising Happiness: A Global Perspective, 1981–2007', *Perspectives in Psychological Science*, 3/4: 264–85.
Jackson, K. (1987), *The Dilemma of Parliament*, Wellington, Allen & Unwin.
James, C. (ed.) (2000), *Building the Constitution*, Wellington, Institute of Policy Studies.
James, C. (2014), 'Poll of Polls', Radio New Zealand website, 22 September, http://www.radionz.co.nz/news/election-2014/columns/255163/poll-of-polls-with-colin-james (accessed 28 October 2014).
Janis, I. L. (1983), *Groupthink: Psychological Studies of Policy Decisions and Fiascoes*, Boston, Houghton Mifflin.
Jesson, B. (1987), *Behind the Mirror Glass: The Growth of Wealth and Power in New Zealand in the Eighties*, Auckland, Penguin.
Jesson, B. (1989), *Fragments of Labour: The Story Behind the Labour Government*, Auckland, Penguin.
Jesson, B. (2001), 'To Build a Nation', in R. Miller (ed.), *New Zealand Government and Politics*, Melbourne, Oxford University Press, 2nd edn: 3–13.
Johansson, J. (2005), *Two Titans: Muldoon, Lange and Leadership*, Wellington, Dunmore Press.
Joyce, S. (2010), 'National', in S. Levine and N. S. Roberts (eds), *Key to Victory: The New Zealand General Election of 2008*, Wellington, Victoria University Press: 65–74.
Karvonen, L. (2010), *The Personalisation of Politics: A Study of Parliamentary Democracies*, University of Essex, Colchester, ECPR Press.
Katz, R. S. and P. Mair (eds) (1994), *How Parties Organise: Change and Adaptation in Party Organisations in Western Democracies*, London, Sage.
Kavanagh, D. and P. Morris (1994), *Consensus Politics from Attlee to Major*, Oxford, Oxford University Press, 2nd edn.
Keating, M. and M. Harvey (2014), *Small Nations in a Big World: What Scotland Can Learn*, Edinburgh, Luath Press.
Keating, M. and M. Harvey (2014), 'The Political Economy of Small European States: And Lessons for Scotland', *National Institute Economic Review*, 227: R54–R66.
Key, J. (2002), Maiden Speech, New Zealand Parliament, 29 August, http://www.scoop.co.nz/stories/PA0208/S00297.htm (accessed 9 June 2014).

Key, J. (2012), Opening Address, New Zealand Political Science Association Annual Conference, 26 November, Victoria University of Wellington.

Key, V. O. (1966), *The Responsible Electorate*, Cambridge, Mass., Harvard University Press.

Kriesi, H. (2012), 'Personalization of National Election Campaigns', *Party Politics*, 18/6: 825–44.

Kumarasingham, H. (2010), *Onward with Executive Power: Lessons from New Zealand, 1947–57*, Wellington, Institute of Policy Studies.

Lange, D. (2005), *David Lange: My Life*, Auckland, Penguin.

Langer, A. I. (2006), *The Politicisation of Private Persona: The Case of Tony Blair in Historical Perspective*, London, London School of Economics and Political Science.

Langer, A. I. (2011), *The Personalisation of Politics in the UK: Mediated Leadership from Attlee to Cameron*, Manchester, Manchester University Press.

Lau, R. R. and D. P. Redlawsk (2006), *How Voters Decide: Information Processing During Election Campaigns*, New York, Cambridge University Press.

Laws, M. (1998), *The Demon Profession*, Auckland, Harper Collins.

Lawson, K. and P. H. Merkl (eds) (1988), *When Parties Fail: Emerging Alternative Organisations*, Princeton, Princeton University Press.

Levine, S. and N. S. Roberts (eds) (2005), *The Baubles of Office: The New Zealand General Election of 2005*, Wellington, Victoria University Press.

Lijphart, A. (1984), *Democracies: Patterns of Majoritarian and Consensus Government in Twenty-One Countries*, New Haven, Yale University Press.

Lijphart, A. (1999), *Patterns of Democracy: Government Forms and Performance in Thirty-Six Countries*, New Haven, Yale University Press.

Lindlom, C. (1977), *Politics and Markets: The World's Political-Economic Systems*, New York, Basic Books.

Lindsey, D. (2006), 'Conscience Voting', in R. Miller (ed.), *New Zealand Government and Politics*, Melbourne, Oxford University Press, 4th edn: 186–98.

Lipson, L. (1948), *The Politics of Equality: New Zealand's Adventures in Democracy*, Chicago, University of Chicago Press.

Lundberg, T. and R. Miller (2014), 'Democracy and Representation: Mass-Elite Opinion and the MMP Review', in J. Vowles (ed.), *The New Electoral Politics in New Zealand: The Significance of the 2011 Election*, Wellington, Institute for Governance and Policy Studies: 199–216.

Lupia, A. and J. G. Matsusaka (2004), 'Direct Democracy: New Approaches to Old Questions', *Annual Review of Political Science*, 7: 463–82.

MacGregor Burns, J. (2010), *Leadership*, New York, Harper Perennial Political Classics.

MacKuen, M. B. and G. Rabinowitz (eds) (2003), *Electoral Democracy*, Ann Arbor, University of Michigan Press.

Maor, M. (1997), *Political Parties and Party Systems: Comparative Approaches and the British Experience*, London, Routledge.

Māori Party (2004), 'Māori Party Tiriti O Waitangi/Treaty of Waitangi Policy', 10 July, http://maoriparty.org/wp-content/uploads/2013/12/Maori-Party-Policy-2004.pdf (accessed 5 September 2014).

Māori Party (2008), 'Policy Priorities: He Aha Te Mea Nui', 4 October, http://maori-party.org/wp-content/uploads/2013/12/Maori-Party-Policy-2008.pdf (accessed 5 September 2014).

Marquand, D. (2004), *Decline of the Public: The Hollowing-out of Citizenship*, Cambridge, Polity Press.

Marsh, I. and R. Miller (2012), *Democratic Decline and Democratic Renewal: Political Change in Britain, Australia and New Zealand*, Cambridge, Cambridge University Press.
Martin, J. E. (2004), *The House: New Zealand's House of Representatives 1854–2004*, Palmerston North, Dunmore Press.
Mazlish, B. (1972), *In Search of Nixon: A Psychohistorical Inquiry*, New York, Basic Books.
McIlwain, C. H. (1939), *Constitutionalism and the Changing World*, Cambridge, Cambridge University Press.
Michels, R. (1962), *Political Parties*, New York, Free Press.
Miller, R. (2005), *Party Politics in New Zealand*, Melbourne, Oxford University Press.
Miller, R. (2006), 'Minor Party Leadership Under Proportional Representation', in R. Miller and M. Mintrom (eds), *Political Leadership in New Zealand*, Auckland, Auckland University Press: 113–32.
Miller, R. and H. Catt (1993), *Season of Discontent: By-Elections and the Bolger Government*, Palmerston North, Dunmore Press.
Miller, R. and J. Curtin (2011), 'Counting the Costs of Coalition: The Case of New Zealand's Small Parties', *Political Science*, 63/1: 106–25.
Mills, C. W. (1956), *The Power Elite*, New York, Oxford University Press.
Ministry of Business, Innovation and Employment (2011), *Permanent and Long Term Migration: The Big Picture*, http://www.dol.govt.nz/publications/research/plt-migration-big-picture/03.asp (accessed 17 December 2014).
Ministry of Foreign Affairs and Trade (2015), http://mfat.govt.nz/Trade-and-Economic-Relations/2-Trade-Relationships-and-Agreements/index.php (accessed 20 January 2015).
Mitchell, A. (1966), *Government by Party: Parliament and Politics in New Zealand*, Auckland, Whitcombe & Tombs.
Muldoon, R. D. (1977), *Muldoon*, Wellington, A. H. & A. W. Reed.
Mulgan, R. (1989a), *Democracy and Power in New Zealand: A Study of New Zealand Politics*, Auckland, Oxford University Press, 2nd edn.
Mulgan, R. (1989b), *Maori, Pakeha and Democracy*, Auckland, Oxford University Press.
Mulgan, R. (1994), *Politics in New Zealand*, Auckland, Auckland University Press.
Mulgan, R. (2004), *Politics in New Zealand*, Auckland, Auckland University Press, 3rd edn.
Muller, W. C. and K. Strom (eds) (1999), *Policy, Office, or Votes? How Political Parties in Western Europe Make Hard Decisions*, Cambridge, Cambridge University Press.
Nagel, J. (1994), 'How Many Parties will New Zealand Have Under MMP?', *Political Science*, 26/2: 139–60.
New Zealand Companies Office (2013), 'Union Membership Return Report 2013', www.societies.govt.nz/cms/registered-unions/annual-return-membership-reports/union-membership-return-report-2013.
New Zealand Electoral Commission (n.d.), http://www.elections.org.nz/events/past-events/general-elections-1890-1993 (accessed 20 August 2014).
New Zealand Electoral Commission (n.d.), http://www.elections.org.nz/elections/2011-general-election-and-referendum/report-on-the-2011-general-election-and-referendum.html (accessed 15 January 2013).
New Zealand Electoral Commission (2002), *The New Zealand Electoral Compendium*, Wellington, New Zealand Electoral Commission, 3rd edn.
New Zealand Electoral Commission (2013), 'Results of 2013 Maori Electoral Option', 29 July, http://www.elections.org.nz/news-media/results-2013-maori-electoral-option (accessed 6 October 2014).

Bibliography

New Zealand Electoral Commission (2014a), 'Advance Voting Statistics', http://www.elections.org.nz/events/2014-general-election/election-results-and-reporting/advance-voting-statistics (accessed 25 January 2015).

New Zealand Electoral Commission (2014b), 'Election Results 2014', 17 October, http://www.electionresults.govt.nz/electionresults_2014/splitvote_index.html (accessed 20 December 2014).

New Zealand Government (2008), *Cabinet Manual*, Wellington, Department of Prime Minister and Cabinet.

New Zealand Government (2013), 'PM Releases Report into GCSB Compliance', 9 April, http://www.beehive.govt.nz/release/pm-releases-report-gcsb-compliance (accessed 14 January 2015).

New Zealand Election Study (1993–2014), Auckland, University of Auckland.

New Zealand Parliament (1999), 'Background Note: Information Briefing Service for Members of Parliament', Parliamentary Library, Wellington, 5 October.

New Zealand Parliament (2011), 'Standing Orders of the House of Representatives', Parliament Buildings, Wellington, 5 October.

Newman, M. (2010), 'An Idea Whose Time Has Come', *NZCPR Weekly*, 5 April, http://www.nzcpr.com/NewsletterArchive.htm

O'Brien, T. (2014), 'Immigration Figures Pose Tripwire for Labour', TV3 News, 21 May, http://www.3news.co.nz/politics/immigration-figures-pose-tripwire-for-labour-2014052117#axzz3M73fGSyx (accessed 17 December 2014).

OECD (2014), Income Distribution Database, June, http://www.oecd.org/els/soc/OECD2014-Income-Inequality-Update.pdf (accessed 31 December 2014).

Ott, D. (2000), *Small is Democratic: An Examination of State Size and Democratic Development*, New York, Garland Publishing.

Palmer, G. (1979), *Unbridled Power?: An Interpretation of New Zealand's Constitution and Government*, Wellington, Oxford University Press.

Palmer, G. (2008), 'The New Zealand Bill of Rights Act and the Police', Wellington, New Zealand Law Commission, http://www.lawcom.govt.nz/media/speeches/2008/new-zealand-bill-rights-act-and-police: 4.

Palmer, G. (2012), 'Democracy Neglected in Canterbury', 21 December, http:/stuff.co.nz/the-press/opinion/8107084 (accessed 11 December 2013).

Palmer, G. and M. Palmer (1997), *Bridled Power: New Zealand Government Under MMP*, Auckland, Oxford University Press, 3rd edn.

Palmer, M. (2006), 'Resolving the Foreshore and Seabed Dispute', in R. Miller and M. Mintrom (eds), *Political Leadership in New Zealand*, Auckland, Auckland University Press: 197–214.

Panckhurst, J. (chair), *Royal Report on the Pike River Coal Mine Tragedy*, 28 September 2012, http://pikeriver.royalcommission.govt.nz/About-the-Commission.

Panebianco, A. (1988), *Political Parties: Organisation and Power*, Cambridge, Cambridge University Press.

Parkinson, J. (2010), 'Decision-making by Referendum', in R. Miller (ed.), *New Zealand Government and Politics*, Melbourne, Oxford University Press, 5th edn: 571–84.

Putnam, R. D. (2000), *Bowling Alone: The Collapse and Revival of American Community*, New York, Simon & Schuster.

Representation Commission (2013), 'Proposed Electoral Districts', Wellington, New Zealand Electoral Commission, November, http://www.elections.org.nz/sites/default/files/bulk-upload/documents/proposed_electoral_districts_2013_report.pdf (accessed 23 January 2015).

Research New Zealand (2014), 'Special Report on the 2013 Census of New Zealand's Population and Dwellings', Wellington, 11 March, http://www.researchnz.com/pdf/Special%20Reports/ResearchNZ%20Special%20Report%20-%202013%20Census.pdf (accessed 22 December 2014).

Robinson, C. (2010), '2008: Images of Political Leadership in the Campaign', in S. Levine and N. S. Roberts (eds), *Key to Victory: The New Zealand General Election of 2008*, Wellington, Victoria University Press: 137–50.

Roper, B. (2001), 'Neo-Liberalism: A Radical Critique', in R. Miller (ed.), *New Zealand Government and Politics*, Melbourne, Oxford University Press, 2nd edn: 578–89.

Sartori, G. (1987), *The Theory of Democracy Revisited*, Chatham, Chatham House Publishers.

Savage, J. and F. O'Sullivan (2014), 'Collins Resigns', *Herald on Sunday*, 31 August, http://www.nzherald.co.nz/adam20feeley203120august202014/search/results.cfm?kw1=Adam%20Feeley%2031%20August%202014&kw2=&st=gsa (accessed 27 January 2015).

Saward, M. (1998), *The Terms of Democracy*, Cambridge, Polity Press.

Schumpeter, J. A. (1976), *Capitalism, Socialism and Democracy*, London, Unwin University Books.

Seidman, L. (2012), 'Let's Give Up on the Constitution', *New York Times*, 31 December, http://www.nytimes.com/2012/12/31/opinion/lets-give-up-on-the-constitution.html?pagewanted=all&_r=0 (accessed 2 October 2013).

Sharples, P. (2007), 'The Maori Party', in S. Levine and N. S. Roberts (eds), *The Baubles of Office: The New Zealand General Election of 2005*, Wellington, Victoria University Press: 283–87.

Sinclair, K. (ed.) (1961), *Distance Looks Our Way: The Effects of Remoteness on New Zealand*, Auckland, Paul's Book Arcade for the University of Auckland.

Sinclair, K. (1980), *A History of New Zealand*, Auckland, Penguin.

Smith, K. (2010), 'Māori Party', in R. Miller (ed.), *New Zealand Government and Politics*, Melbourne, Oxford University Press, 5th edn: 509–21.

Sorrenson, M. P. K. (1986), 'A History of Maori Representation in Parliament', in J. Wallace (Chair), *Report of the Royal Commission on the Electoral System: Towards a Better Democracy*, Wellington, Government Printer: B1–B82.

Sorrenson, M. P. K. (2014), *Ko Te Whenua Te Utu/Land is the Price: Essays on Maori History, Land and Politics*, Auckland, Auckland University Press.

Srebrnik, H. (2004), 'Small Island Nations and Democratic Values', *World Development*, 32/2: 329–41.

Statistics New Zealand (released annually), http://www.stats.govt.nz/browse_for_stats/population/estimates_and_projections/dem-trends-landing-page.aspx (accessed 18 January 2015).

Statistics New Zealand (1998), *New Zealand Official Yearbook 1998*, Wellington, GP Publications.

Statistics New Zealand (2013), 2013 Census, www.stats.govt.nz/census/2013-census (accessed 18 January 2015).

Stern, G. (1993), *Leaders and Leadership*, London, London School of Economics and Political Science.

Stoker, G. (2006), *Why Politics Matters: Making Democracy Work*, Houndmills, Basingstoke, Palgrave Macmillan.

Street, M. (2003), 'Trade Unions', in R. Miller (ed.), *New Zealand Government and Politics*, Melbourne, Oxford University Press, 3rd edn: 378–87.

Stuart, S. (2014), 'Twelve Questions: Steven Joyce', *New Zealand Herald*, 6 March,

http://www.nzherald.co.nz/nz/news/article.cfm?c_id=1&objectid=11214535 (accessed 24 November 2014).
Sullivan, A. (2010), 'Māori Participation', in R. Miller (ed.), *New Zealand Government and Politics*, Melbourne, Oxford University Press, 5th edn: 538–47.
Sullivan, A., M. von Randow and A. Matiu (2014), 'Māori Voters, Public Policy and Privatisation', in J. Vowles (ed.), *The New Electoral Politics in New Zealand: The Significance of the 2011 Election*, Wellington, Institute for Governance and Policy Studies: 141–60.
Theakston, K. (2012), 'Winston Churchill, 1945–51', in T. Heppell (ed.), *Leaders of the Opposition: From Churchill to Cameron*, Houndmills, Basingstoke, Palgrave Macmillan: 7–19.
Trent, J. S. and R. V. Fruedenberg (1991), *Political Campaign Communication: Principles and Practices*, New York, Praeger, 2nd edn.
Trevett, C. (2010), 'Government Backtracks on Electoral Finance Law', *New Zealand Herald*, 23 November, http://www.nzherald.co.nz/business/news/article.cfm?c_id=3&objectid=10689429 (accessed 27 January 2015).
Trevett, C. (2014), 'Maori Party Co-leader Well Ahead in Waiariki Electorate', *New Zealand Herald*, 1 September, http://www.nzherald.co.nz/nz/news/article.cfm?c_id=1&objectid=11317473 (accessed 7 September 2014).
Uhr, J. (2008), 'Distributed Authority in a Democracy: The Lattice of Leadership Revisited', in P. 't Hart and J. Uhr (eds), *Public Leadership: Perspectives and Practices*, Canberra, ANU Press: 37–44.
Vasil, R. (2000), 'Indigenous Rights and the Constitution', in C. James (ed.), *Building the Constitution*, Wellington, Institute of Policy Studies: 214–18.
Vowles, J. (2002), 'Parties and Society in New Zealand', in P. Webb, D. Farrell and I. Holliday (eds), *Political Parties in Advanced Industrial Democracies*, Oxford, Oxford University Press: 409–37.
Vowles, J. (ed.) (2014), *The New Electoral Politics in New Zealand: The Significance of the 2011 Election*, Wellington, Institute for Governance and Policy Studies.
Vowles, J., P. Aimer, H. Catt, J. Lamare and R. Miller (1995), *Towards Consensus? The 1993 Election in New Zealand and the Transition to Proportional Representation*, Auckland, Auckland University Press.
Vowles, J. and P. Aimer (2004), 'Political Leadership, Representation and Trust', in J. Vowles, P. Aimer, S. Banducci, J. Karp and R. Miller (eds), *Voters' Veto: The 2002 Election in New Zealand and the Consolidation of Minority Government*, Auckland, Auckland University Press: 167–83.
Waldron, J. (2008), *Parliamentary Recklessness: Why We Need to Legislate More Carefully*, Auckland, Maxim Institute.
Walker, R. (1983), 'The Genesis of Maori Activism', Auckland, University of Auckland.
Walker, R. (1984), 'The Political Development of the Maori People of New Zealand', Auckland, University of Auckland.
Walker, R. (1990), *Ka Whawhai Tonu Matou: Struggle Without End*, Auckland, Penguin.
Walker, R. (2006), 'Maori Conceptions of Leadership and Self Determination', in R. Miller and M. Mintrom (eds), *Political Leadership in New Zealand*, Auckland, Auckland University Press: 134–52.
Wallace, J. (Chair) (1986), *Towards a Better Democracy: The Report of the Royal Commission on the Electoral System*, Wellington, Government Printer.
Ward, A. (1999), *An Unsettled History: Treaty Claims in New Zealand Today*, Wellington, Bridget Williams Books.
Ware, A. (1996), *Political Parties and Party Systems*, Oxford, Oxford University Press.

Ware, A. (2009), *The Dynamics of Two-Party Politics: Party Structures and the Management of Competition*, Oxford, Oxford University Press.
Watson, R. P. and C. C. Campbell (eds) (2003), *Campaigns and Elections: Issues, Concepts, Cases*, London, Lynne Rienner Publishers.
Webb, P. (2000), *The Modern British Party System*, London, Sage.
Weber, M. (1978), *Economy and Society: An Outline of Interpretive Sociology*, Berkeley, University of California Press, volume 2.
Winiata, W. (2000), 'How Can or Should the Treaty by Reflected in Institutional Design?', in C. James (ed.), *Building the Constitution*, Wellington, Institute of Policy Studies: 205–6.
Wlezien, C. and R. S. Erikson (2002), 'The Timeline of Presidential Election Campaigns', *The Journal of Politics*, 64/4: 969–93.
Young, A. (2014), 'National Accepts the Risks in Going Back to NZ First', *New Zealand Herald*, 22 January, http://www.nzherald.co.nz/nz/news/article.cfm?c_id=1&objectid=11189985 (accessed 10 February 2014).
Young, A. (2014), 'Greens Spring in Polls as National Takes Hit', *New Zealand Herald*, 22 August, http://www.nzherald.co.nz/nz/news/article.cfm?c_id=1&objectid=11312481 (accessed 27 January 2015).

Further Electronic Sources

Democracy Ranking Association, http://democracyranking.org/wordpress/?page_id=738 (accessed 24 December 2014).
Department of the Prime Minister and Cabinet, Ministerial List, http://www.dpmc.govt.nz/cabinet/ministers/ministerial-list (accessed 27 January 2015).
Department of the Prime Minister and Cabinet, 'Cabinet Committees', http://www.dpmc.govt.nz/Cabinet/committees (accessed 27 January 2015).
Inter-parliamentary Union, 'Women in National Parliaments', http://www.ipu.org/wmn-e/classif.htm (accessed 1 December 2013).
New Zealand Electoral Commission, Election Results 2011, http://www.electionresults.govt.nz/electionresults_2011/referendum.html (accessed 21 January 2014).
New Zealand Parliament, http://www.parliament.nz/en-nz/ (accessed 18 December 2013).
Transparency International, http://www.transparency.org/cpi2014/infographic#compare (accessed 20 December 2014).
World Atlas, http://www.worldatlas.com/aatlas/populations/ctypopls.htm (accessed 3 December 2014).

Index

Note: General institutional and other references apply to New Zealand, unless otherwise indicated. Entries to footnotes are indicated by an 'f' after the page number.

Abbott, Tony, 22–23, 42
Accident Compensation Corporation (ACC), 122
Act Party, 64, 67, 89, 116, 237; and Epsom electorate, 91f, 92, 102, 103, 173, 211–12, 227; and Māori representation, 200; and parliamentary representation, 102, 105, 166; and 'Teapot Tape' affair, 103; and voters, 102; as support party, 107, 110, 112, 125, 194, 196, 217, 225, 229, 237; collapse of, 158; formation of, 165–66, 168; funding of, 177, 178; internal organisation of, 181; leadership of, 152; membership of, 175–76; policies and attitudes of, 112, 168, 169, 173, 174, 178, 194, 198, 200, 203, 220; voting rates for, 165, 225; see also Association of Consumers and Taxpayers (ACT); Banks, John; Brash, Don; Hide, Rodney; National Party, and Act Party; Seymour, David; Whyte, Jamie
Adams, Amy, 94, 115, 120f
adoption, controversies over, 73
advertising agencies, and political parties, 142, 175, 212–13; see also campaigns: and advertising
advisers, government, 22, 126, 128, 142–43, 145, 175, 207
advisory panels, 46, 196–97; see also Constitutional Advisory Panel; Policy Advisory Group
Afghanistan, US invasion of, 109
Aimer, Peter, 210
Alcohol Advisory Council (ALAC), 233
alcohol: abuse, 193; controversies over consumption and legislation, 62, 73, 233, 240
All Blacks, 15, 23, 218
Alliance Party, 64, 72, 164, 190; as support party, 109, 110, 112, 144, 177; collapse of, 158; formation of, 153; voting rates for, 165; see also Anderton, Jim; Labour–Alliance coalition government

Anckar, Carsten, 12–13
Anderson, Virginia, 95
Anderton, Jim, 89, 109, 111f, 151, 161f
anti-apartheid movement and protestors, 135, 164, 195, 234
anti-free-market parties, 164
anti-nuclear movement, 164, 234; see also France: New Zealand's relationship with; nuclear tests; nuclear-armed and -powered ships; South Pacific, nuclear testing in
anti-smacking legislation, 62, 140, 174, 241–42, 246; see also Crimes (Substituted Section 59) Amendment Bill 2007
ANZUS alliance, 21
Aoraki electorate, 93, 226
Ardern, Jacinda, 92, 94
Asia-Pacific Economic Cooperation forum (APEC), 7
Asian community: representation of in Parliament, 10–11, 92, 197; stereotyping of, 173; see also Chinese MPs
Association of Consumers and Taxpayers (ACT), 165
Association of Southeast Asian Nations (ASEAN), 7; and trade with New Zealand, 6
Atmore, Harry, 33
Attorney-General, role of, 31, 119, 143; see also Finlayson, Chris
Auckland, 15, 31, 38, 40, 122, 127, 177, 180, 222, 243; as super city, 36; electorates in, 91, 92, 205, 226; housing in, 12, 219; population and ethnicity of, 10–11, 205; representation of in Parliament, 120–21; two-party results in, 226, 227; see also East Coast Bays electorate; Epsom electorate; Helensville electorate; Kelston electorate; Māngere electorate; Manukau East electorate; Manurewa electorate; Mt Albert electorate; Mt Roskill electorate;

Index

Auckland *(cont.)*, New Lynn electorate; North Shore electorate; Pakuranga electorate; South Auckland electorate; University of Auckland; Waitakere electorate; West Auckland electorate
Auckland Central electorate, 92, 135–36, 190
Australia: and alliances with, 21; and democracy in, 13; and discrimination against Aboriginal population, 184; and imperial awards, 22–23; and judiciary, 27; and leadership choice in, 148; and leadership style in, 154; and New Zealand, 5, 20; and New Zealanders in, 8; and Parliament in, 79; and representation in, 16, 16f, 74, 76; and representation of women in, 97; and senate in, 82; and Statute of Westminster, 21; and trade with New Zealand, 5–6, 41; and women's vote, 1f; government system of, 13, 76, 154, 159; republicanism in, 42; *see also* Liberal coalition (Australia)
awards, imperial, 19, 22–23
Awatere, Donna, 186

backbenchers, 63, 65, 114, 150, 166, 171, 189
Bagehot, Walter, 81
Bakshi, Kanwaljit, 94
Balfour Report, 21
Banks, John, 103, 122–23, 173, 180, 211–12
Barry, Maggie, 94, 115
Bassett, Michael, 132
Beaumont, Carol, 94
Beetham, B. C., 161f
Belgium, and government system of, 159
Bellamy's, 63
Bennett, David, 94
Bennett, Paula, 90, 94, 115, 116, 203f
Beyer, Georgina, 201
biculturalism, 173, 186
Bill of Rights, 24, 45, 232, 245
Bill of Rights 1688 (England), 54
Bill of Rights Act: 1990, 35, 36, 46, 52–53, 60, 67; 1993, 54, 57, 58, 60
biographies, political, 132–33, 138, 145
Bishop, Chris, 94
Blair, Tony, 169, 245

Bloxham, Jenny, 182
Blundell, Sir Denis, 37
Boag, Michelle, 136
Bolger, Jim, 44, 117, 124, 131, 147, 208; leadership style of, 134
Borrows, Chester, 94
Bowen House, Lambton Quay, 63
'brain drain', 8
Brash, Don, 51, 72, 137, 140, 173, 212; and Exclusive Brethren, 140, 211; and Orewa Rotary Club speeches, 12, 186, 198–99, 208; communication style of, 150; leadership style of, 134; popularity of, 141
Brazil, and voting ages, 2f
Bridges, Simon, 94, 115, 120f, 203f
briefing papers, 118, 128
British Commonwealth, 7, 21, 27, 37, 40, 234
British Empire, 4, 5, 19
Brown, Gordon, 245
Brownlee, Gerry, 94, 115, 116, 119, 127f
Buck, Peter (Pita Te Rangi Hīroa), 187, 187f
Bush, Jeb, 208
Business Roundtable, 8
Business Committee (of Parliament), 68, 69
by-elections, 103, 124, 164–65, 189, 192–93, 195, 225, 229; *see also* Northland by-election

Cabinet, 28, 31, 33, 34, 63, 65, 72, 93, 112, 113–18, 126–27, 130, 137, 143, 147, 208; and forming a government, 108–13; appointment to, 29, 30, 71, 76, 111, 114, 116–17, 118–20, 121, 136, 143; composition of, 120–21, 126–27, 183, 187; curbing of, 77, 83–84, 144; dismissals from, 29, 72, 121, 123–24, 143, 144, 192; portfolios, 114, 121, 127; power of, 126–27, 142, 156; representation in, 120–21, 203; reshuffles, 121, 122; resignations from, 29, 121–23, 144, 221–22; responsibility, 55, 121–24, 127; roles of, 34, 61, 78, 106–8, 113–18, 127–28; shadow, 137, 149; size of, 30, 113–14, 119, 126–27; *see also* Department of the Prime Minister and Cabinet; Policy Advisory Group (of Cabinet); select committees
Cabinet Legislation Committee, 117

Index

Cabinet Manual, 55, 106, 123–24, 143
Cabinet Office, 128
Cameron, David, 145
campaigns: advertising, 8, 109, 142, 134, 162, 178, 183, 206, 207, 211, 218–19; educational, 100; political, 17, 18, 24, 38, 78, 93, 142, 145, 146, 151, 153–54, 155, 158, 163, 165, 168, 174–75, 179, 180, 183, 205, 206–14, 216–24, 227–28, 231, 233, 247; *see also* funding issues: of campaigns; United States: and election campaigns in
Campbell, John, 211
Canada, 5; and democracy in, 13, 245; and government system of, 82, 159, 245; and judiciary, 27; and New Zealand and New Zealanders, 8, 20; and political campaigns in, 209; and representation in, 16, 16f, 74, 76; and representation of women, 97; and Statute of Westminster, 21; and term of government in, 79; constitution of, 46, 53; *see also* Charter of Rights (Canada); Quebec
Canterbury Earthquake Recovery Act 2011, 248
Canterbury earthquakes, 41, 205, 206f, 248
Canterbury, population of, 10–11, 205
Caribbean, 12; government system of, 32
Carroll, James, 187, 187f, 188, 201
Carter, Chris, 72
Carter, Daniel, 15
Carter, David, 94
Carter, Jimmy, 239
Catalonia, and independence movement, 7
caucuses, party, 34, 65, 70–71, 72, 73, 77–78, 82, 96–97, 114, 118, 119, 120, 127, 136, 137, 148–49, 156, 176, 187, 188, 189, 194, 219, 229
celebrity culture, 15, 129–30, 138, 209, 218; *see also* personality politics
Chal, Kelly, 3f
Chapman, Robert, 135, 214, 215
Charter of Rights (Canada), 53
charter schools, 171,
Chauvel, Charles, 90
child poverty, 12, 152, 170, 196
China: and government of, 159; and Judith Collins, 123; and trade with New Zealand, 6, 7, 41, 92, 125, 140; immigrants from, 180

Chinese MPs, 92
Christchurch: housing in, 12; population movements in, 205; two-party results in, 227; *see also* Canterbury earthquakes; Sydenham electorate; Wigram electorate
Christian Coalition Party, 89, 177
Christian Democrats, 166; *see also* United Future Party
Christian Heritage Party, 72
Churchill, Winston, 147
Citizens' Initiated Referendums Act 1993, 60, 242
citizens' juries and assemblies, 244–45
civil liberties, 49, 54
civil rights movement, 234
Civil Unions Bill 2005, 73, 73f
Clark, David, 94
Clark, Helen, 7, 15, 114, 125, 131, 135, 142, 146, 149, 178, 191, 208, 211, 217, 245; and government formation under, 107, 109–10, 112, 120–21; and Māori, 120, 191–92, 194; decisions and policies of, 22, 124; leadership style of, 117–18, 119, 131–32, 133–34, 137–39, 140, 144–45, 209; political background of, 131–32, 135–36; popularity of, 140, 141, 209; *see also* foreshore and seabed controversy; government, Clark/Key model of
Clerk of the House, 63, 65
climate change, debate on, 244
Clinton, Bill, 49f, 169
Clinton, Hillary, 130, 208
coalition governments, 24, 26, 35, 36, 42, 43, 52, 57, 61, 70, 74, 85, 98, 106–10, 111, 124, 125, 154, 196f, 232; majority, 106, 107, 109, 110, 111; minority, 24, 26, 29, 36, 43, 61, 70, 85, 98, 106, 107–8, 109, 110, 111–12, 125–26, 144, 191, 192, 231; *see also* Labour–Alliance coalition government; Labour–Progressives coalition government; mixed-member proportional electoral system (MMP); National–New Zealand First coalition government; Reform–Liberal coalition government
Coates, Gordon, 132
Coffey, Tamati, 94
Coleman, Jonathan, 94, 115
Collins, Judith, 94, 105, 123, 127f, 221–22

Index

colonial era, 5, 7, 19, 47; government during, 19–21, 27, 52, 201; hangovers from, 22–23, 27, 58
Colonial Office (UK), 19
common law, 50, 54–55, 192
communications advisers, and political parties, 142–43, 145–46, 150, 175, 207, 213, 221
confidence and supply agreements, 62, 70, 108, 109–10, 154, 194, 196–97, 217
conscience issues, 53, 62, 72–73, 83
Conservative–Liberal Democrat coalition government (UK), 35
Conservative Party, 112, 152, 166, 217, 225; funding of, 153, 177; policies and values of, 169, 198, 203; voting rates for, 165, 225; *see also* Right of Centre Party
Conservative Party (UK), 214
Constitution Act: 1852, 20; 1986, 52, 78–79
constitution, 27, 46–50, 63, 143, 231, 240, 245; codification of, 45, 55–60, 185; entrenched, 27; reform of, 42, 57, 58, 60, 75, 79–80, 86–87, 134, 170, 193, 231–32, 247–48; structure of, 50–55; written or unwritten, 45, 45f, 47–48, 50, 52, 55–60, 80, 240f; *see also* common law; conventions, constitutional; statutes; India: constitution of; petitions, constitutional; Treaty of Waitangi; United States, constitution of
Constitutional Advisory Panel, 57, 59–60, 75, 79, 185–86, 197, 202, 203
constitutional issues: historical, 19–22, 25, 200; contemporary, 28–29, 30, 31, 35, 36, 38, 42, 44, 45–55, 59–60, 193, 196–97, 200–1, 203
constitutional supremacy, 36
conventions, constitutional, 24, 50, 48, 55, 123, 125, 127, 143, 193
Cosgrove, Clayton, 95
Costa Rica, representation in, 76, 77
Council of Trade Unions, 237; *see also* trade unions, and political parties
Court of Appeal, 31, 50–51, 54, 192
courts, functioning and roles of, 31, 46, 50, 54–56, 58, 194; *see also* Court of Appeal; District Court; Family Court; High Court; Supreme Court; Youth Court
Cracknell, V. F., 161f
Craig, Colin, 152, 153, 177

Craig, Liz, 94
Crimes (Substituted Section 59) Amendment Bill 2007, 241f
Cullen, Michael, 64, 117, 119
Cunliffe, David, 71, 72, 94, 142, 148–49, 168–69, 170, 179–80, 220, 223, 226; leadership style of, 218–19; popularity of, 141

Dahl, Robert, 239
Davis, Kelvin, 95, 195
de Tocqueville, Alexis, 184
Dean, Jacqui, 94
decentralised state, 36, 44, 170
defence, 20, 21, 24, 30, 69, 115, 116, 170, 234
democracy, 1–2, 12–13, 16, 24, 26, 76–77, 163, 178, 184, 224, 228, 230–32, 248–49; associative, 242–43; deliberative, 243–46; direct, 12, 35–36, 173, 238–43, 244; indirect or representative, 2, 15, 35–36, 44; neo-pluralist, 236–37, 238; pluralist, 32, 35–36, 44, 159, 232–38; representative, 2, 26, 35–36, 83–84; social, 169–70, 174; *see also* Westminster system, of democracy
Democracy Ranking Association, 13
Democrats, 88, 164
Denmark: government system in, 125; representation in, 76, 77
Department of Labour, 122
Department of the Prime Minister and Cabinet, 28, 30, 117, 128, 143
'dirty politics', 18, 123, 219, 221–24, 228, 231; *see also* Hager, Nicky
District Court, 31, 146
Dominion, status of, 20–21
donations, to political parties, 123, 140, 142, 177, 178–80, 183; *see also* Banks, John; Brash, Don; Cunliffe, David; Dotcom, Kim; Exclusive Brethren; funding issues; Labour Party, donations to; SkyCity casino
Dotcom, Kim, 59, 123, 142, 151, 153, 177, 212, 222, 228, 229
Douglas, Roger, 165, 173, 236
Downs, Anthony, 166, 171–72, 215
Dryzek, John, 244
'Duke and Duchess of Cambridge effect', 39, 42

Index

Dunedin, two-party results in, 227
Dunedin electorate, 226
Dunleavy, Patrick, 35, 244
Dunne, Peter, 90, 109–10, 115, 122, 152, 153–54
Durie, Mason, 201
Duverger, Maurice, 32, 43, 161
Dyson, Ruth, 68

Eagleson, Wayne, 145
East Coast Bays electorate, 64, 161f
Eastern Maori electorate, 187f, 188f, 190
Ede, Jason, 221
Eden Park Trust Amendment Bill 2009, 66
election results 2014, 64, 165, 195, 200, 224–27, 250–51
elections, 160, 204; 1935, 81, 163; 1943, 188, 190f; 1946, 189, 190; 1949, 79f, 81, 108, 190; 1951, 79f, 190; 1957, 81, 189, 190; 1960, 81, 190; 1972, 81, 163, 189, 190, 224; 1975, 81, 136, 168, 190; 1978, 32, 64, 87, 108, 164, 190, 247; 1981, 17, 32, 87, 88, 94, 95, 108, 136, 164, 190, 247; 1984, 17, 34, 52, 64, 79f, 81, 136, 161f, 164, 190, 229; 1987, 17, 87, 164, 190; 1990, 17, 81, 161f, 164, 190, 200; 1993, 17, 29f, 33, 88, 160f, 165, 190; 1996, 17, 81, 91, 96, 107, 110, 160, 165, 166, 172, 182, 190, 205; 1999, 17, 74, 81, 86, 89, 109, 110, 140, 148, 165, 191; 2002, 17, 79f, 109, 110, 136, 137, 140, 142, 157, 165, 223; 2005, 17, 72, 104, 110, 137, 140, 165, 178, 194, 195, 208, 211, 217; 2008, 17, 55, 74f, 81, 107, 110, 119–20, 140, 146, 165, 186, 194, 208, 223–24, 225, 246; 2011, 17, 86, 91f, 96, 98f, 105, 110, 111, 142, 149, 157, 165, 182, 194, 202, 206, 211, 216, 217, 220, 223–25, 227, 248; 2014, 17, 18, 24, 67–68, 91, 103, 105, 110, 111, 123, 143, 157, 165, 175, 194, 195, 196f, 205, 206, 207, 212, 216–17, 220, 224–27, 231, 250–51
elections: early, 44, 79f; 'snap', 34f, 78–79, 79f, 109
Electoral Act 1993, 53, 86, 90, 92–93, 180–81, 193, 200
Electoral Amendment Act 2010, 178
electoral boundaries, 53, 90, 92, 205–6
Electoral Enrolment Centre, 206

Electoral Finance Act 2007, 245
Electoral (Finance Reform) Bill 2005, 178
Electoral Integrity Act 2001, 71–72
Electoral (Reduction in Numbers of Members of Parliament) Amendment Bill 2006, 75f
electorate seats, 64, 65, 74, 88–89, 90–92, 93, 94–97, 98f, 104, 173, 182, 205
Emissions Trading Scheme, 246
English, Bill, 60, 72, 94, 115, 116, 119, 127f, 137, 137f, 140, 142, 149; popularity of, 141
Environment Canterbury Act 2010, 248
environmental movement, 164, 174, 182, 232–34
Epsom electorate, 89, 91f, 92, 102, 103, 173, 205, 211–12, 227
Esler, Gavin, 145
European Economic Community (EEC), 5, 21, 40, 164
European Parliament, 35
European systems of government, 4, 13, 33, 59, 76, 77, 79, 97, 125–26; *see also* Belgium, and government system of; Denmark; Finland, representation in; France; Germany; Ireland; Italy, and government system of; Northern Ireland; Norway; Scandinavian countries; Scotland; Switzerland, and democracy in; United Kingdom; Wales
executive, 13, 22, 27, 30–31, 33, 35, 47–48, 55, 56, 61, 64, 76, 78, 106, 113, 116, 121, 135, 142, 143–44, 146, 185, 203, 248; curbing of, 77, 80, 82–84; powers of, 27, 28, 29, 32, 34, 36, 43, 57, 58, 61–62, 77, 80, 81–82, 98, 126; size of, 114
Executive Council, 29

Falwell, Jerry, 146
Families Commission, 110
Family Court, 31
federal government, 16f, 44, 48, 76, 80, 160, 239; *see also* Australia: government system of; United States, government system of
Federated Farmers, 237
Feeley, Adam, 123, 222
feminist movement, 164
Finance and Expenditure Select Committee, 68f, 69

267

Index

Finland, representation in, 76, 77
Finlayson, Chris, 94, 115, 143
first-past-the-post electoral system (FPP), 32, 33, 75–76, 86, 88, 90, 98, 98f, 99, 100, 108, 126, 160, 160f, 182–83, 204–5, 213, 232; *see also* plurality voting systems
first-term ministers and MPs, 78, 80, 114, 120–21, 137
Fishkin, James, 245
Fitzsimons, Jeanette, 154
'Five Eyes' surveillance network, 5
flag, national, 19, 23, 240
Flavell, Te Ururoa, 115, 152
foreign policy, 5, 21, 125, 135, 163–64
Foreshore and Seabed Act 2004, 55, 69, 192–93, 194
foreshore and seabed controversy, 54, 69, 124, 192, 201
Foss, Craig, 94, 115
Foster-Bell, Paul, 94
France: and representation in, 76; and term of government in, 79; French Revolution, 49; New Zealand's relationship with, 5, 21, 40–41; *see also* anti-nuclear movement; nuclear tests
Fraser, Peter, 108, 131, 132, 189
free market economics, 24, 112, 160, 167, 170, 172; reforms, 87, 147, 165, 173, 236; *see also* anti-free-market parties
free trade agreements, 5–7; *see also* China: and trade with New Zealand
Freer, Warren, 136
Freyberg, Lord Bernard, 37f
funding issues, 8, 53, 195, 213; of campaigns, 24, 158, 175, 177–78, 207; state vs private funding, 178–80, 183; *see also* Act Party, funding of; Conservative Party, funding of; donations, to political parties; Green Party, funding of; National Party, funding of; parties, political, funding of

gay rights, 73, 73f; *see also* Civil Unions Bill 2005; Marriage (Definition of Marriage) Amendment Bill 2012; same-sex marriage
Gaylor, Penny, 95
Geddis, Andrew, 198
General roll, 91, 185, 198, 206

General seats, 91, 96, 190, 199, 200, 201, 202, 206, 226
Genesis Energy, 248
Germany: and democracy in, 13; and representation in, 76, 88; and term of government in, 79; constitution of, 46
Giddens, Anthony, 7
Gisborne electorate, 187
globalisation, economic, 7
Goff, Phil, 72, 95, 125, 142, 145, 148–49, 226; popularity of, 140, 141
Goldsmith, Paul, 92, 94, 115
Goodfellow, Peter, 176f
Goodhew, Jo, 93, 94, 115
Government Administration Committee, 68, 69
Government Communications Security Bureau (GCSB), 18, 59, 122, 143
government, Clark/Key model of, 110–27
Governor-General, 113, 115, 119, 143; role of, 22, 28–29, 30, 31, 37–38, 42, 55, 144, 207; *see also* Blundell, Sir Denis; Freyberg, Lord Bernard; Holyoake, Keith; Porritt, Sir Arthur; Reeves, Sir Paul; Tizard, Dame Catherine
Great Depression, 162
Green Party, 18, 40, 42, 64, 70, 88–89, 98f, 104, 107, 109, 110, 111, 112, 140, 152, 153, 156, 160, 166, 170, 179, 217, 224–25, 228; advertising campaigns of, 218–19; and National, 154; and representation of women, 97; formation of, 164; funding of, 177, 213; internal organisation of, 93, 181; policies, attitudes and initiatives of, 73, 102, 169, 174, 196, 199, 200, 220–21, 245; visibility of, 152, 210; voters, 199
Greenwald, Glenn, 222
Greer, Christine, 95
Grey, Sir George, 20
Groser, Tim, 64, 78, 94, 115
Grover, Frank, 72
Gustafson, Barry, 14, 132
Guy, Nathan, 94, 115, 180

Hager, Nicky, 123, 210–11, 212, 221–22, 223, 224, 228–29; *see also* 'dirty politics'
Hailsham, Lord, *see* Hogg, Quintin
Halbert, Shanan, 95
Hamilton East electorate, 226

268

Hamilton West electorate, 226
Hamilton, Peter, 41
Harawira, Hone, 72, 151, 152, 153, 194–95, 228f
Harré, Laila, 152, 153
Hauraki-Waikato electorate, 91
Hawke, Bob, 138
Hawkesby, John, 142
Haworth, Nigel, 176f
Hayes, Joanne, 94
health care, 10, 12, 14, 47, 69, 92, 171, 188, 193, 194, 219, 221, 233, 242, 243
Heke, Hone, 187, 187f
Helensville electorate, 136
Henare, Tau, 160f, 190
Hide, Rodney, 89, 173
High Court, 31, 123
Hillary, Sir Edmund, 138
Hills, Richard, 95
Hipkins, Chris, 95
history and its effect on democracy, 19–23
Hobson electorate, 64, 161f
Hobson, Captain William, 19, 186
Hogg, Quintin, 34
Holland, Harry, 188
Holland, Sidney, 131, 137f
Holyoake, Keith, 14, 38, 131, 132, 139, 145, 224
home-insulation agreement, 154
honours, *see* awards, imperial
Horan, Brendan, 72
Horomia, Parekura, 191
House of Lords (United Kingdom), 61, 82
housing, 9, 11, 12, 14, 36, 47, 189, 218, 219, 220, 243
Hudson, Brett, 94
Human Rights Act 1993, 35, 46
Huo, Raymond, 95
Hutt City Council (Graffiti Removal) Bill 2012, 66
Hutt South electorate, 226

identity, collective and national, 3, 5, 7, 10, 13–14, 25, 27, 45, 58, 90, 127, 163–64, 204
Ikaroa-Rāwhiti electorate, 91, 191, 195
independence movements, 2, 2f, 7
Independent MPs, 72, 165, 187f
India: and British Commonwealth, 37; constitution of, 47

international bodies and connections, 6, 7, 21, 23–24, 28
Internet Party, 152, 153, 177, 195, 228f
Internet/Mana Party, 151, 195, 225, 228, 228f; *see also* Mana Party
Invercargill electorate, 226
Ireland: and representation in, 77; and senate in, 82; constitution of, 46
Islamic State, 23
Israel, 45f, 88; and government system of, 159
Italy, and government system of, 159

James, Colin, 222–23
Japan, and trade with New Zealand, 6, 7, 41
Jesson, Bruce, 58, 235
Johansson, Jon, 132
Jones, Rachel, 95
Jones, Shane, 174
Joyce, Steven, 64, 78, 94, 115, 119–20, 127f, 170, 209
judicial review, 36, 48, 56, 58
judiciary, 27–28, 29, 31, 48, 53, 54, 56, 57, 58, 60

Kaushal, Sunny, 95
Kavanagh, Denis, 133
Kaye, Nikki, 92, 94, 115, 120f
Kelston electorate, 226
Key, John, 8, 15, 22–23, 62, 67, 94, 103, 110, 115, 116, 125, 131, 135, 142, 146, 208, 210, 221, 245; and anti-smacking law, 242; and *Dirty Politics*, 221–22, 228; and government formation under, 107, 112, 119–21, 125–26; and 'Teapot Tape' affair, 211–12; composition of Cabinet under, 120–21, 127f, 126–27, 143; communication style of, 146, 150; decisions and policies of, 97–98, 140, 240; leadership style of, 117–18, 119, 131–32, 133–34, 138, 139–40, 144–45, 149, 209, 210f, 217–19; political background of, 136–37; popularity of, 137–38, 140, 141, 224, 228; *see also* government, Clark/Key model of
Key, V., O. 215
King George VI, 144
King Movement, 188
King, Annette, 94
King, Michael, 132, 138
Kirk, Norman, 131, 137f, 139

KiwiSaver Homestart, 219–20
Knapp, G. T., 161f
Kopu, Alamein, 72
Korako, Nuk, 94

Labour–Alliance coalition government, 81, 109, 110, 112, 144, 191
Labour government, 8, 131, 163; 1935, 81, 162–63; 1957, 81; 1972, 81, 163–64; 1984–87, 81, 114f, 136, 229; 1987–90, 81, 229; 1999–2008, 81, 93, 109, 191, 210–11; 2002–5, 109, 111f, 202–3, 217, 227; 2005–8, 77, 110, 111, 111f, 112, 125, 178, 194
Labour Party, 3, 29f, 32, 38, 66, 78, 108, 111f, 134, 135–36, 139, 140, 144, 151, 157, 159–60, 160f, 165, 173, 174, 195, 216, 224–25, 247; advertising campaigns of, 218–19; and election defeat, 148–49, 224–25, 226–27; and leadership choice, 147–48; and Māori, 159–60, 160f, 187–90, 191–93, 195, 196, 196f, 199–200, 201, 202; and representation of women, 97; defections from, 124, 164; dismissals from, 124, 192; donations to, 142; formation of, 162–63; in opposition, 64, 69, 70, 87, 90, 92, 140, 229; internal organisation of, 71, 78, 118–19, 147–48, 163, 176f, 181–82; leadership of, 71, 72, 142, 148f, 180, 229; list, 93, 94–95, 218; loyalty to, 149, 156, 182; membership of, 33, 43, 163, 175f, 212f, 212–13, 214, 234, 237; policies and attitudes of, 42, 54, 60, 71, 73, 86–87, 102, 112, 163–64, 165, 168–71, 172, 173, 182, 199, 219–20, 229; resignations from, 189; support for, 16–17, 18, 33, 164, 182, 223–24, 226–27, 228, 248; voters, 40, 100, 103, 156, 165, 199, 214, 227; *see also* Clark, Helen; Cunliffe, David; Fraser, Peter; government, Clark/Key model of; Kirk, Norman; Lange, David; Māori: and electoral alliance with Labour; Nash, Walter; Palmer, Geoffrey; Rātana–Labour alliance
Labour–Progressives coalition government, 81, 109, 110
Lange, David, 87, 114, 117–18, 119, 131, 136, 137f, 147, 150, 169, 208; leadership style of, 15, 117, 132, 134, 144, 146

Langer, Ana Inés, 138, 139
law, entrenched, 46, 52, 53, 57, 58–59, 60, 67, 78, 200, 245; *see also* Māori seats, entrenchment of; Treaty of Waitangi, entrenchment of
Leader of the Opposition, 131, 136, 137, 139, 140; role of, 147–51, 154, 208; *see also* opposition parties
leaders' debates, televised, 130, 153–54, 155, 210, 210f, 223; *see also* television, and political campaigning, publicity and information-spreading
leadership and leaders: 129–34, 134f, 209–10; choosing of, 147–48; contests and disputes, 72; populist, 130–31, 155; public perceptions about, 138–39, 141–42, 152; qualities of, 137–42, 154; roles of, 142–47; styles of, 117, 131, 154, 156, 217–19; types of, 134–35; *see also* Clark, Helen, leadership style of; Cunliffe, David, leadership style of; Lange, David, leadership style of; Key, John, leadership style of; Leader of the Opposition; Muldoon, Robert, leadership style of; prime minister: leadership styles of; small parties, leadership of
Lee, Melissa, 94
Lee, Sandra, 190, 191
Lees-Galloway, Iain, 95
Legislative Council, 29f, 43, 62, 63, 82
legislature, 27–28, 29–30, 58
Levine, Stephen, 215
Liberal coalition (Australia), 42
Liberal Party, 20, 162, 163, 187
libertarianism, 164, 165, 167–68, 173
Libertarianz, 168
Lindlom, Charles, 236–37
Lipson, Lesley, 1
list MPs, *see* party lists
Little, Andrew, 71, 95, 148f, 150
Liu, Donghua, 180
Local Electoral Act 2001, 122–23
local government, 32, 35, 36, 154, 160, 233, 248; constitutional role of, 58
Lotu-liga, Peseta Sam, 94, 115
loyalty, to party, 33, 93, 119, 149, 155, 157–58, 214, 216; *see also* Labour Party, loyalty to

Index

MacGregor Burns, James, 132, 133
Macindoe, Tim, 94
Mackey, Moana, 95
Magna Carta 1297 (England), 54
Maharey, Steve, 134, 169
Mahuta, Nanaia, 94, 192, 201
Major, John, 133
Malta, and voting ages, 2f
Mallard, Trevor, 226
Mana Motuhake movement, 159, 164, 185, 189, 191
Mana Party, 91f, 112, 152, 153, 159, 165, 169, 177, 185, 191, 194, 195, 196, 200, 202; *see also* Internet/Mana Party
Māngere electorate, 226
Manukau East electorate, 226
Manurewa electorate, 226
Māori: and colonisation, 19, 50–51, 186; and Crown, 19–20, 45, 51, 54–55, 58, 113, 192, 200–1; and disengagement from voting, 17; and electoral alliance with Labour, 159, 162, 187–90, 191–93, 195, 196f, 202, 214, 234; and National Party, 194, 203f; and the vote, 1, 20, 184, 185; development, 124; independent tribal movements, 186–87; land loss, 54–55, 186, 187, 188; politicians, 187, 187f, 199, 203; population, 11, 11f; representation of, 37, 94–96, 120–21, 159–60, 185f, 185–87, 191–93, 196–98, 199, 200, 201–2, 203, 234; rights of, 52, 54, 184, 198, 203, 234; sovereignty, 174, 186, 189, 201; *see also* Act Party, and Māori representation; Foreshore and Seabed Act 2004; foreshore and seabed controversy; Labour Party, and Māori; minority rights and provisions; mixed-member proportional electoral system (MMP), and Māori electoral politics; National Party, and Māori; Parliament: representation of Māori and ethnic minorities in; Rātana–Labour alliance; Rātana movement; referenda: on Māori representation and seats; Treaty of Waitangi; Whānau Ora
Māori Affairs Committee Room, Parliament, 63
Māori Council, 51
Māori Electoral Option, 197, 202, 206f
Māori electorates, 73, 186, 190, 206, 227

Māori Land Court, 54, 69, 192
Maori Land March 1975, 234
Māori Party, 12, 44, 64, 67, 72, 74f, 79, 91f, 105, 107, 110, 112, 125, 126, 152, 153, 156, 159, 165, 185–86, 196, 202, 203, 217, 225, 229, 237; and constitutional review, 45–46, 79; and foreshore and seabed controversy, 55, 124, 193; and formation of, 191–96; and partnership with National, 194–97; defections from, 72, 194–95; formation and development of, 106f, 124, 153, 191–96; policies and attitudes of, 102, 169, 193, 199, 200; representation of in Parliament, 105, 106; voters, 102, 199; *see also* National Party, and Māori Party
Maori Representation Act 1867, 186
Māori roll, 3, 91, 185, 190, 198, 206
Māori seats, 1, 3, 91, 91f, 94–96, 103, 160, 160f, 184–86, 185f, 188–91, 193, 194, 196–202, 203, 206, 228f; entrenchment of, 186, 193
Marine and Coastal Area (Takutai Moana) Act 2011, 55, 194, 195
Marlborough District Council, 54
Marriage (Definition of Marriage) Amendment Bill 2012, 62, 66, 73, 83
Marshall, John, 131
Marxism, 235–36
mass-membership parties, 17, 26, 43, 163, 212, 237–38
Massey, William, 130
Mauri Pacific Party, 72
Maxim Institute, 79
McCaw, Richie, 15
McClay, Todd, 94, 115
McCready, Graham, 123
McCully, Murray, 94, 115, 116, 127f
McDonald, Robyn, 182
McDouall, Hamish, 95
McKelvie, Ian, 94
McKinnon, Don, 7
McLay, Jim, 168
McLay, Todd, 68f
media, role of, 129–30, 142, 145–46, 150, 155–56, 206–7, 247; *see also* campaigns, advertising; social media, importance and use of; television, and political campaigning, publicity and information-spreading

Members of Parliament (MPs), roles of, 65–68
Meridian Energy, 248
Michels, Robert, 235
Mighty River Power, 51–52, 52f, 248
migration, from New Zealand, 8; to New Zealand, 4f, 8–9, 19
Mika, Jerome, 95
military alliance, with the US, 4; *see also* ANZUS alliance; Australia: and alliances with; United States: and alliances with
Milne, Tony, 95
mining exploration, protests over, 233
ministers outside Cabinet, 30, 34, 110, 114–17, 120, 125, 183, 194
ministers, roles of, 63–64, 64, 113–14, 116–17
Ministry of Education, 121–22
Ministry of Health, 30
Ministry of Justice, 30
Ministry of Māori Development, 243
Ministry of Social Development, 30
minorities, representation of, 73, 94–95, 98, 184, 187, 197, 198
minority government, *see* coalition governments, minority
minority rights and provisions, 11–12, 46, 50, 53, 54, 58–59, 198–99, 203
Minto, John, 195
Mitchell, Austin, 70
Mitchell, Mark, 94
mixed-member proportional electoral system (MMP), 2, 15f, 17, 25, 26, 27, 43, 68, 70, 79, 87–90, 98f, 99, 103, 106, 106f, 131, 133–34, 154, 161f, 182, 194, 198, 224, 237, 247; and government formation under, 107–13, 125, 144, 166; and Māori electoral politics, 197–98, 199, 201–3; and representation under, 74–75, 94–95, 96, 197; debate about and review of, 102–5, 244; impacts of, 27, 57, 64, 71–72, 74–75, 81–82, 85–86, 89, 94–95, 114–15, 130, 131, 155, 156, 157, 166, 204–5, 213–14, 217, 228, 232; introduction of, 74, 86–88, 108–9; opposition to, 99–100, 101, 102, 165, 232, 247–48; pros and cons of, 97–100; *see also* coalition governments; referenda: on electoral system

monarch, British, 21–22, 26, 27, 28–29, 30, 38, 40f, 55, 234
monarchy, retention or removal of, 19, 20, 21–22, 23, 36, 37–42, 57, 170; *see also* 'Duke and Duchess of Cambridge effect'; Queen Elizabeth II
Moore, Mike, 7, 131, 136, 147
'Moral Majority', 168
Moroney, Sue, 95
Morris, Peter, 133
Morrison, N. J., 161f
Mt Albert electorate, 136, 226
Mt Roskill electorate, 205, 226
Muldoon, Robert, 14–15, 34f, 52, 114, 117, 120, 130, 131, 132, 208, 234; leadership style of, 134, 144, 150, 168
Mulgan, Richard, 168, 198, 233–34
multi-party systems and parliaments, 15f, 27, 33, 36, 43–44, 64, 68, 70, 83, 107, 108–9, 117, 131, 133, 144, 154, 158, 159, 160–61, 164–66, 182–83, 205, 213, 217, 224, 232

Nash, Walter, 131, 142–43, 189
National government, 32, 38, 108, 117, 126–27, 131, 149, 163, 170; 1960, 81, 163; 1978, 81, 87; 1981, 81, 87; 1984, 34; 1990–93, 81, 87; 1993–96, 29f, 33, 66, 81; 2008–11, 60, 86, 97–98, 111, 119–20, 125, 127f, 140, 154; 2011–14, 67, 68, 68f, 81, 104–5, 111, 125, 126, 127, 170, 172, 248; 2014–17, 5, 64, 67–68, 69, 70, 81, 91–92, 111, 115, 120, 125, 216–17, 224–27, 229
National–New Zealand First coalition government, 15f, 74, 81, 107, 108–9, 110, 116, 134, 191
National Party, 12, 32, 33, 40, 42, 64, 68, 72, 78, 79, 98, 105, 108, 110, 136, 142, 151, 157, 164, 165, 176, 179, 181–82, 202, 208, 228, 247, 248; advertising campaigns of, 217–19; and Act Party, 110, 125, 165, 173, 217, 220, 229; and constitutional review, 45–46, 79, 104–5; and election defeat, 148, 229; and foreshore and seabed controversy, 55; and Māori, 60, 186, 194–95, 196, 196f, 198–99, 200, 202, 203f; and Māori Party, 55, 107, 110, 112, 194–95, 196–97, 203, 217, 229;

and New Zealand First, 110, 126, 134, 172, 217, 229; and representation of women, 96–97; and United Future, 110, 126, 217, 229; defections from, 164; dismissals and suspensions from, 72, 124, 137f; formation of, 64, 163; funding of, 178, 180, 211; in opposition, 163, 208; internal organisation of, 71, 117, 118–19, 176, 181–82; leadership of, 72, 131, 136–37, 209; list, 91, 94, 182; membership of, 16–17, 33, 43, 70, 156, 163, 175f, 212f, 214, 234, 237; policies and attitudes of, 3, 5, 40, 42, 44, 45–46, 57, 60, 73, 83, 87, 100, 102, 112, 125f, 163, 168, 169, 170–71, 172, 181, 182, 198–99, 202, 219–20, 228; support for, 18, 199, 223, 224–26, 227; voters, 100–1, 102, 103, 156, 182, 214; *see also* Bolger, Jim; Brash, Don; 'dirty politics'; English, Bill; Holyoake, Keith; Key, John; Māori: and National Party; Muldoon, Robert; Shipley, Jenny; 'Teapot Tape' affair
nationalism and patriotism, 27, 159
Naylor, Jonathan, 94
Nelson, 33
neo-conservative ideologies and parties, 168
neo-liberal ideologies and parties, 167, 168, 169–70
neutrality, political, 30, 237
NewLabour Party, 161f, 164
New Lynn electorate, 226
New Plymouth electorate, 226
New South Wales, 19
New Zealand–China Free Trade Agreement 2008, 125f
New Zealand Defence Force, 30
New Zealand Election Study, 15, 86, 100, 215, 246–47
New Zealand Electoral Commission, 17–18, 53, 88, 102–5, 175, 178, 207, 248
New Zealand First Party, 64, 72, 74–75, 88, 89, 104, 107, 110, 112, 126, 127, 151, 153, 159–60, 165, 188, 205, 210, 212, 217, 229; advertising campaigns of, 218–19; and Māori, 190–91, 192, 200, 202; and representation of women, 97; formation of, 165; internal organisation of, 182; policies and attitudes of, 73, 102, 169, 172–73, 174, 198–99, 221; *see also* National Party, and New Zealand First;

National–New Zealand First coalition government; Peters, Winston
New Zealand Law Commission, 233
New Zealand Law Society, 31, 178
New Zealand Party, 164, 168
New Zealand Police, 30
Ngaro, Alfred, 94
Ngata, Āpirana, 187, 187f, 188, 201
Nixon, Richard, 49f, 138
Norman, Russel, 152, 154
North Island, representation of in Parliament, 90, 91, 119
North Shore electorate, 226
Northern Ireland, 35
Northern Maori electorate, 160f, 187f, 188, 189–90
Northland by-election 2015, 64, 70, 126, 152, 229
Norway: government system in, 125; representation in, 76, 77
'Novopay' payroll system, 121
nuclear tests, 5, 40–41; *see also* South Pacific, nuclear testing in
nuclear-armed and -powered ships, 5, 21, 40–41

Obama, Barack, 15, 49, 56, 130, 145
O'Connor, Damien, 95
O'Connor, Simon, 94
Office of the Clerk of the House, 63
Office of the Prime Minister, 128, 143, 221
Official Information Act 1982, 35
Ōhāriu electorate, 90, 91f
Ohariu-Belmont electorate, 89
one-New Zealand policy, 198
one-party government, 32, 36, 43, 159, 204; *see also* single-party majority government; single-party minority government
opposition parties, 8, 29, 30, 62, 64, 80, 81, 121, 149, 150–51, 154, 196, 203, 208, 209, 218, 219, 229, 248; *see also* Leader of the Opposition
Orewa Rotary Club, 12, 186, 198–99
overhang, 28, 74, 74f, 91f
Oxford Union Debate, 1985 146

Pakuranga electorate, 64, 137, 161f
Palmer, Geoffrey, 25, 27, 52, 54, 86–87, 105, 131, 134, 145, 147, 247f, 247–48

Index

Palmer, Matthew, 54–55
Parata, Hekia, 94, 115, 120f, 121–22, 203f
Parata, Tame, 187, 187f
Parker, David, 94, 220
Parliament: dissolution of, 144;
  independence and powers of, 58, 79–81;
  physical setting of, 63–65; reform of,
  81–84; representation of Māori and
  ethnic minorities in, 94–96, 98, 197,
  198; representation of women in,
  96–97, 98; roles of, 61–62, 65–68; size
  of, 46, 60, 62, 74–78, 83, 85, 90, 103,
  240f, 242; term of, 46, 52, 60, 62, 78f,
  78–81, 82, 83; *see also* legislature; select
  committees; upper house
Parliament House, 63; layout of, 64
Parliamentary Library, 63
Parliamentary Press Gallery, 63, 118, 122
Parliamentary Service, 30, 63
parliaments: provincial, 26; sovereign, 36,
  43, 55–56, 61; two-house, 26, 43–44
Parma, Parmjeet, 94
participation, public, 1, 12, 15–17, 24, 53,
  83, 148, 174–75, 186, 202, 204, 210,
  214–16, 230–31, 235–36, 244, 247; and
  voter disengagement, 4, 17–18, 24, 175,
  224, 231
parties, political, 70–73, 157–58; funding
  of, 177–80, 183; membership of, 238; *see
  also* Act Party, membership of; funding
  issues; Labour Party, membership of;
  National Party, membership of; United
  Future Party, membership of
party hopping, 33, 71–72, 124, 162, 194,
  225; *see also* Labour Party, defections
  from; Māori Party, defections from;
  National Party, defection from
party lists and seats, 16, 64–65, 71–72,
  74–75, 82, 85–86, 89, 91f, 91–97, 99f,
  99–100, 103–4, 182, 200, 202; *see also*
  Labour Party, list; National Party, list
party system, 1, 158–66; and candidate
  selection, 180–82; development of,
  161–66; ideological model of, 166–71,
  172; organisational structure of, 155,
  176–77; values and policies of, 166–74;
  see also funding issues; multi-party
  systems; participation, public; small
  parties; two-party systems; vote-
  maximisation model of party system

party vote, 40, 64, 72, 74f, 85, 88, 91, 98f,
  102, 196, 204, 213, 218, 220, 226–27
Pasifika community, 92; representation of
  in Parliament 120–21, 176, 197, 234
Perry, Katy, 15
personality politics, 129–30, 139, 151–52,
  154, 155–56, 171–72, 182, 209–10,
  217–19, 227; *see also* celebrity culture
Peters, Winston, 72, 107, 108, 124–25, 127,
  151–52, 164–65, 172, 182, 190–91, 200,
  208–9, 212, 217, 219, 229
petitions, 44, 68, 231, 240, 241;
  constitutional, 240f
Pike River mining disaster, 122
pluralist democracy, *see* democracy,
  pluralist
plurality voting systems, 32–33, 35, 43–44,
  160f, 204, 232; *see also* first-past-the-
  post electoral system (FPP)
politics of the Third Way, 169–70
Policy Advisory Group (of Cabinet), 128
polls: deliberative, 244, 245–46; internal,
  172; opinion, 18, 149, 153–54, 196f,
  205, 208, 212, 213, 216–17, 222–23,
  223f, 224–25, 229, 245, 247, 248; *see also*
  Colmar Brunton polls
Pōmare, Māui, 187, 187f, 201
population factors: ageing, 10–11, 12;
  ethnicity of, 10–11; growth of, 9; life
  expectancy, 11
population size, and its effect on form of
  democracy, 4, 8–19, 23, 24, 76–77, 127,
  230–31, 249
pornography, controversies over, 73
Porritt, Sir Arthur, 37
post-election negotiations, 46, 98, 126,
  127, 186, 194, 237
Power, Simon, 105, 135
Prebble, Richard, 135–36, 165, 173
preferential voting, 99, 100
presidential style of leadership and
  politics, 42, 129–31, 142, 155; elections
  under, 18, 22, 37–38; *see also* United
  States, and presidential style of
  leadership
prime minister: leadership styles of,
  117–18, 131, 154–55; power of, 155–56;
  roles of, 117–19, 142–47
Prime, Willow-Jean, 95
Prince Charles, 41

Prince George, 41
Prince William, 41
privatisation, 7, 87, 170, 232, 248
Privy Council (United Kingdom), 22, 31, 53
professional marketers and fundraisers, and political parties, 175, 212–13
Progressive Coalition, 89, 109, 111f, 112, 151, 225
proportional representation, 35, 36, 43, 88–89, 107, 160–61, 247f; *see also* mixed-member proportional electoral system (MMP)
prostitution reform Bill, 62
provincial government, 20, 26, 32, 239
public service, 28, 30–31, 55, 107, 113, 121, 126, 127–28, 143
Pullar, Bronwyn, 122
Putnam, Robert, 237

Quebec, 7
Queen Elizabeth II, 22, 28, 38, 40, 41, 42
Queen Victoria, 51
Quigley, Derek, 165, 168

Radhakrishnan, Priyanca, 95
Rahman, Anjum, 95
Rangitīkei electorate, 64, 161f
Rata, Matiu, 189–90
Rātana–Labour alliance, 188f, 188–90, 190f, 193
Rātana movement, 187–88, 191–92, 193
Rātana, Tahupōtiki Wiremu, 162, 188–89, 201
Reagan, Ronald, 168
Reeves, Sir Paul, 37
referenda, 240–42, 241f; citizens'-initiated, 24, 26, 36, 44, 62, 74, 173, 231, 240, 241, 246, 247, 248f; government-initiated, 79, 83, 86, 240, 247–48; on electoral system, 25, 46, 52, 53, 54, 60, 79, 87–88, 97–101, 161, 165, 240, 247–48; on flag, 23, 240; on Māori representation and seats, 203; *see also* Citizens' Initiated Referendums Act 1993; United States of America: democracy in
reform: electoral, 85–88, 240, 245; legislative, 62–63, 81; top-down, 232–32; *see also* constitution, reform of; free market economics, reforms; Parliament, reform of; Resource Management Act, reform of

Reform–Liberal coalition government, 162–63
Reform Party, 162, 163, 187
remoteness, and its effect on form of democracy, 3–8, 23
representation, 1, 16, 24, 76, 85, 87, 89, 94–95, 119, 134, 181; *see also* Asian community: representation of in Parliament; Māori: representation of; Māori Party: representation of in Parliament; minorities, representation of; Pasifika community, representation of; women: representation of
Representation Commission, 90, 90f, 205–6
republicanism, 22, 36, 37–42
Reserve Bank Act 1989, 36
Resource Management Act, reform of, 219, 220
responsibility, *see* Cabinet, responsibility
Right of Centre Party, 166; *see also* Conservative Party
rights, individual and minority, 2, 24, 46–50, 53, 54, 58–59, 168, 184, 234, 236, 242; *see also* Māori: rights of; women: rights of
Roberts, Nigel, 215
Robertson, Grant, 94, 148f
Roper, Brian, 235–36
Rose, Richard, 37
Ross, Jami-Lee, 94, 180
Rotorua electorate, 226
Rowling, Wallace, 131
Royal Commission on the Electoral System, 3, 74, 79–80, 87, 89, 103, 105, 197, 198, 201–2, 203, 247f
Royal Commission on Pike River, 122
Russell, Deborah, 95

Sabin, Mike, 94
Salesa, Jenny, 94
same-sex marriage, 174
Savage, Michael Joseph, 132, 138, 144
Scandinavian countries: and democracy in, 13; and representation of women in, 97; and term of government in, 79; *see also* Denmark; Norway
Scotland: and independence movement, 7; and representation in, 76, 77; and voting ages, 2; devolved parliament in, 35

Index

Security and Intelligence Service (SIS), 30, 143
select committees, 29–30, 65, 66, 67, 68–70, 71, 75, 77, 81, 83–84, 144, 244; *see also* Finance and Expenditure Select Committee; Government Administration Committee; Social Services Committee
Sepuloni, Carmel, 90, 94
Serious Fraud Office, 123, 222
Seymour, David, 92, 115, 116, 126, 227
Sharples, Pita, 193, 195, 203f
Shearer, David, 72, 95, 148, 150, 226
Shipley, Jenny, 30, 124, 131, 135, 140, 141, 142, 191, 208; leadership style of, 134; popularity of, 141
Simpson, Heather, 145
Simpson, Scott, 94, 180
Sinclair, Keith, 11
single-party majority government, 26, 43, 98, 108, 109, 133; *see also* one-party government; single-party minority government
single-party minority government, 109; *see also* one-party government; single-party majority government
single-transferable vote (STV), 98, 99, 100
Singapore: and representation in, 76, 77; and trade with New Zealand, 6
Sio, Sua'a William, 95
SkyCity casino, 123
Slater, Cameron, 123, 221–22
small parties, 27, 30, 33, 35, 44, 64, 68, 70–71, 82, 83, 86, 88–89, 93, 98–99, 103, 106, 106f, 108, 108f, 109, 111, 112–13, 125, 126, 131, 158f, 164–65, 166, 171, 172–73, 175, 180, 183, 213, 217, 225, 232, 234; future of, 158, 159–61; leadership of, 151–56, 208–9, 210f; organisation of, 176–77
Smith, Nick, 94, 115, 122
Snowden, Edward, 222
Social Credit Association, 162
Social Credit Political League, 64, 88, 160, 161, 164, 247f
'social laboratory', New Zealand as, 24
social media, importance and use of, 46, 142, 145, 150, 152, 213
Social Services Committee, 68f
Solomon, Tipene, 195

Sorrenson, Keith, 184–85, 187
South Africa: and British Commonwealth, 37; and representation of women, 97
South Auckland electorates, 226
South Island, representation of in Parliament, 90, 91, 93, 119, 120–21
South Pacific, 5, 12, 17, 21, 164; nuclear testing in, 5, 41
Southern Maori electorate, 187f, 188
Speaker, role of, 29f, 29–30, 65–66, 69, 114f, 120
Springbok tours, opposition to, 234
standing committees, 69–70, 116–17
Standing Orders and Privileges Committees, 70
Standing Orders of Parliament, 65–66, 68
state-owned assets and enterprises, 7, 28, 51–52, 87, 143–44, 170, 232, 248
State Services Commission, 30, 128
statutes, 35, 46, 50, 52–54, 192
Statute of Westminster, 21
Street, Maryan, 95
student loans, 171
submissions, to Parliament, 67, 68, 69, 81, 103, 105, 231, 233, 244
Suisuiki, Anahila, 95
'super city' model, 36
supplementary-member system, 98, 98f, 99, 100
support agreements and parties, 67–68, 82, 105, 110, 112–13, 114
support parties, 118, 119, 125–26, 194, 196, 220, 225, 229
Supreme Court, 22, 31, 45, 52f, 53–54, 232
Supreme Court Act 2003, 53–54, 54
Sutton, Jim, 93
Switzerland, and democracy in, 13
Sydenham electorate, 161f
Sykes, Annette, 195
Syria, 49
Szabo, Claire, 95

Tainui electorate, 191, 201
Tainui/Hauraki-Waikato electorate, 195
Tāmaki electorate, 164
Tāmaki Makaurau electorate, 91, 191, 195
Tapsell, Peter, 29f, 66
Taupō electorate, 226
Tauranga electorate, 96, 164–65
Te Rangi Hīroa, *see* Buck, Peter

Te Rūranga o Kirikiriroa, 243
Te Tai Hauāuru electorate, 91, 124, 191, 192–93, 195, 201
Te Tai Tokerau electorate, 91, 191, 194, 195, 228f
Te Tai Tonga electorate, 91, 191, 195
Te Whānau o Waipareira Trust, 243
'Teapot Tape' affair, 103, 211–12
television, and political campaigning, publicity and information-spreading, 14, 17, 129, 142, 145–46, 150, 155–56, 174–75, 207, 209, 218, 238, 247; *see also* leaders' debates, televised
Thatcher, Margaret, 41, 133, 168
thresholds, 88–89, 98, 103–5, 161, 161f, 173, 195, 202, 212, 228f
Tirikātene, Eruera, 188
Tisch, Lindsay, 94
Tizard, Dame Catherine, 37, 38
Tolley, Anne, 94, 115
trade, 5–7; *see also* Association of Southeast Asian Nations (ASEAN), and trade with New Zealand; Australia, and trade with New Zealand; China: and trade with New Zealand; Japan, and trade with New Zealand; Singapore: and trade with New Zealand; United Kingdom, and trade with New Zealand; United States, and trade with New Zealand
trade agreements, 23, 125, 140; *see also* New Zealand–China Free Trade Agreement 2008; Trans-Pacific Partnership Agreement
trade unions, and political parties, 33, 71, 127, 148, 148f, 162, 175, 175f, 179, 212, 214, 216, 232–33, 234, 237; *see also* Council of Trade Unions
Trans-Pacific Partnership Agreement, 7, 28
Transparency International, 230f
Treasury, 30, 118, 128
Treaty of Waitangi, 19, 188–89, 200–1, 203; and its importance under the law, 54–55; and the constitution, 50f, 50–52, 58, 60; articles of, 51; entrenchment of, 193; settlement process, 36, 45–46; *see also* Waitangi Tribunal
Turia, Tariana, 124, 191, 192–93, 195, 201, 203f

Turei, Metiria, 152, 154, 179, 194
Turkey, 88
Twain, Mark, 3
two-party systems and mindset, 16, 26, 32, 33–34, 36, 43, 44, 57, 64, 70, 82, 85, 108, 156, 157, 159–61, 163, 164, 171, 183, 203; survival of, 157f, 157–58
Twyford, Phil, 94

unicameral legislatures, 62–63, 76
unitary government, 32, 36, 43, 154
United Future Party, 3f, 64, 67, 89, 90, 91, 105, 107, 109–10, 112, 125, 126, 152, 153, 165, 217, 225, 229, 237; collapse of, 158; formation of, 166; membership of, 175–76; policies and values of, 169; *see also* Christian Democrats; Dunne, Peter; National Party, and United Future
United Kingdom: and democracy in, 13, 245; and New Zealanders in, 8; and representation in, 16, 16f, 76; and surveillance network, 5; and term of government in, 79; and trade with New Zealand, 5; and voting ages, 2; and voting in, 214; and women's vote, 1; constitution of, 45f; government system of, 32, 45, 114, 121, 159; governments in, 35; New Zealand's relationship with, 21, 58, 164; opposition leaders in, 147
United Nations, 7
United Nations Declaration on the Rights of Indigenous Peoples, 50
United States: and alliances with, 21, 234; and democracy in, 13, 239–40, 244–45, 246; and election campaigns in, 129–30, 179; and New Zealanders in, 8; and party system in, 159; and political campaigns in, 179, 207–8; and presidential style of leadership, 48–49, 56–57, 129–30, 132, 155, 207–8; and representation in, 74, 76; and representation of women in, 97; and role of president, 143; and surveillance network, 5; and term of government in, 79; and trade with New Zealand, 6, 7, 41, 164; and voter disengagement, 24; and voting ages, 2; and women's vote, 1f; constitution of, 28, 31, 46, 47–50, 56–57, 59, 63; government system of, 13, 28, 32, 49, 49f, 68, 70, 76, 181, 239, 245–46;

Index

United States *(cont.)*, judiciary in, 31, 48–49; New Zealand's relationship with, 21, 40–41
United Party, *see* United Future Party
universal suffrage, 1, 2
University of Auckland, 135
upper house, 160; abolition of, 24, 26, 44, 45, 232; reinstating of, 81–82, 83
Upston, Louise, 94, 115
Uruguay, representation in, 77

Victoria University of Wellington, 215
Vietnam War, opposition to, 135, 164, 234
violent crime, penalties for, 242
voluntary organisations, 175, 177, 237, 242–43
vote-maximisation model of party system, 171–74
vote splitting, 164, 227
voting ages, 2–3
voting choice, 34, 214–16
Vowles, Jack, 210, 215

Wagner, Nicky, 94, 115
Waiariki electorate, 91, 191, 195
Waiapu electorate, 187f
Wairarapa electorate, 201, 226
Waitakere electorate, 90
Waitangi Tribunal, 51–52, 203
Waldron, Jeremy, 81
Wales: and devolved parliament in, 35; and representation in, 76, 77
Walker, Janette, 95
Walker, Ranginui, 185f, 189–90, 193
Wall, Louisa, 66, 95
Ware, Alan, 157, 166–67
Waring, Marilyn, 168
Watene, Puti Tipene (Steve), 188f
welfare state and system, 11, 14, 24, 47, 50, 163, 167, 168, 170, 188, 194, 216, 234, 242–43
Wellington: electorates in, 91, 226; population of, 11; two-party results in, 227; *see also* Te Tai Tonga
West Auckland electorates, 226
West Coast-Tasman electorate, 227

Western Maori electorate, 187f
Westminster Parliament, 20
Westminster system, 1, 3, 21–22, 26–27, 30, 32f, 32–34, 37, 42–44, 52, 63, 64, 121, 155, 160; durability of, 35–36
Whaitiri, Meka, 95
Whānau Ora, 12, 194, 203, 243, 243f
Whanganui electorate, 226
Whips, party, roles of, 70–71, 114f, 117, 120
Whyte, Jamie, 152, 153, 173
Wilkinson, Kate, 122
Williams, Arena, 95
Williams, Poto, 94
Williamson, Maurice, 72, 94, 137, 180
Wigram electorate, 89
Wilson, Clare, 95
Wilson, Margaret, 78
Wilson, Woodrow, 49
Winiata, Whata, 201
women: and the vote, 1; representation of, 73, 94–97, 98, 120–21, 135, 176, 181, 182; rights of, 174, 234; *see also* Australia: and representation of women; Canada, and representation of women in; feminist movement; Green Party, and representation of women; Labour Party, and representation of women; National Party, and representation of women; New Zealand First Party, and representation of women; South Africa: and representation of women; United Kingdom, and women's role
Wood, Michael, 95
Woodhouse, Michael, 68f, 94, 115, 120f
Woods, Megan, 95
Working for Families scheme, 171
World Trade Organization, 7
Wright Mills, C., 235

Yang, Jian, 94
Young, Jonathan, 94
Youth Court, 31
youthfulness of a country, and its effect on form of democracy, 19–23